D0786768

Patrimonialism
and Political Change
in the Congo

Jean-Claude Willame

Patrimonialism
and Political Change
in the Congo

Stanford University Press, Stanford, California
1972

Stanford University Press
Stanford, California
© 1972 by the Board of Trustees of the
Leland Stanford Junior University
Printed in the United States of America
ISBN 0-8047-0793-6
LC 79-153821

To my friends in Berkeley for the exciting years I spent with them

Contents

1. Patrimonialism and Congolese Politics   1

2. Appropriation of Offices   8

3. The Politics of Centrifugal Relations   34

4. Private Armies   57

5. Conditions for Political Change   77

6. The Breakdown of Patrimonialism   102

7. Toward a Caesarist Bureaucracy   129

8. Alternatives to Patrimonialism   159

   Appendix: Social Profiles and Career Patterns
     of the Political Class   167

   Chronology of Events   179

   Notes   185

   Bibliography   205

   Index   213

Tables

1. Net Income of Industrial Enterprises in Belgium and in the Congo   11

2. Self-Employed Persons in the Congo in 1959   27

3. Salaries of Statutory and Auxiliary Personnel in the Civil Service, 1960   28

4. Statutory Positions in the Congo in June 1960 and June 1963   30

5. Political and Territorial Division of the Congo as Proposed at the Tananarive and Coquilhatville Round Tables   38

6. Themes of Parliamentary Debates on New Provinces   44

7. Profile of the New Provinces at the Time of Their Creation   46

8. Patrimonial and Cliental Relations in the Congo, 1962–65   49

9. Distribution of Shares and Votes on the Board of UMHK   88

10. Distribution of UMHK Shares and Votes in February 1965   92

11. Increase in Wages and Salaries by Socioeconomic Category, 1960–65   104

12. Combined Volume of Congolese Exports and Domestic Turnover of Goods, 1958–64   105

13. Congolese GNP, 1958–68, in Millions of Zaires   133

14. Real Income of Selected Occupational Groups   134

15. Assignments of Governors and Provincial Commissioners During 1967   137

16. Ministerial Reshuffles, 1965–70   142

Preface

This study is the unfinished product of field research carried out in the Congo between 1962 and 1966. When I arrived in the Congo in October 1962 as a research assistant at the Institut de Recherches Economiques et Sociales (IRES) of Lovanium University, I was assigned the task of studying provincial politics in the Congo. This research was a collective enterprise from the start. The Centre d'Etudes Socio-Politiques of IRES had just been created, and its prime objective was to study Congolese political processes after independence. The Congolese Parliament had just created 21 new provinces, and at the time was considered one of the most significant political phenomena of the postcolonial period. Accompanied by Benoit Verhaegen and Laurent Monnier, I toured the Congo in order to gather all available material on political life in the provinces. This preliminary step resulted in a series of political monographs on the new provinces, published by IRES between 1964 and 1965.*

The monographs were aimed at providing the student with raw material on Congolese politics rather than with a ready-made interpretive framework. The members of our research team had always believed that the researcher's prime task in Africa was to gather as many data as possible before attempting any kind of generalization. Such an attitude was based on the belief that as far as the Congo was concerned, it would be very difficult to capture the dynamics of contemporary events within a static frame of reference. The rapid disintegration of provincial politics between 1963 and 1965 was the most convincing proof that we had chosen the right approach.

* Monnier and Willame.

During my stay in the Congo, I became aware of three methodological obstacles facing historians and social scientists investigating African politics. These obstacles are related to the distinctiveness of the subject matter, the written documentation available, and the strength and weakness of oral information.

The first problem arises from the fact that political scientists are concerned with structures and events still in flux, or "ultracontemporaneous," to use Verhaegen's terminology. Most African states are barely ten years old, and the lack of temporal reference points in the brief postcolonial era impedes the clear organization of historical facts. Which among today's political events are merely peripheral, and which represent meaningful trends? Which among a multiplicity of forces and institutions are destined to make history? There can be no clear answers to these questions, for the political, social, and cultural boundaries of Third World countries are not yet defined.

No matter how limited his perspective, though, the social scientist is invaluable in his role as eyewitness to contemporary events. Such a role affords him immediate intuitions and perceptions that strongly affect his selection of data. Over a four-year period I recorded my own intuitions as frequently as possible in notebooks or on tape, and these notes became valuable aids to my understanding of Congolese politics.

Still, the researcher must support his intuitions with solid evidence. In the Congo, such evidence was often provided by official documents, for even after independence most government employees followed their exact preindependence routines in blind emulation of their European predecessors, though some did seem aware that their work would serve a higher purpose. Though political documents were more easily available than they might have been elsewhere, my search for information was still somewhat hampered by administrative confusion. Typists, bureaucrats, and officials of all ranks spent half their time writing and dispatching various documents, many of which ended up in wastebaskets or in rooms with "lost" keys. So it was that information on the period immediately following Congolese independence was gathered partly from documents found in litter cans at the capital in Léopoldville. Similarly, I was able to analyze the workings of the rebel Stanleyville regime from the thousands of documents that still littered "President" Gbenye's residence two whole months after the city's recapture by the Congolese army.

Through my contacts with Congolese politicians I had free access to private and public archives that elsewhere would have been kept secret for 50 years or more. In fact, many Congolese politicians paid unwitting tribute to the impartiality of historical and political science by providing me with written accounts of their activities, even while some of them were still engaged in political struggles. The most striking instance was that of the local politician (later a minister in the central government) who gave me the personal memoranda, letters, public statements, and petitions that he and his party had been holding for several months. His mail was frequently handed to me unopened in my office at the Centre d'Etudes Socio-Politiques.

Still, this situation had a distinct disadvantage: each statement or document taken by itself represented some individual or factional interest. Though I succeeded in collecting a wide variety of documents from all groups and factions in the Congo, such information alone could not provide an overall view of the fluid and unstable political situation. Hence the necessity of frequent direct contact with important political figures. Most valuable in this respect was the use of interviews to obtain biographical information about politicians and political insiders. This practice placed the written documents into a referential framework and brought patrimonial rulers and regional leaders into sharper focus by highlighting the details of their careers. However, this technique had limitations of its own. As politicians and insiders spoke, they inevitably distorted and exaggerated their own roles and actions. There were few deliberate attempts to mislead, but not many politicians could remain objective when speaking of political contests in which their own survival was at stake.

I do not think there is any simple way to overcome the kinds of difficulty I encountered in my study of Congolese politics; it may well be vain to expect exactitude in the study of political events anywhere. Moreover, the quest for scientific validity demands not only that we accumulate facts, but that we place them in an interpretive framework that allows for the diversities and ambiguities inherent in politics.

In 1966 I left the Congo for the U.S. in order to find such a framework. I began a Ph.D. program at the University of California, Berkeley. This program brought me into contact with the vast array of contemporary literature in political science and related disciplines, notably political sociology, political anthropology, comparative politics, and the politics of development. It was during my stay at Berkeley that I developed the first hypotheses for my dissertation. From the outset, I was drawn to the historical method of Karl Marx and the political sociology of Max Weber. I felt strongly that these two approaches were extremely relevant to political events in the Congo, an impression that was confirmed in the seminars, coursework, and discussions that I had during my stay at Berkeley.

I said at the beginning that this study is an unfinished product. Indeed, my research has only produced some basic outlines, and these should be developed (and possibly reappraised) through more detailed empirical investigation. Such a preoccupation with basic data does not come from a desire to arrive at some ultimate scientific truth, but from the simple realization that we still know very little about the political history of the Congo, especially at the local and regional levels. Accordingly, on my return to the Congo in May 1970 I joined forces with four graduate students at Lovanium University to undertake interdisciplinary field research aimed at investigating in depth the recent sociopolitical history of the Kasangulu territory near Kinshasa. The Department of Political Science at Lovanium University has long been firmly committed to the idea that any research on political processes in the Congo should be intensive rather than extensive in scope. We encourage students in political science to do research on one province, one territory, one *secteur*, or one chieftaincy because we feel that there have been considerable local variations in political phenomena in the Congo, both before and after independence. An awareness of such variations might adequately correct the rigidity inherent in most theoretical explanations.

(Though I speak throughout of "the Congo," in November of this year the name "Republic of Zaire" was officially adopted.)

I would like to acknowledge here that the present study was made possible by a special grant from the Centre de Recherche et d'Information Socio-Politique in Brussels, and by a grant-in-aid from the Institute of International Studies in Berkeley, California.

I am indebted to Benoit Verhaegen, Ilunga Kabongo, and Laurent Monnier, whose theoretical reflections and studies contributed many ideas to my analysis. I also wish to express my appreciation to Professors Carl G. Rosberg, Michael Leiserson, and Martin Klein, who all read my manuscript at various stages and offered many valuable suggestions and criticisms.

J.-C.W.

Lubumbashi, December 1971

Patrimonialism
and Political Change
in the Congo

The Democratic Republic of the Congo

 CHAPTER 1

Patrimonialism and Congolese Politics

IN THE CONCLUSION to his *Politics in the Congo,* Crawford Young writes:

> At the present stage of knowledge, . . . the primary challenge to the student of Congolese politics remains the basic task of providing a conceptual framework adequate to order the mass of disparate data available. . . . The very nature of the Congolese political community is not entirely defined. Both colonization and decolonization created profound disequilibria in the evolution of Congolese society. In this environment, the task of seeking comprehension of the dynamic could seem to merit priority over the rigorous analysis of the static.[1]

As an example of decolonization and its aftermath, Congolese politics has often been considered atypical, if not aberrant. Recently, however, it has become increasingly clear that political events in Africa will not conform to any preconceived pattern. Such concepts as "nationalism," "Pan-Africanism," "African socialism," the "one-party state," or "mobilization and reconciliation systems" are mere rationalizations for the artificial facades that African political leaders have erected around themselves in the wake of independence. After all, as Aristide Zolberg points out, our information about African politics is grossly deficient, consisting only of declamatory statements from the political elite.[2]

The decolonization process in the Congo was perhaps atypical in that no such facades could be built. Within a month after independence, the colonial administration had collapsed with the departure of its 10,000 Belgian civil servants, the major political parties and coalitions were disintegrating, and the Force Publique, the military

arm of colonial domination, was in full-scale rebellion. This does not
mean, however, that any conceptual framework is necessarily inadequate or that these chaotic events preclude any understanding at all
of Congolese politics. This study is, in fact, an attempt to relate the
Congo to contemporary political experience, to challenge the commonly held assertion that the Congo is politically unique, and to
establish order where order seems never to have existed. In brief, the
metaphor with which Tocqueville explained his approach to democracy in America may serve equally well to illustrate my own purpose:

> My present object is to embrace the whole from one point of view; the re-
> marks I shall make will be less detailed but they will be more sure. I shall
> perceive each object less distinctly but I shall descry the principal facts with
> more certainty. A traveler, who has just left the city, climbs the neighboring
> hill. As he goes farther off, he loses sight of the men whom he just quitted;
> their dwellings are confused in a dense mass; he can no longer distinguish
> the public squares and can scarcely trace out the great thoroughfares; but
> his eyes have less difficulty in following the boundaries of the city and for
> the first time he sees the shape of the whole. . . . The details of the immense
> picture are lost in the shade, but [he] conceives a clear idea of the entire
> subject.[3]

My analysis of Congolese politics starts from the concept of patrimonialism. Following the lead of Max Weber, who invented the term,
I am defining patrimonialism as a system of rule incorporating three
fundamental and related elements: appropriation of public offices as
the elite's prime source of status, prestige, and reward; political and
territorial fragmentation through the development of relationships
based on primordial and personal loyalties; and the use of private
armies, militias, and mercenaries as chief instruments of rule.

I have chosen these three aspects of patrimonial politics neither
randomly nor with an eye to certain isolated characteristics of Congolese politics. Rather, I propose to use patrimonialism here as a
system-related concept: each of its three components refers to an essential part of the Congolese political experience. Thus, the first chapter
of this study deals with the distribution of political power; the second with the geopolitical basis of political leadership and the relationships among members of the political elite and their followers;
and the third with the military, the main instrument of political
domination in the Congo as it is in most patrimonial states.

The concept of patrimonialism has recently been advanced as a substitute for the much-abused notion of charismatic leadership. Thus, Zolberg said that although charismatic political leadership prevailed in periods of militancy, the style of leadership in African one-party states now appears more patrimonial than charismatic.[4] Similarly, Guenther Roth argues that in the new states of Africa and Asia, patrimonial elements may outweigh both charismatic appeal and belief in legal or bureaucratic nationality. According to Roth, neglect of patrimonial elements has led scholars to interpret all political leadership in new states as charismatic, thus obscuring the difference between a charismatic system of authority and charismatic leadership, and taking the international propaganda claims of the new rulers at face value.[5]

Both models of patrimonialism, Zolberg's and Roth's, remain inadequate. Zolberg believes wholeheartedly in the one-party system, "in spite of its failure to bring about fundamental change," and in spite of his agreement with Fanon that the leaders of one-party states have become "chairmen of the board of a society of impatient profiteers."[6] Roth, in his efforts to transcend the dichotomy between tradition and modernity, does not clearly differentiate patrimonial rule in industrialized countries, whether totalitarian or pluralistic, from patrimonialism in the new states. I should stress here that the structures to which the concept may be applied differ radically in the two cases. In developed countries, established political and governmental hierarchies, advanced industrial organizations, and sophisticated communications networks all combine to produce a highly integrated society by which the effects of patrimonialism are quite easily diffused. In the new nations, patrimonialism implies not only personalistic leadership in government, but a type of social relationship that makes itself felt everywhere. This relationship arises where authority is dispersed, the scope of government activity limited, and intense power politics often the only channel of social mobility.[7]

My interpretation of patrimonialism might give rise to three objections. The first objection deals with the way Max Weber utilized his ideal type, which differs from mine on at least one central point; the second is related to the meaning one should attach to the ideal-typical method in general; and the third concerns the relevance of any Western analytic tool to African politics.

In Weber's view, patrimonialism, together with the related concepts of patriarchalism and feudalism, was part of a political system based on traditional authority, i.e., on what "has always existed":

> Traditionalism . . . refers to the psychic attitude set for the habitual worka-day and to the belief in the everyday routine as an inviolable norm of con-duct . . . . It is characteristic of patriarchal and of patrimonial authority, which represents a variety of the former, that the system of inviolable norms is considered sacred; an infraction of them would result in magical or re-ligious evils.[8]

If, as Weber says, the patrimonial system of rule stems from tradi-tional authority, a serious question arises: can one justify speaking of a political regime that is still in its infancy as being based on tradi-tional authority? Perhaps the notion of tradition has hitherto been used in the too-narrow sense of "things and activities of time im-memorial," and traditionalism defined more in terms of long duration than of an unchanging order. Zolberg points out that in Africa

> tradition . . . does not merely refer to pre-European times. Many political in-stitutions created during the colonial period have become, in the eyes of liv-ing men, part of the natural order of things: district commissioners, provin-cial commissioners, commandants and governors are offices hallowed by time; the African occupants of these offices derive their authority from the fact that they are legitimate successors to the original charismatic founders.[9]

Traditions, in other words, are more likely to be drawn from recent history than from the remote past, and the Congo's recent history has largely been one of bureaucratic, authoritarian, and paternalistic structures and behavior. These, then, were the traditions adopted by the Congolese political elite.

Let me add, however, that the concept of patrimonialism can stand by itself without reference to past traditions, especially if we do not view it as excluding all other forms of legitimacy. Weber himself indicated that respect for ancient norms was not an absolute requisite of patrimonial authority. Immediately after emphasizing the impor-tance of tradition to patrimonialism, he adds: "Side by side with this system there is a realm of free arbitrariness and favor of the lord, who in principle judges only in terms of 'personal,' not 'functional,' relations. In this sense, traditionalist authority is irrational."[10] This last remark points to another fundamental question, the exact limits and meaning of the ideal type. Max Weber defines his analytical con-struct as a "one-sided accentuation . . . by the synthesis of a great num-

ber of . . . diffuse, discrete, more or less present and occasionally absent concrete individual phenomena, which are arranged . . . into a
unified analytical construct. In its conceptual purity this mental
construct cannot be found anywhere in reality."[11] The analyst who
uses such ideal constructs must be fully aware that he cannot apply
them equally to all aspects of reality without some distortion or irrele-
vance. In my analysis of the nationalist army of Stanleyville, for instance, I have grouped this army with the other private militias (the
South Kasai army and the South Katangese constabulary), deliberately exaggerating its importance as an instrument of personal rule.
To compensate, I have either avoided or reinterpreted certain factors
in order to maintain a consistent vision of political reality. Thus
in this study I have not dealt with the familiar problem of national
identity. The concept of ethnicity as I have used it refers not to political competition between tribes, but to a type of political interaction
that takes place between rival patrimonial rulers, and between them
and their respective followers. In other words, tribal identifications
are treated as an object of class analysis rather than as an obstacle to
national integration.

One final question regarding my use of patrimonialism stems from
the familiar argument that theoretical concepts borrowed from Western political sociology are irrelevant to supposedly alien experiences.
This assertion is based on the widespread but erroneous belief that
study of developing areas requires methods quite different from those
used in the analysis of European sociopolitical forms. Herbert Spiro
correctly points out that this belief has moved modern area studies
toward overspecialization, which hampers intellectual exchange between students of the world's major areas.[12]

It is even more disturbing that recent critiques of the "establish-
mentarian" character of African studies—i.e., the close connection
between governmental agencies and universities—seem to follow the
same trend. Legitimate claims regarding the development of channels for radical scholarship are enmeshed with the implicit assumption that "Africa can be explained by Africans (or blacks) only,"[13]
and that the African experience is unique and must be distinguished
from other political experiences. Unless one totally discounts human
nature, there is no reason to deny certain experiences, structures, and

behavior to some people and not to others. Significant differences do indeed exist between men and nations, but in fact most of these differences arise in a specific historical context.

Emphasis on the contextual framework introduces another fundamental point needing further elaboration, notably the appraisal of the total setting in which the polity operates. I venture to say that such an approach is imperative to an understanding of the dynamics of social and political change in the Congo. Social change is not a self-induced process rooted in abstract causes; it is determined both by the propensities of a given social system and by the relationship of that system to its historically determined environment. This view of change coincides with the recent efforts of the so-called genetic-structuralist school to formulate a new version of historical materialism. In Lucien Goldmann's words:

Actually, the structures that make up human behavior are neither basic nor universal; rather, they are specific entities, created at a particular moment in the past and now in the process of undergoing transformations that suggest a future evolution. At any given stage, the structure's internal dynamics result not only from the contradictions which it contains within itself, but from the dynamics, closely linked to these contradictions, of the larger structure surrounding it. This structure is moving toward an equilibrium of its own, a fact that makes it necessary to add that no state of equilibrium, at whatever level, can be more than temporary. In the case of human behavior, the very acts that transform the environment create new conditions that upset the old equilibrium, which becomes contradictory and inadequate.[14]

One fact is fundamental to an analysis of the dynamic relationship between the political system and its environment: the lack of autonomy of the national polity vis-à-vis outside influences. A glance at the literature on colonization and decolonization in Africa suggests that most scholars have consistently ignored the vulnerability of African political systems. Colonization is too often regarded as a special case of modernization whose destructive effects (disruption of tradition, loss of political autonomy, cultural dependency) are offset by such positive gains as the introduction of schools, economic corporations, cities, churches, and hospitals.[15] Similarly, newly independent states are generally considered autonomous units within the international order, though continual outside intervention, both political and military, has already invalidated this assumption in regard to the Congo.

The recognition that new states are not fully autonomous allows a clearer understanding of colonization and decolonization. Colonization denotes total political, social, and economic domination, and decolonization may be understood as continuing this domination by less direct means. Decolonization takes place within the larger context of an imperialism that, as far as the Congo is concerned, has been shaped by the transformation of mercantilism into industrial capitalism, by Cold War tensions and conflicts, and by the dominance of Western democratic ideologies in world politics.

Let me emphasize here that my critique of imperialism is not derived from ethical or dogmatic principles but from essentially human and practical considerations.[16] The difficulties that Third World countries have experienced in economic development and, more importantly, in nation building, have hitherto been explained by purely internal causes: lack of human and material resources, absence of entrepreneurial capabilities, lack of political support, etc.[17] However, other political experiences suggest that the key to genuine national development lies in isolation from outside influences. Thus the Enclosure Movement in eighteenth-century England, the iron curtain of Stalinist Russia, and Japan's relative isolation during the Meiji era all exemplify national consolidation following a period of closure and self-reliance. The Congo, by contrast, has been continuously open to outside influences since the beginning of her colonial era. It is this fact, perhaps, that makes Western analytical concepts germane to the study of Congolese politics. At any rate, an awareness of such outside influences is essential to a complete understanding of contemporary political events in the Congo.

 CHAPTER 2

Appropriation of Offices

ACCORDING to Max Weber, the appropriation of public office tends to be the process most crucial to the patrimonial authority system, and it is the prime incentive to the system's elite

in all states resulting from conquest which have become rationalized to form permanent structures; also of parties and other movements which have originally had a purely charismatic character. With the process of routinization the charismatic group tends to develop into one of the forms of everyday authority, particularly the patrimonial form in its decentralized variant or the bureaucratic. Its original peculiarities are apt to be retained in the *charismatic standards of honor attendant on the social status acquired by heredity or the holding of offices.* This applies to all who participate in the process of appropriation, the chief himself and the members of his staff.[1]

In the Congo, the appropriation process was determined neither by routinization of charismatic leadership nor by conquest, but by the dramatic and abrupt increase in political activity during July 1960. This intense politicization manifested itself in heavy competition for the public offices that independence had made available. It is impossible to determine why the scope of political activity expanded so dramatically, or how and in what context competition for public offices took place, without first briefly examining the structures and traditions that constitute the Congo's colonial legacy.

The Economic Variable in Belgian Colonization

Georges Balandier defines the "colonial phenomenon" as the domination of a native majority by a minority of foreigners in the name of racial and cultural superiority.[2] As a particular form of cultural contact, colonialism also implies the imposition of a modern, indus-trialized society with a dynamic economy and a fast tempo of life upon a nonindustrial society whose pace of life is much slower; a fundamentally antagonistic relationship between the two societies due to the subservient role of the native majority; and a readiness to use force in maintaining the colonial relationship.[3]

This approach, which follows a tradition begun by Emile Durk-heim and Marcel Mauss and which centers on an appraisal of social reality in its total context, was very useful some years ago when the bulk of the sociological, political, and anthropological literature sys-tematically ignored those elements that could produce psychocultural tensions and conflicts within colonial systems. Indispensable as Balan-dier's analysis is to an understanding of the colonial situation, how-ever, it needs further elaboration if it is to explain how a colonial society operates within its concrete historical setting.

Within its own setting, Belgian colonization was not only an insti-tution that would use coercion against any resistance it might en-counter, but also one aimed at establishing a system of authority vir-tually devoid of a political sphere.[4] The "colonial behemoth," to use Young's expression, aimed to purge the colonized population of all political structures, activities, or ideologies through physical and psy-chosocial constraints premised on economic efficiency.

The Mercantilist and Capitalist Aspects of Colonization. Roland Oliver and J. D. Fage point out that the colonization of Africa was not begun by the great European powers, but by small powers whose economic growth depended on expansion beyond their own borders: "In so far as there was an economic motive for partition of the kind suggested by Marxist writers, it was a motive which appealed to those European powers which had no colonies and little commercial influence in Africa rather than to those whose influence was already established there, [namely, France and England]."[5]

The first of those small powers to enter the African scene was not strictly a power but rather a European sovereign, acting as an individ-ual, whose own imperial ambitions made the colonial venture in the Congo possible: King Léopold II of Belgium. From his youth, this ambitious and energetic king, whose power was strictly limited by the principles of constitutional monarchy, interested himself in Bel-gium's expansion abroad, and specifically in the acquisition of a colo-

nial outlet for Belgian manufactured goods. King Léopold reasoned
that

if the country were to consult its best friend . . . and if it were to ask this
friend how to develop the material and moral wealth of the kingdom to its
fullest, this friend would reply: "Imitate your neighbors, extend yourself
abroad whenever you can. There you will find commercial outlets with new
demand for your products, . . . a useful solution to the population surplus,
and new sources of revenue. . . . This will allow the government to lower
taxes, as has been done in Holland, . . . to augment its power, and to better
its position in the great European family."[6]

However, very few Belgian businessmen showed initial enthusiasm
for these grand designs, and since the major Belgian banks did not
want to involve capital in what they considered a hazardous venture,
Léopold was long dependent on limited aid from such private bank-
ers as Nagelmackers, Philippson, Cassel, and Lambert. With their
help, he founded, in March 1887, the Compagnie pour le Congo du
Commerce et de l'Industrie (CCCI), responsible for all industrial,
financial, agricultural, commercial, and public works administration
in the colony. After initial difficulties, commercial exploitation of
Congolese natural resources began to yield increasing benefits to the
king. By 1900, the value of goods exported from the Congo greatly
exceeded that of imports, and by 1903 exports were valued at 54
million Belgian francs against 20 million francs in imported goods.[7]
However, Léopold's commercial venture did not prove viable in the
long run. High transport costs, huge land concessions, a policy of
forced labor, the emergence of commercial monopolies, and the systematic plunder of the most accessible natural resources were all
symptomatic of an outmoded and unprofitable form of colonization.
As R. J. Lemoine points out:

We are dealing here with a system of exploitation referred to in classical
terminology as "Raubwirtschaft." Thus on the eve of the twentieth century,
a historical form of colonization practiced by Spain in America during the
sixteenth century appears again; there is no development here, but only
commercial exploitation of natural wealth.[8]

The annexation of the Congo Free State by Belgium in March 1908
fundamentally changed the orientation of the Congolese economy
by opening the door to Belgian and foreign investments and by stimu-
lating industrial development. The argument for annexation went
unchanged: a colony would be profitable as an outlet for excess popu-

lation, surplus capital, and manufactured goods, while the value of Congolese ivory, rubber, and mineral deposits would offset the cost of colonial development. At the same time two principles, the fostering of free trade and the release of new labor potential through education of the native population, were advanced to rationalize this new form of colonial exploitation.[9] Thus the new administration undertook to reorient the Congolese economy toward a capitalist system based on free labor, low transport costs, and smaller land concessions. The result was a more modern and rational use of resources, producing increased capital investment and industrial development. As a Belgian fiscal expert later noted: "Investment in the Congo decreased until 1908 . . . [and increased from 1909 on]. . . . There was a tendency to deemphasize commercial exchanges with the natives, and to concentrate on the exploitation of raw materials."[10]

Contradictions arose, of course, between the two systems of production. Older corporations, still based on an outdated economy, continued to exploit the Bakongo railways and most waterways. However, it was various newly arrived international cartels, including SHCB, Forminière, Union Minière, Société Générale, Empain, Nagelmackers, Lever, Williams, Ryan, and Guggenheim, that received the strong political support of such colonial administrators as Louis Franck and Georges Moulaert. By 1920, financial and industrial capitalism had won the battle and, as Table 1 shows, revenue from colonial investments was soon to exceed profits from metropolitan industries.

The fact of mercantilist and capitalist penetration in the Congo

TABLE 1

Net Income of Industrial Enterprises
in Belgium and in the Congo
(*Percent earned on investments*)

Year	Enterprises in Belgium	Enterprises in the Congo
1936–39	7.00%	10.10%
1947–50	6.88	15.07
1951–54	8.20	21.48
1955	8.19	18.47
1956	9.40	20.16
1957	9.49	21.00

SOURCE: Joye and Lewin, p. 57.

does not by itself explain the primacy of economic variables as determinants of the colonization process. As Nicolas Poulantzas stresses, a given mode of production is characterized not only by its specific economic relationships, but also by "a typical combination of structures and ideologies determined by the preponderance of those relationships."[11] Thus, to demonstrate the direct relationship between colonialism and capitalism, it is indispensable to analyze not only the structures of European capitalist enterprises operating in the Congo, but also the interrelationship of those structures with the institutions and ideologies of the colonial government. For instance, capitalist participation in the colonization of the Congo produced a distinct ideology based on purely economic considerations. The gradual evolution of this ideology is evident in many documents and statements issued over the years by colonial authorities. At first, ideological premises were almost completely absent, and colonization was presented flatly, with no attempt at justification, as an act of economic exploitation. As King Léopold so bluntly stated in 1901: "To say that what the white man produces in Africa must be spent in Africa for the benefit of Negroes only is simply a heresy, an injustice, and a mistake."[12] More often, though, the colonists' real designs were masked by humanitarian statements. Official circulars of the early 1920's, for instance, continually stressed that the natives should not remain idle once taxes were paid and other legal obligations met. In these terms, idleness was considered a sign that the colonists were neglecting their duty toward their black subjects.

Throughout the whole colonial period, the colonial government consistently advanced the argument that the civilization of the native population promoted cheap labor, and that taxes were a basic civilizing influence. In the words of Thomas Hodgkin, the Belgian colonial rule was based on the principle that "the prime interest of the mass is in welfare and consumer goods, . . . not liberty, and on the conviction that it is possible, by expert administration, to arrest social and political change."[13] This ideological postulate implied a close interdependence between economic structures and activities on the one hand and the Catholic missions and the colonial administration on the other. The missions were entrusted with an educational system tailored to the maintenance of law and order and the smooth functioning of the colonial economy. Stressing the importance of missionary work in central Africa, Monsignor Roelens asserted, in agreement with the "entire colonial elite," that "only the Christian Catholic religion, based on sacred authority, is capable of changing the natives' views, of giving our Africans a clear and intimate consciousness of their duties, and of inspiring in them respect for authority and a spirit of loyalty toward Belgium."[14] However, official documents make it clear that the Congolese educational system, of which the missions were a key element, was aimed primarily at forwarding the colony's economic and industrial expansion:

The better educated a person is, the stronger his economic performance, and thus the higher his income. Mass education will have a beneficial effect on the population's productivity; a worker or peasant who can read or count is more likely to progress than one who cannot. It is plain that the entire Congolese economy will be affected by [mass education].[15]

Unlike Protestant missions, which were strictly limited to educational activities due to their meager financial resources, Catholic missions were able to extend large-scale efforts to the community as a whole. In addition to evangelical activities, Catholic missions organized isolated, self-sufficient communities in which education and agricultural work were combined in order to meet the operating cost of the missionary stations.[16] Such practices were consistent with the underlying assumption of the colonial educational policy, an assumption that vocational training, limited to a few technical skills, would best serve the interests of the colony. Thus normal schools inculcated in future schoolteachers "a love of work, the habit of a continuous effort . . . and respect for the authorities"; commercial schools trained clerks, accountants, and typists; and vocational schools trained carpenters, metalworkers, and printers.[17] The only institutions offering any literary education were the seminaries established by the Catholic Church to train African priests and a school for medical assistants in Léopoldville.

Two further examples show how capitalism dominated colonial society. First, increased prosperity brought significant changes in the role of the territorial administrator. In the beginning, this official had acted as a kind of paterfamilias, dispensing justice, arbitrating local disputes, regulating taxes, researching customary laws, and even writing ethnographic essays on the people of his constituency; in sum, the authority of the territorial administrator corresponded to his deep involvement with the native population.[18] From 1933 onward, however, a growing bureaucratization at the highest administrative levels, accompanied by an increase in the administrative and economic tasks assigned to the lower levels, caused a decline in the importance of such intermediary officials as district commissioners.[19] After the war effort of 1940–44, numerous local officials expressed complaints like the following:

> We are no longer governing the natives, or administering for them. We are administering for the Europeans and exploiting the blacks with a false colonial philanthropy. . . . Conditions are worsening as civil servants become mere agricultural agents, producers of cotton, builders of bridges and roads, and commercial expeditors for the production of rubber, oil, coffee, gold, and copper. The act of administration has lost all meaning, for though the economic instinct is the lowest of all political instincts, it has nonetheless received universal primacy. [Our] policy toward the natives is degenerating rapidly, [and] signs of this decline are to be found in the basic principles of Belgian colonization, [principles] aimed more at exploitation than at civilization.[20]

Also worth noting are the interlocking directorates of Belgian corporations and the colonial administration. The colony held an impressive investment portfolio that included shares in many parastatal (semipublic) corporations, chartered companies,* mineral industries, and transport enterprises. In principle, ownership of this portfolio should have allowed the colonial administration nearly full control over key enterprises, and thus considerable influence on the whole Congolese economy. In practice, the Belgian colonial authorities always left effective direction of these enterprises to representatives of private corporations. Thus management of Forminière, Vicicongo, and the Katanga Special Committee (CSK) was assigned to Société Générale, Cominière, and Union Minière. Interpenetration of private and official functions reached such extremes, in fact, that most top colonial officials were given high posts in the private sector upon retiring from government service. This tradition, begun with Albert Thys, Léopold's aide-de-camp and creator of the Congo's first industrial complex, continued with Emile Francqui (governor of the Société Générale), Pierre Orts (Bank of Brussels), Georges Moulaert (Kilo-Moto), Gaston Heenen (administrator of fifteen corporations), Alfred Moeler (Forminière, Cotonco), and Pierre Cornelis (Forminière).[21]

---

* The chartered companies were holding corporations created at the same time as the Congo Free State.

The same held true for most high officials and congressmen who had served in the metropolitan administration, or who were otherwise considered experts in colonial affairs.[22]

The Colonial Bureaucracy. The primacy of economic concerns in the colonial venture allowed the development of a centralized, structurally immobile bureaucracy that incorporated neither internal counterbalances nor open channels for political expression—a system of government, in short, devoid of all political vision. From its inception, the colonial government's institutional framework remained essentially unchanged. King Léopold alone held all legislative and executive power in the Free State until the Belgian Parliament promulgated the Colonial Charter in March 1908.[23] Though the new Charter was intended to eliminate the crude absolutism of Léopold's rule, Jean Stengers asserts that it served only to reinforce an established centralism:

> This may seem paradoxical at first glance. After all, what could have been more centralized than the system practiced by Léopold II . . . [in which] all initiative emanated from the king himself? But . . . this was not a structural, organic centralism; nothing could have prevented the king from delegating considerable power to the governor or other top officials. Under the Colonial Charter, centralism became organic, and the governmental apparatus and all agencies of control were established at Brussels. Since the Parliament and the Colonial Council had to exercise their control from Brussels, . . . it was no longer possible to implement political authority . . . within the colony without changing the whole system. In other words, decentralization became impossible without modifying the structure of the Charter itself.[24]

Though the proliferation of Léopoldville's administrative bureaucracy after World War II[25] and the creation of such new control institutions as the Governing Council allowed the colonial administration greater freedom in decision making, the Congo never reached the point of political takeoff.

The centralization of political power is often assumed to be the product of rationality and efficiency. However, such was not the case in the Belgian Congo, where centralization existed together with an incredibly clumsy decision-making and procedural apparatus. For instance, any decision concerning the colony was made in the following manner:

> A draft project had first to be prepared, often by a special commission. Interested departments of the Ministry, often more than one, then had to have an opportunity to study and propose changes. When this was completed the

draft was sent to Léopoldville, with an explanatory memorandum. The services of the Governor-General then studied the project. It next had to be sent to the provincial councils, which met once a year. The next stage was submission to the Council of Government. Finally there followed a reexamination by the Governor-General, an expression of his definitive opinion and retransmission to Brussels. There the draft returned to the relevant departments, was filtered through the Minister's cabinet, and put before the Minister for his decision. It had then to be submitted to the Colonial Council which often, if the problem was important, designated an ad hoc subcommittee to give it thorough study. At each step in the process, progress of the decree was at the mercy of vacations, absences in Africa, changes of ministers; not only that, but the whole process had to take place in two languages.[26]

Excessive centralization and clumsy decision-making procedures were not the only factors limiting the political sphere within the Belgian colonial system. Also crucial was the absence of an imperialist tradition in Belgium, which prevented either internal or external review of colonial policies. Leon Trotsky's analysis of the Belgian colonial enterprise is quite relevant on this point:

The Belgians [are] the archetype of a totally commercialized people, worthy, industrious, stable indeed, but of a people who [have] renounced all national visions, dreams, ideals; of a people whose almost universal ambition [has] become individual wealth and comfort. Such a people have in a sense given up; they have given up because altogether too much has happened to them; they have endured too many disasters, humiliations and defeats, too many enemy occupations, too many alien armies marching across them. Such a people receives a thoroughgoing impression of its own impotence to decide its fate. Even its boldest and most energetic spirits are apt to opt for personal comfort and security at all costs. In politics they become neither left nor right, neither progressive nor reactionary, neither nationalist nor internationalist; they become "Belgianized."[27]

Belgian colonial policy was subject to none of the metropolitan controls that normally governed British or French ventures. Annual reports of colonial officials to the Parliament and speeches by the Governor-General before the Governing Council both constantly stressed the basically sane and pragmatic nature of the Belgian colonial system. The Belgian public was quite content to bask in reflected colonial glory, while, as Young stresses, few of Belgium's formal political institutions had any real control over colonial policy:

The Belgian Parliament was required to vote on the Congo budget but this became a strictly pro-forma ritual. Not only did the administration have authorization to transfer items from one budget category to another but the budget itself frequently was not submitted for parliamentary discussion until six months after the start of the fiscal year. Until the appearance of nationalist stirrings, the Congo was only a matter of concern to Parliament when it required a Belgian subsidy. Debates were brief and perfunctory; the large portion of public investment which went through the sundry parastatal organizations entirely escaped scrutiny.[28]

An attitude of complacency also typified those political parties from which sharp criticism of colonial policy might have been expected. Although the Belgian Socialist Party (PSB) constantly invoked the principle of self-determination for Congolese peoples, it did so mostly from electoral and domestic considerations.[29] Specifically, by demanding decentralization and more effective parliamentary control over colonial affairs, the PSB was merely attempting to retrieve the colonial ministerial portfolio that it had held briefly during a protracted governmental crisis in 1946. Expression of concern for colonial affairs was limited to piecemeal criticism of paternalism,[30] labor problems,[31] excessive land concessions,[32] and the delegation of authority to private interests in Katanga.[33] Joseph Van Bilsen, head of the Marzorati research team that as late as 1955–56 was the only group to forward a plan for Congolese independence, was shunned by all administration figures in Belgium and the Congo.

The Belgian colonial system was as remarkably free of internal restraints as it was immune to outside criticism. Censorial and consultative institutions like the Colonial Council in Brussels, the Governing Council in Léopoldville, and the Committee for the Protection of Natives never performed central roles in determining policy and goals. The Colonial Council could discuss details but never overall policy, and it had no legislative authority at all.[34] The Governing Council was a mixed body whose chief purpose was to supply an open forum to various European pressure groups; in fact, all of these groups attended the meetings with widely varying objectives.[35] The Committee for the Protection of Natives, originally intended as a sort of moral ombudsman, did make important contributions in the Congo Free State. However, it later compromised much of its moral potential when it became a captive body of the colonial administration.[36]

To sum up, all aspects of the Belgian colonial venture were subordinated to purely economic considerations. The educational system produced the skilled and semiskilled workers needed for the exploitation of the Congo, while missionary organizations instilled in these same workers a morality based on order and authority. The cumbersome administrative apparatus functioned at the command of commercial and industrial trusts, affected neither by the politics of distant Brussels nor by urgent problems close at hand. Only once, at the Economic Round Table of 1960, did a cogent dialogue take place between native Congolese and representatives of Belgian trusts. It is not surprising that European economic interests prevailed again at this meeting. Nor is it surprising, given such a total lack of communication between rulers and their subjects, that colonial authorities were eventually overwhelmed by the demands of aggressive Congolese nationalists.

Independence and the Emergence of Political Discourse

The coming of Congolese independence was a process that can be divided into three stages. By the end of the first stage, it had become clear that the values on which the colonial institutions rested were chiefly those of economic rentability and economic exploitation. In the second stage, questions of a distinctly political nature arose both inside and outside the colonial system. The third stage saw the politically rigid colonial system become totally helpless in the face of the contradictions it had created. With the collapse of the colonial system, power politics took over. I have already dealt with the first of these stages; in the following section I shall be concerned with the two remaining.

It would be useful to determine at the outset exactly which groups and social forces first introduced political discourse into the Congo. In current analyses of African politics, the combination of forces inherent in westernization is often seen as producing a social category new to Africa, that of the educated elite whose members, after absorbing Western culture, are able to lead their countries to independence.[37] It is rarely stressed that colonialism contains the seeds of its own destruction, and that African nationalism itself bears the stamp of a highly unstable political system. A colonial society may undertake to create a modernizing elite, acting on the assumption that the native population will accept a modernizing social system based on universalism and efficiency and will perform economic and administrative roles within this system. Such an assumption may prove invalid, though, as the racism inherent in the colonial situation makes it impossible for the native population to establish a functional relationship with the white minority or to enjoy the social rewards of modernization.

The first blows against the colonial structure in the Congo came not from any native intelligentsia, but from diverse elements within, or associated with, the Belgian administration. At the end of World War II, signs of discontent appeared among some groups of Europeans in the Congo, and for the first time voices were raised expressing profound disillusionment with the ends and means of colonization. One of the clearest expressions of this discontent was a series of articles and pamphlets, later gathered and published by Antoine Rubbens under the title *Dettes de Guerre* (War Debts). This book made clear some basic contradictions of the colonial system as junior civil servants directed harsh criticism toward excessive centralization and bureaucracy, and toward the demoralized state of the territorial administration. In the book's conclusion, Rubbens stressed that "there can be no easy solution to this situation. An extensive effort is needed [to solve] political problems arising from the Congo's relationship with Belgium, its administrative institutions, and its native organizations. This massive task can only be achieved through close collaboration between those who are in touch with the facts of the situation; that is, between true colonials."[38]

At the same time, European settlers, associated since 1944 in the Colonization Union (UCOL), were exerting strong pressure on the government to "take all possible steps in order to obtain for the white population in the Congo the liberties granted by the Belgian constitution to its nationals, and to promote, by all available means, the growth of European colonization."[39] Addressing the Settlers' Commission in Brussels in 1946, a UCOL spokesman told of the Belgian settlers' anger: "They do not want to be regarded as foreigners in what is now their own country. The Congo must therefore remain Belgian, perhaps with a status similar to that of a British dominion."[40]

Catholic missionaries, too, grew disenchanted with a policy whose stress on the expansion of capitalism increasingly interfered with the task of civilizing the African population.[41] Finally, pressure was felt from an international community that, as former Governor-General Pierre Rijkmans put it, "had decided to put an end to colonial regimes."[42]

The colonial government became cautious when faced with these sometimes contradictory pressures. Governor Pétillon, for instance, felt that the subject of political emancipation would involve so many delicate problems and arouse such intense emotions that it would be best not to broach it at all.[43] Until the end of the colonial period, an attitude of distrust toward political expression was widespread in the colonial administration, in both Brussels and Léopoldville. As late as August 1958, Auguste Buisseret, a former colonial minister, declared: "There is a large body of verbal and literary expression in the Congo that is distinct from tangible facts and realities, and that does not represent the overall state of mind of the Congolese people."[44]

Reforms aimed at eventual decolonization still betrayed their authors' complete lack of political acumen, as these reforms incorporated substantively irrational changes that were structurally incompatible with the system to which they were applied.[45] To assuage new political demands, the Belgian administration offered the principle of "controlled gradualism"; in answer to the political impatience of the Congolese intelligentsia, it proposed a total restructuring of the administrative apparatus; to solve the problem of the native elite, it produced the same matriculation decree that had been implemented by the Free State in May of 1895; and though Belgium lacked any imperial tradition, the administration hastily formulated a plan for a Belgo-Congolese community.

By 1955, the colonial regime had reached a point beyond which the explosive political tempo[46] of radical nationalism, with its demand for immediate independence, could only clash with the balky pace of a colonial bureaucracy no longer able to integrate or direct the forces of political change. The key event of 1955 was the publication in Brussels of Joseph Van Bilsen's proposed thirty-year plan for the political emancipation of the Congo. As soon as they appeared, Van Bilsen's proposals were enthusiastically seconded by Congolese intellectuals in the eloquent Manifesto published in the July-August issue of *Conscience Africaine*. This demand to the Belgians for a straightforward statement on decolonization and independence served to intensify the politicization and revolutionary potential of the whole Congo. According to *Africa Special Reports*, "the response was electric. Word swept Léopoldville's African city and filtered deep into the Congo bush. . . . Africans who couldn't read posted treasured copies on their walls. The Manifesto was sold at a football game, and amazed Europeans watched African fans buy it up like pieces of chickwanga bread."[47] A similar statement was made by M. C. C. Debacker, head of the information service in Léopoldville: "Its publication . . . had the same effect as a thunderstorm from out of a clear blue sky, and gave rise to impassioned comment. . . . It was no longer possible to doubt that the Congo had been drawn into the same great historical and political revolution that was sweeping all of Africa."[48]

The Bakongo Alliance (ABAKO) answered the Manifesto with a countermanifesto of its own, distinguished by its more radical tone, its lucid critique of the colonial regime, and its advocacy of democratic struggle between ethnic groups.[49] The Bangala leaders' uncompromising attitude toward the Catholic Bangala intellectuals who wrote the *Conscience Africaine* Manifesto has sometimes been viewed as an expression of Bakongo tribal fears that the Bangala would claim the leading role in the emancipation struggle. It is far more likely, however, that ABAKO originated in direct opposition to Belgian colonial rule.[50] In fact, not long after issuing its countermanifesto, ABAKO became the leading popular organization engaged in the struggle for independence.

ABAKO became the champion of nationalist aspirations in two stages. First, ABAKO candidates won 78 percent of elective seats in the Léopoldville communal elections of 1957. Since the Bakongo constituted only 46.5 percent of Léopoldville's total population, this victory demonstrates overwhelming support for ABAKO among ethnic blocs from Equateur, Kwango-Kwilu, and Kasai.[51] ABAKO was then able to expand and consolidate its position in the Bakongo region, though it lacked organization and leadership after the arrest of party leaders in the 1959 Léopoldville riots. While these election results demonstrated the political awareness of city dwellers, noteworthy examples of intense and spontaneous politicization were observed firsthand in rural areas of the Congo as well. A confidential report by acting Governor-General Schoeller, who had just completed a trip through the Bakongo area, warned of the serious situation there: "It is universally agreed that political contact with the population has become impossible. . . . Any advice, dialogue, or attempt at persuasion on the part of the administration, Europeans, or Congolese who are considered collaborators with the white regime is rejected out of hand."[52]

In many respects the Bakongo region now behaved as though it were already independent, and thus withheld tax payments, boycotted the 1959 elections, and substituted newly created ABAKO chapters for local elements of the colonial administration:

Unlike what occurred in the Léopoldville commune, the installation of these [party] chapters was overwhelmingly spontaneous. Each center, from the village to the district headquarters, organized its own chapter and reported its composition to the Léopoldville central committee, which had no choice but to endorse it. . . . The chapters were largely autonomous, depending primarily upon the initiative of local populations and their leaders.[53]

A similar movement arose, though in a different form and to a lesser degree, in the neighboring region of Kwango-Kwilu. Here, a well-trained, well-educated elite organized the African Mutual Party (PSA), and successfully established its influence in rural areas. The emphasis on leadership as the guiding principle of the party was made clear in its motto: "The intellectuals conceive, the old support, and the young execute."[54] Disciplined PSA leaders were indeed able to accomplish an enormous task of political education among the masses.

The hostility between the PSA and colonial administrators in the key Kwango-Kwilu region assumed a pattern determined largely by popular political sentiment: intrusions by Belgian civil servants into political meetings caused mob violence. Such violence in turn forced PSA leaders into open, if not always willing, opposition to the administration in order to draw the support of the radicalized local population.[55] As in the area controlled by ABAKO, taxes went unpaid and rural elections organized by the colonial administration were widely boycotted: "People refused to appear for the census, or mothers refused to appear with their children for medical examinations, or they asked that they be paid for bringing their children for medical examinations on the argument that the Belgians would not have insisted on doing this all these years if it did not bring them some advantage."[56] In contrast to Bakongo leaders, the Kwilu elite constantly stressed the necessity for organization, discipline, and hierarchy. As Weiss puts it: "They [the leaders] desired to prove that they could make the administrative system work just as well as the Belgians . . . but every move in that direction inevitably sustained the system which was so obnoxious to the masses."[57]

Civil disobedience was not limited to these two regions of Léopoldville province, but spread through territory controlled by Lumumba's Congolese National Movement (MNC-Lumumba). Here again, protests took a different form from that in the Kwango-Kwilu or Bakongo regions. In Orientale Province and the district of Maniéma, the charismatic figure of Patrice Lumumba dominated the politicization of the masses. Lumumba's name alone was enough to cause mass unrest in the provincial capital of Stanleyville, and his arrest and trial there in October 1959 caused widespread violence against European cars, welfare centers, public buildings, and all other symbols of colonial domination.[58] In the Maniéma district, district chiefs, paramount chiefs, ushers, and soldiers faced public wrath as Congolese servants of the hated colonial regime. Early in 1959, the MNC-Lumumba set up the popular tribunals that were to reappear during the 1964–65 rebellions in the eastern provinces.[59]

In brief, the coming of independence was marked by a remarkable growth of political consciousness among the masses, in which the Congolese people not only backed their leaders, but forced them to take a more radical stance than they might otherwise have taken. Whatever its roots—nationalism as in the case of ABAKO, organizational efficiency as in the case of the PSA, or charismatic leadership as in the case of the MNC-Lumumba—this political awakening was largely responsible for the abrupt end of colonial rule. The exclusively political nature of these protest movements is illustrated by the fact that none of them offered any concrete economic programs, structural reforms, or plans for the future. It was felt that once freedom and self-determination had been achieved, all else would follow.

Independence and the Emergence of Power Politics

Another basic aspect of Congolese independence was the progressive emergence of a political class of petty bureaucrats. This class in fact dominated the politicization of the Congo after independence. In this section, I will analyze the origin of this political class, and show the importance of bureaucratic officeholders to Congolese social structures and political processes.

The Evolués. From the end of World War II, there existed in the Congo a small bureaucratic intelligentsia whose position in the colonial hierarchy was highly ambivalent. The *évolués* (lit. "those who have emerged") knew very well that they could never cross the racial barrier established by their colonial benefactors. Yet they did wish to be regarded as members of an elite group distinct from the Congolese masses; in fact, just as widespread criticisms and reappraisals of colonialism were appearing toward the end of World War II, the évolués were trying to barter their loyalty and obedience to the colonial regime for a special status within it. The conservative, even timid, manner in which the évolués expressed their grievances is revealed in one of the lesser-known documents of the period, a memorandum presented to the district commissioner in March 1944 following the mutiny of the Luluabourg garrison. After praising the "great work of civilization" undertaken by the Belgians, the representative of the Kasai évolués went on to say:

Apart from all these kind things, Sir, some small errors still remain that the government could easily correct. The first and most important of these is that the existence of the évolué class is not recognized. . . . The Europeans have kept such a distance from the évolués . . . that even the best administrator today is unaware of what the natives are doing. . . . The backward masses have more direct relations with the évolués than with the Europeans, [and] the évolués are, in a way, mediators between the white man and the native. . . . It is in everybody's interest that we request: that we be heard weekly by an agent who will investigate our claims . . . (although our intentions are good, we are still treated as savages); decent housing conditions . . . and second-class ship and train tickets; that the penitentiary system not be applied indiscriminately to the évolués; [that attention be given the fact that] insults like "monkey" and "macaque" are frequently used, though prohibited by administrative regulations. Before ending, Sir, the évolués would like to deny rumors according to which we instigated [the mutiny] at Luluabourg. . . . It is very sad that the Europeans will not acknowledge what we have done to demonstrate our attachment, and this in spite of the numerous proofs that we have given. . . . To those Europeans who are unaware of it . . . we say, Sir, that of the two factions formed [in the mutiny], all of the évolués chose the European side."[60]

Thus the évolués were asking neither reforms nor equality of opportunity, but rather acknowledgment of their role as mediators between white men and "savages." The deferential tone of the évolué memorandum was more the result of tactical considerations than an awareness of their isolated situation, for the évolués believed that as long as they expressed themselves with restraint the white establishment would value them as trusted interlocutors, but that if they grew aggressive in their demands the Europeans would lump them together with other self-seeking minorities. Ten years later, Patrice Lumumba was to use the same tone of polite mediation in his book, *Congo, My Country*:

> It is important that the Congolese elite who enjoy the confidence of their fellow Congolese and can communicate freely with them without any mental reservation, should work in a close collaboration with the Belgian people to enlighten them on . . . the conduct of the native affairs. It is through the Congolese elite that the Belgians will plunge into the depths of the African soul. . . . The native elite, whose loyalty has been officially acknowledged by a decision of the High Court, should be regarded as a genuine ally of the Belgians; it should form with them a united and dynamic team in order to continue the work of civilizing [the Congolese]. . . . The elite must be closely associated to the goals of the Belgo-Congolese community and act as an intermediary between their people and the colonizer by taking an adequate share in the conduct of public affairs.[61]

The attitude of Congolese évolués can better be understood in the context of a sociological phenomenon that Michel Crozier identifies as typical of bureaucratic organizations. Crozier asserts that any such organization gives rise to areas of psychological or political ambiguity that can be eliminated neither by the introduction of new regulations nor by constraints inherent in the bureaucratic structure. It is in response to such ambiguities that informal power relationships, together with their subdependencies and power conflicts, develop parallel to the formal hierarchy. Individuals who gain control in these areas of ambiguity will wield considerable power over those at the bottom of the hierarchy, says Crozier, and it is in the very bureaucratic organizations where the areas of ambiguity are the fewest and the formal structure the most rigid that these parallel power relationships become crucial.[62]

In the Congo, the bureaucratic hierarchy was not merely rigid, but physically and politically oppressive. The specific institutional manifestation of parallel power relations within this hierarchy was the emergence of évolué clubs and associations. These groups insulated the évolués from the harmful effects of colonization by helping them maintain their petty privileges, and by reinforcing their feeling that they formed a special group distinct from the Congolese masses.

One of the most notable attempts to classify Congolese political groups is that of René Lemarchand, who uses the language of structural-functional analysis in order to distinguish "functionally diffuse organizations" involving the "cooperation of individuals drawn from one or several ethnically related groups" from "functionally specific organizations" in which activities, rights, and membership are precisely defined.[63] However, Lemarchand and others generally fail to distinguish the manifest from the latent functions of such associations; i.e., they do not examine the specific roles of such organizations within the colonial system. Unfortunately, we have at our disposal very few studies of associational life in the Congolese urban setting. The main sources on this topic are a doctoral dissertation on African leadership at Elisabethville,[64] an essay on the political role of regional associations in Léopoldville,[65] and the weekly journal of the Léopoldville évolués, *La Voix du Congolais*.

The Congolese press of the preindependence period reveals an impressive growth in the number of tribal and regional associations, and of évolué clubs in particular. By 1947, some 110 clubs with a total of 5,609 members had been organized in various Congolese cities. Between 1952 and 1956, the number of clubs increased from 131 to 317, and their membership from 7,661 to 15,345.[66] The number of territorial, tribal, and regional associations grew also, with 85 new ones officially registered in Léopoldville in 1956.[67] The proliferation of these clubs was due partly to the rapid growth of the évolué population and partly to the implementation of a matriculation decree that granted special privileges to "loyal and civilized servants of the colony." It also demonstrated the pressing need, caused by tentative reforms affecting the status of the Congolese intelligentsia, for new opportunities to demonstrate leadership potential.[68] Thus the plethora of titles and offices in associations of every kind, all of which had a president, two vice-presidents, a "founding" president, and several commissioners and advisors with the word "notable" included in their titles.

In many respects, the political life of the clubs and associations exhibited patterns that were to emerge later on a larger scale. Competition for the presidencies of these associations was keen, and the nominations or confirmations of committee members were accompanied by political intrigues and recognizable electoral campaigns. Indeed, victory in a presidential campaign within a club could open the door to a similar post on the outside. Paul Caprasse notes that the majority of club members joined specifically to be considered civilized by the Europeans, and that Europeans in fact served as associate presidents and vice-presidents in most clubs. Such a strong yearning for power and respect accounts for the proliferation and growth of these associations, and for the practice of one person's joining several clubs whose goals and principles might conflict.

The Prominence of the Petty Officeholder. No precise definition of the term "évolué" has been offered here because this term was highly ambiguous even when used by colonial authorities. As Young notes, misunderstandings arose in the Congo about the precise criteria for matriculated status, the procedures for granting it, and the exact benefits it was to bring.[69] More significant was the eventual incorporation of many évolués into a group of petty functionaries in the governmental, missionary, and corporate bureaucracies of the colony. This group of bureaucrats was to supply the majority of Congolese political leaders in the postindependence era.[70]

The relative importance of the functionary within the colonial social structure is shown indirectly by the small numbers of the Congolese engaged in business or professional activities. In the last years of the colonial regime, a small African trading class began to appear in major cities. For instance, a 1955 survey showed that Léopoldville had 8,331 self-employed persons, half of whom were engaged in commercial and banking activities.[71] By 1959, their number had increased to 19,000.

TABLE 2

Self-Employed Persons in the Congo in 1959

Occupation	Congolese	Europeans
Planters	2,481	1,900
Artisans	3,567	1,125
Traders	11,113	3,636
Small businessmen	1,576	1,451
Liberal professions	29	750
Other	297	585
TOTAL	19,063	9,447

SOURCE: Jacques Ceulemans, "Le Rôle social de la classe moyenne africaine," in "Journées d'Etudes Africaines," *Le Rôle du secteur privé dans l'expansion actuelle de l'économie africaine* (Foire Internationale de Gand, 1959), p. 57.

In evaluating the figures in Table 2 it should be borne in mind that the great majority of the African enterprises were modest, one-man operations.[72] Moreover, the would-be Congolese entrepreneur faced formidable obstacles, including the establishment of regional monopolies by Portuguese and Greek traders, the colonial government's policy of denying Africans access to credit or the right to own land, and the generally tight bureaucratic control of any Congolese who might seek to escape the heavy hand of colonial domination.

The prominence of the petty bureaucrat in the Congolese social structure is more directly indicated by the great number of officeholders in the colony. In 1960, more than 100,000 Congolese, or about one-seventh of urban wage earners, were employed by the colonial administration. This group was divisible into two major categories, that of civil servants with administrative status, who were permanent employees subject to all regulations of the administration; and that of auxiliary agents, usually recruited on an ad hoc basis.[73] In 1960, some 22,880 persons were permanently employed in the colonial administration. Of these, 12,600 were Belgians occupying the highest positions in the civil service, the army, and the educational institutions (the top nine categories in Table 3). Before 1959, when a group

TABLE 3

Salaries of Statutory and Auxiliary Personnel
in the Civil Service, 1960

Position	Number of Europeans	Number of Congolese	Annual salary in Belgian francs
Positions carrying salary of more than 500,000 francs	40	—	500,000+
Director General	90	—	500,000
Director	380	—	424,000
Assistant Director	390	—	365,000
Principal Bureau Chief	2,200	—	317,000
Assistant Bureau Chief	2,800	—	259,100
First Principal Supervisor	1,690	9	216,500
Principal Supervisor	1,976	24	163,200
Supervisor	1,774	726	115,300
Chief Clerk	—	1,078	97,550
Principal Clerk	—	1,157	78,600
Clerk	—	1,340	67,400
Principal Assistant Clerk	—	1,435	62,100
Assistant Clerk	—	1,911	56,800
Auxiliary Clerk	—	2,125	51,500
Auxiliary Clerk (2d category)	—	1,745	40,300

SOURCE: Dupriez.

of 750 Congolese attained the rank of supervisor, none of the 10,000 African clerks employed by the administration could advance beyond the grade of head clerk.

At the same time, more than 90,600 Africans were hired as auxiliary agents. Of these, 23,000 constituted the rank and file of the colonial army, 9,000 were semiqualified workers employed in medical services, 28,000 were roadmen working in the countryside, and 30,600 were teachers. In the main the two categories of civil servant consumed about one-fourth of the Congolese GNP, which reached 48 million Belgian francs in 1958.[74]

An ordinance that took effect in January of 1959 definitively separated statutory from auxiliary workers by establishing a uniform wage scale for the entire colony, and by setting the wages of statutory bureaucrats at more than double those of auxiliary personnel with similar qualifications.

Thus an auxiliary clerk at the lowest permanent rank in the civil service hierarchy, married and the father of two children, earned about 3,400 Belgian francs in January 1960. His opposite number, a semiqualified typist with the same number of dependents, but who was employed on a contractual basis, earned 1,950 francs in Léopoldville, or 1,225 francs at Feshi or Kahemba in the district of Kwango.[75]

A report by the International Labor Office confirmed the gross distortions in the ordinance: "The wages of the least qualified administration employees have been . . . made as comparable as possible to the wages of non-African employees."[76] Private companies relied as heavily upon these bureaucrats as did the colonial administration, and the disparity in pay between bureaucrats and other workers was as great in business as it was in government: "It is common to find a typist with no qualifications but a relatively good knowledge of French and typing whose wage is twice that of an experienced mechanic or an able truck driver."[77]

The Congolese elite was molded almost entirely by the structure of colonial society, becoming what Georges Balandier calls an "administrative bourgeoisie." As Young points out:

The nature of elite recruitment has crucial significance in determining the political perspectives of the Congo's leadership. The political resources available to the elite did not include economic power. The prospect of a transfer of political authority to this elite implied, at least for a long transitional period, a policy where the economic and political structures would be . . . completely divorced. The new Congolese elite had virtually no vested interest in the economic and social status quo. . . . From its bureaucratic genesis, [it] had derived one real vested interest: the state.[78]

It must be added that the administrative bourgeoisie that Young describes consisted entirely of incompetent clerks, and had no top level of administrative experts. This fact was to have disastrous implications for the social stratification and administrative capabilities of the independent Congolese state.

The coming of independence had little organizational effect on the Congo's bureaucratic machine; the distinction between statutory and auxiliary employees was retained, though some low grades previously classified as auxiliary were made statutory after 1960. Until Mobutu's takeover, however, the Congolese civil service was plagued by sharp increases in personnel and, more significantly, by the heavy drain this new personnel imposed on the national budget. Between June 1960 and June 1963, for instance, 8,000 statutory positions were added to the civil service rolls, partly because of the creation of 21 new provinces between August 1962 and May 1963. As Table 4 indicates, the increase in statutory posts was greatest in the lowest ranks of the administration, where pressure upon patronage-oriented political institutions was most keenly felt; indeed, the number of clerks

TABLE 4

Statutory Positions in the Congo in June 1960 and June 1963

Position	Number in June 1960	Number in June 1963
Secretary General	1	1
Provincial Secretary	10	14
Director (central government)	70	44
Provincial Director	41	57
Assistant Director	239	275
Principal Bureau Chief	10	25
Bureau Chief	501	580
Assistant Bureau Chief	825	814
Principal Supervisor	980	645
Supervisor	1,230	1,199
Assistant Supervisor	1,590	2,004
Chief Clerk	—	1,358
Principal Clerk	1,321	1,604
Clerk	3,618	9,709
Assistant Clerk	1,406	499
Principal Usher	—	1
Usher	—	33
TOTAL	11,842	18,862

SOURCE: Verhaegen, "Traitements"; CEP-IRES, *Archives*, doc. MF 160/21/1.

in one category leapt from 3,618 to 9,709 between 1960 and 1963. The bulk of the statutory employees remained in the areas of public health, transportation, police, and administration of the interior, all of which had been organized by the colonial administration.[79] However, not all of the new employees remained in Léopoldville, as would have been the case before independence. In 1963, 4,373 statutory agents were working in various departments of the central government and 1,860 in the Léopoldville city hall, while the rest were employed in provincial administrations at Bukavu, Luluabourg, Stanleyville, Elisabethville, and Coquilhatville.[80] Some 10,000 European civil servants employed by the colony before June 1960 fled the Congo during the unrest following independence. They were later replaced by 2,500 Belgian and other foreign technicians whose salaries were partly subsidized by the Belgian government and partly by the UN, UNESCO, and other international agencies.[81]

It is considerably more difficult to find reliable statistics on the auxiliary employees in the Congolese civil service. According to some estimates, their number increased substantially after independence, and their distribution by qualification was as follows:[82]

Highly qualified	5,000
Qualified	10,000
Semiqualified	15,000
Specialized	20,000
Semispecialized	25,000
Manual workers	30,000
TOTAL	105,000

According to Alois Kabangi, who became civil service minister in 1962, there were some 300,000 auxiliary workers in the beginning of that year, three times more than in 1960. Since the local officials who hired the majority of auxiliary workers were often reluctant to give precise information about their employment practices, more reliable estimates than these are impossible. Available statistics do suggest, however, that pressure from familial, tribal, and personal client groups was greatest at the local level, and that it was at this level that most employment abuses took place. Here are some examples of employment practices in provincial administrations after December 1962:

In the province of South Kasai, long torn by political feuds, there were 625 statutory and 5,593 auxiliary agents at the end of January 1963, five times more than before June 1960. In the province of Cuvette Centrale, politically dormant after independence, 884 statutory and 3,776 auxiliary agents were working in the administration in April 1963, three times more than before June 1960.

In some provincial departments at Bukavu, it was not unusual for an auxiliary agent to kick back part of his salary to the patron-politician who found him his position in the civil service.

In almost all the provinces the author visited, complaints were heard that the provincial government was still paying former auxiliary agents who had not been working in the administration for as long as two years. In spite of repeated demands from the central government, no list of contractual agents paid by the provinces was ever produced. In most cases, these agents had been hired by influential ministers or cabinet members rather than by any department itself.[83]

Substantial increases also occurred in the number of ministers, members of Parliament, provincial legislators, and others directly linked to Congolese political institutions. In July 1962, this group was made up of about 1,844 high-ranking civil servants, 438 provincial assemblymen, and 235 congressmen and senators.[84] The creation of 21 new provinces in 1962 increased the number of local assemblymen to 500 and that of provincial ministers to 252. After the 1965 elections, there were 644 provincial assemblymen and 299 members of Parliament.

The steady increase in Congolese administrative personnel demanded an increasingly large portion of the new country's total budget. At the end of 1962, expenditures for political and administrative personnel were as follows (in billions of Congolese francs):[85]

Army and police	2.5
Political personnel	1.6
Statutory agents	2.5
Auxiliary agents	3.95
TOTAL	10.55

The sum of 10.55 billion Congolese francs represented 62 percent of total government expenditures in 1962. Moreover, the pay scale for the various civil service categories was far from uniform. If the 1960 wage scale is used as a base, the wages of auxiliary workers rose 90 percent in 1962, and those of statutory workers 130 percent. In the same year, politicians' wages rose 400 percent, and those of the army rank and file 410 percent.[86] By 1963, wages and salaries in the public sector had reached 22 billion Congolese francs out of a total budget of 28 billion, while the treasury deficit had increased from 13.9 to 16 billion Congolese francs.[87] In November 1963, after a year of trade-union agitation, salaries of statutory agents were raised. However, the 13 percent increase for workers with high qualifications compared unfavorably with the 60 percent hike in the pay of the least qualified, lowest-ranking functionaries, and reflected the deterioration of public finance in the newly independent Congo. This deterioration reached startling extremes during Moise Tshombe's administration. "While the government did have relative success in balancing its budget during 1964, there was no budget at all in 1965, or at least not until September 17. This did not prevent the government from spending 53.6 percent more than it had in previous years, while its revenue increased by only 12 percent."[88] Such fiscal irresponsibility inevitably caused the violent inflationary trend that Hughes Leclerq summarized at the end of 1962:

Credit advanced to the government by the Central Bank caused more money to be poured into the economy in the form of wages and other payments to the army and civil service. While raising the income of some 150,000 privileged individuals, this deficit financing led to increased demand [for consumer goods] and, consequently, to a rise in prices. . . . Inflation in the Congo is no longer a simple monetary fact; it is increasingly becoming an institutional phenomenon that affects behavior, destroys economic institutions, disrupts the flow of trade, and saps the country of its resources and moral values.[89]

The rush to appropriation of public offices in the first years of the Congo's independence, then, was fraught with wholesale waste, both of the human energies expended in political struggles and of economic resources lost through runaway inflation.

 CHAPTER 3

The Politics of Centrifugal Relations

A SECOND BASIC characteristic of patrimonialism is the privatization of political relationships. According to Weber, in patrimonial politics

the object of obedience is the personal authority of the individual, which he enjoys by virtue of his traditional status. The organized group exercising authority is, in the simplest case, primarily based on relations of personal loyalty cultivated through a common process of education. The person exercising authority is not a "superior" but a personal "chief." His administrative staff does not consist primarily of officials but of personal retainers. Those subject to authority are not members of an association but are either his traditional "comrades" or his "subjects." What determines the relations of the administrative staff to the chief is not the impersonal obligations of office, but personal loyalty to the "chief."[1]

In most studies of African politics, such relations are considered to be tribal and ethnic in origin. However, the formation of personal clientages and territorial estates in the Congo did not arise from any popular support organized on an ethnic basis. Congolese regional leaders and key figures in the central government were able to pursue their own political goals without much interference from the groups they supposedly represented.

Weber further asserts that patrimonial rulership is an inherently decentralized system of government.[2] Indeed, in the Congo the rush to appropriate public offices coincided with a process of centrifugal fragmentation that totally undermined the coherence and primacy of the central government. The only real centers of political power were various competing paramount suzerains backed by shifting clienteles of local followers and personal retainers.

Independence and Fragmentation

Political dissidence and threats of secession first arose in the Congo with the coming of independence on June 30, 1960. By the end of that year, centrifugal pressures had produced the separatist movements of ABAKO (Bakongo Alliance), ABAZI (Bayanzi Alliance), and RDLK (Democratic Assembly of Lac-Kwango-Kwilu) in the province of Léopoldville; the proclamation of the "Mining State" of South Kasai; the secession attempts of Equateur province; and the creation of an autonomous government in the Maniéma district.[3] Most of the dissident groups were limited to the formation of paper governments that could not seriously threaten the territorial integrity of the Congo. South Kasai, South Katanga, and Kongo Central, though, were able to create functioning local governments and thus establish their independence from Léopoldville.

Though officially forbidden by the Congo's provisional constitution, the more successful autonomist movements held a certain fascination for Léopoldville's journalists, intellectuals, and politicians, many of whom viewed the movements as presenting model answers to urgent Congolese socioeconomic questions. Thus the South Katangese secession was frequently cited as having solved crucial problems of unemployment, medical care, social security, and tax relief that Léopoldville seemed unable to face.[4] Moise Tshombe, the president of South Katanga, became legendary throughout the Congo as a "father of prosperity and abundance." At the same time, the "Mining State" of South Kasai was praised for its performance, and "for the courage and determination of the Baluba people who, in spite of . . . hostile conditions, are building a new country."[5] South Kasai was considered exemplary, since, unlike Katanga, the province had declared its independence with very limited foreign support in the midst of a bloody civil war. It was widely felt that "[South Kasai] . . . serves as a model by which the many new states now mushrooming in the Congo might form a new federation."[6]

One major cause of fragmentation was the widespread debate as to whether the newly independent Congo was to be organized federally, confederally, or as a single unit. This question had arisen prior to independence, particularly at the Belgo-Congolese Round Table in 1960, but it became inflammatory after July of that year.

From December 1960 to April 1961, the Léopoldville press published endless studies and editorials comparing the merits of the three types of organization. These publications frequently linked federalism and confederalism with an increase in the number of provinces in the Congo, while associating single-unit organization with maintenance of the existing provincial structure. Since the arguments of moderate federalists carried the most weight at this time, the multiplication of provinces was increasingly accepted as inevitable. Such debates were premature, however, in view of the disintegration of the Congo's hastily contrived constitutional and governmental structures after independence.

The new Congolese government was headed by Patrice Lumumba as prime minister and Joseph Kasavubu as chief of state, the latter office having been created to approximate the influence previously exercised by the Belgian king. The ambiguity inherent in this dual leadership was aggravated by personal hostility between the two men. Widespread rioting in the Congolese National Army (ANC), with attendant murders of Europeans, the rapid departure of Belgian civil servants, military intervention from abroad, and the series of secessions listed above, all put unbearable pressure on this shaky Léopoldville government. In September 1960, Kasavubu attempted to oust Lumumba and asked Joseph Ileo to form a new government, but the Congolese Parliament quickly ruled Kasavubu's action illegal. A few days later, General Joseph Mobutu issued a press release announcing a coup d'etat by the dispirited and disorganized ANC.

Thus the end of 1960 found the Congo territorially fragmented and its former central government split among warring factions. Not surprisingly, efforts at reunification during the following year were not undertaken within the shattered constitutional framework, but through temporary and extralegal Round Tables of national reunification. These Round Tables produced regional suzerains who, by the exercise of patrimonial rather than constitutional authority, succeeded in transforming the entire territorial and political structure of the Congo.

The Round Tables of National Reconciliation. The first attempt at national reconciliation took place in Léopoldville on January 25, 1961 at the initiative of the Léopoldville government, though at this time the influence of Moise Tshombe's Katangese secession was at its

height and Léopoldville's position in relation to all Congolese separatist movements was extremely weak. Since the Léopoldville conference lacked representatives from Katanga or Orientale provinces,
it constituted neither a parliamentary assembly nor a true Round
Table. The conference was thus doomed from the outset, and its
delegates were able only to set the time and place for a second Round
Table. However, a committee charged with the territorial reorganization of the Congo did prepare a report demonstrating the delegates'
inclination to link the problem of federalism with that of new territorial divisions: "The Committee fully supports federalism. . . . It
is obvious that once the structure of the country is [so] defined, the
political map must necessarily be modified."[7]

The second Round Table was held at Tananarive, Malagasy Republic, in March 1961. Initially aimed at creating a tactical alliance
between Léopoldville, South Kasai, and Elisabethville against the
growing power of Antoine Gizenga's Stanleyville secession, this
Round Table served only to further the confederalist views of Moise
Tshombe.[8] As Table 5 shows, the conference resulted in recognition
of six regional suzerains, Alois Kabangi, Adrien Omari, Joseph Kulumba, Sylvestre Bondekwe, Vital Moanda, and Barthelemy Mukenge, and the creation of the six new states that these men claimed
to head. Only one of the new states, Kongo Central, had implemented
autonomous political institutions, and the states of Maniéma and
Congo Oriental were represented by men who had never before held
positions of authority in their respective regions. The central government was powerless to prevent such territorial fragmentation;[9]
indeed, many Round Table delegates were more than willing to re-
nounce their allegiance to Léopoldville if they could gain recognition
for their own regional suzerainties by doing so.

The Tananarive Round Table greatly complicated the problem
of territorial fragmentation. At the end of March 1961, the *Courrier
d'Afrique* published a list of new "states" created on paper in the
wake of the conference. These included Mayi-Ndombe (formerly the
district of Lac Léopold II), Kwango-Kwilu, Lulonga-Ikelemba (formerly the district of Tshuapa), and North Sankuru. Each one had
its own chief of state or president, about fifteen ministers, and as
many secretaries of state.[10]

During the same period, the central government's efforts to end

TABLE 5
Political and Territorial Division of the Congo as Proposed at the Tananarive and Coquilhatville Round Tables

The provinces before the Round Tables (June 1960)		After the Tananarive Round Table (March 1961)		After the Coquilhatville Round Table (May 1961)	
Province	Provincial president[a]	State	Chief of state	State[b]	Chief of state
KATANGA	M. Tshombe	KATANGA	M. Tshombe	SOUTH KATANGA	M. Tshombe
				NORTH KATANGA	J. Sendwe
LÉOPOLDVILLE	C. Kamitatu	KONGO CENTRAL	V. Moanda	KONGO CENTRAL	V. Moanda
		LÉOPOLDVILLE	C. Kamitatu	KWANGO	L. Mbariko
				MAYI-NDOMBE	V. Koumoriko
				KWILU	F. Kimvay
				SOUTH KWILU	V. Mbwankiem
KASAI	B. Mukenge	SOUTH KASAI	A. Kalonji	SOUTH KASAI	A. Kalonji
		LOMAMI	A. Kabangi	LOMAMI	A. Kabangi
		NORTH KASAI	B. Mukenge	NORTH KASAI	B. Mukenge
				NORTH SANKURU	E. Lutula
				UNITÉ KASAIENNE	G. Kamanga
EQUATEUR	L. Eketebi	EQUATEUR	J. Bolikango	CONGO-UBANGI	J. Bolikango
				UBANGI	M. Denge
				MONGO	E. Ndjoku
ORIENTALE	J. P. Finant	CONGO ORIENTAL	L. S. Bondekwe	CONGO ORIENTAL	L. S. Bondekwe
				UÉLÉ-ITURI	M. Dericoard
KIVU	J. Miruho	KIVU	J. Miruho	KIVU	J. Miruho
		MANIÉMA	A. Omari	MANIÉMA	A. Omari

SOURCES: Gérard-Libois, *Congo 1960*; Verhaegen, *Congo 1961*.
[a] The men listed in this column are the first provincial presidents, elected by the assemblies after the legislative elections of June 1960.
[b] South Kwilu was never officially a province. South Katanga later split into Katanga Oriental and Lualaba; Uélé-Ituri split into Uélé and Ituri; Kivu split into North Kivu and Kivu Central. Likewise, Mayi-Ndombe later became Luluabourg; North Sankuru became Sankuru; Congo-Ubangi became Moyen Congo; Mongo became Cuvette Centrale; and Congo Oriental became Haut Congo.

this centrifugal trend were given tactical support by Jean Bolikango, Justin Bomboko, and Jason Sendwe, all powerful regional leaders who felt threatened by increasing territorial fragmentation. Thus the third Round Table, which took place in Coquilhatville from April 23 to May 30, began with a sharp split of opinion about its very goals. For Léopoldville's Ileo government, this Round Table was meant to modify the decisions made at Tananarive by forming a group of parliamentary leaders capable of neutralizing Katangese influence on regional delegations. Moise Tshombe, by contrast, expected the conference to follow exactly the confederalist principles set forth in the Tananarive resolutions.

Tshombe's adamant refusal to compromise with the central government on the purpose of the talks led to his arrest and imprisonment in Léopoldville; significantly, Tshombe was not removed by the weak and disorganized Léopoldville government but by the Coquilhatville army garrison.[11] Even in Tshombe's absence, the central government was forced into the position of moderator to the several hundred delegates pressing for recognition of their own regional states. The end of the Coquilhatville Round Table saw seven new Congolese states recognized.[12] Here as at Tananarive, however, recognition was extended more to regional leaders than to established political institutions. The 55 delegates whose states were acknowledged included 24 parliamentary representatives, 10 provincial assemblymen, 3 acting provincial ministers, and a group of 18 relatively well-known mayors, former provincial ministers, high civil servants, and paramount chiefs. Most of these men were actually residing in Léopoldville while promoting the autonomy of their respective regions.

In the rush for recognition the exact boundaries of most states were left undefined, and border disputes naturally ensued. In the province of Equateur, for instance, Michel Denge, head of the new state of Ubangi, opposed the state of Congo-Ubangi that Jean Bolikango promoted, since this state would have included some territory claimed for Ubangi. In Kasai, conflicting territorial claims arose between Alois Kabangi's state of Lomami and that of North Sankuru promoted by Mayor Eugene Lutula and Chief Emery Pene-Sengha. Finally, and most significantly, many delegates were not always able to speak for all political factions existing in the states they allegedly represented. The state of Kwango, for example, was sponsored only

by the leaders of two territories within the state, and Laurent Mbariko, the proposed head of state, actually came from the neighboring
district of Kwilu. Cleophas Kamitatu, president of Léopoldville Province, represented himself as a leader of the Kwilu elite, though the
Kwilu delegation was headed by his close political comrade, Felicien
Kimvay. Similarly, the delegation from Kivu-Maniéma was led by
Antoine Omari, who represented only a relatively small faction in
Maniéma, while the delegation from Congo Oriental included no
representatives from Antoine Gizenga's dissident nationalist group.

The Institutionalization of the Fragmentation Process. Though the
Tananarive and Coquilhatville Round Tables took place outside
any regular institutional framework, this fact alone cannot explain
their failure to provide stable channels for the exercise of authority.
In fact, the conferences themselves were marked by the same concentration of power in the hands of regional leaders as the eventual implementation of the Round Table resolutions was to produce. The
resolutions also gave control of legislative procedures to regional
suzerains operating in both houses of the Congolese Parliament.

The centrifugal trend did halt briefly, though, in the wake of the
two Round Tables. Efforts were made to reconstitute central institutions with United Nations help, as the Léopoldville government
grappled with the unresolved problem of the Katangese and Orientale secessions. At the same time, new regional chiefs discovered that
they could not implement the Coquilhatville resolutions in the absence of a higher coordinating body. As a result, most coalitions and
caucuses were willing to join in discussions aimed at strengthening
the central government, and Joseph Kasavubu was able to call the
Congolese Parliament into session after a year's inactivity. Meeting
at Lovanium University in August 1961, the Parliament created a
compromise government in accord with the Congo's provisional constitution, the Fundamental Law. The new government was headed
by Cyril Adoula, a leader acceptable to all who participated in the
session.

Despite the spirit of conciliation surrounding its formation, the
Adoula government was closely bound by the Round Table resolutions.[13] Referring to the article of the Fundamental Law that defined the Congo's territorial composition, Prime Minister Adoula
acknowledged this bond in an address to the combined houses of

Parliament: "My government will take into account the regional diversities that characterize this vast country of ours, and the desire of its inhabitants to achieve . . . local autonomy. . . . Accordingly [the government] pledges to submit to Parliament an amendment modifying the seventh article of the Fundamental Law [heavy applause]."[14] On August 28, 1962, Minister of the Interior Christophe Gbenye presented the House of Representatives with a bill amending the territorial organization of the Congo. In his speech to the congressmen, the minister made clear that the central government would keep the legislative initiative in any territorial reorganization: "It will be necessary to deviate from the seventh article in order to allow . . . the executive branch . . . to set temporary boundaries for new provinces. . . . There is no need to fear arbitrariness on the part of the executive branch, since boundaries will be debated in the Council of Ministers, where all regions and factions are represented."[15]

Despite Gbenye's assurances, his bill was discussed neither in the Senate nor in the House. On October 10, the president of the House, Joseph Kasongo, submitted a bill that differed radically from the government's interpretation of the Fundamental Law. Specifically, Kasongo's bill assigned Parliament the task of "determining the number and boundaries of new provinces, as well as the criteria for their creation."[16] Though many congressmen distrusted Kasongo because he had no territory of his own, the House passed his bill unanimously. Since August, the Senate had been discussing a bill of its own that called for popular referendums to determine the number and borders of new provinces.[17] The bill caused such heated debate that it was only in December that the Senate could muster the quorum needed to defeat it. The Senate also rejected Kasongo's bill of October 10 as involving too lengthy a procedure for creating new provinces.[18] Unable to reach agreement on any proposed amendment to the Fundamental Law, the Senate turned its attention to another bill that the House had passed on October 13, this one dealing directly with the economic and demographic criteria for the establishment of new provinces.

Not surprisingly, protracted debates and procedural confusion totally obscured the issue of territorial reorganization. By passing Kasongo's bill, the House clearly violated established procedures for amending the Fundamental Law, as well as ignoring the government's views in the matter. The Senate in turn rejected both government and House proposals. It finally passed a bill of its own that was patterned on the October 13 House bill, but that specified less stringent criteria for the creation of new provinces and contained its own proposed amendment to the Fundamental Law. Each house had its own Committee on Internal Affairs, and a joint session of both committees was therefore necessary to resolve the impasse. In sum, six months of debate resulted in a single addition to the Fundamental Law: "The Congolese State, in its borders of June 30, 1960, consists of the six provinces of Equateur, Kasai, Katanga, Kivu, Léopoldville, and Orientale, each possessing its own civil identity. *Laws may be enacted creating other provinces.*"[19]

However, the exact legal criteria for the creation of new provinces were yet to be established. Once again, the House and the Senate worked apart from one another, their efforts further hampered by parliamentary leaders seeking provincial status for their own regions. Four months of laborious discussions produced the organic law of April 27, 1962, a law rendered meaningless by the irregularities contained in those of its articles that touched on territorial reorganization. Here are the bills proposed by the government, the House of Representatives, and the Senate on the criteria for new provinces, as well as the relevant articles of the organic law:[20]

GOVERNMENT: The question of criteria will be decided by the constitution itself. (Bill modifying the seventh article of the Fundamental Law.)

HOUSE: *Article 1.* A region wishing to become a province must (*a*) have a population of at least 1,200,000; (*b*) demonstrate economic resources that will allow it to meet routine budgetary demands; (*c*) possess communication networks capable of linking its territory to the other provinces and the central government; (*d*) possess such social institutions as schools, clinics, etc.

Article 2. A request for the transformation of a region into a province will be presented in the form of a petition to the government. This petition will include the signatures of the majority of members of Parliament and provincial assemblymen.

Article 4. Regions whose economies are complementary and whose populations have never demonstrated the desire to form new provinces will keep their present status.

SENATE: *Article 1.* A region wishing to become a province must have at least 500,000 inhabitants.

Article 2. The president of the cabinet will receive the request for the transformation of a region into a province in the form of a petition signed by two-thirds of the representatives of that region.

Article 4. A new province that after at least three years . . . cannot function due to its economic or demographic situation will cease to exist, and will merge with another province . . . after a popular referendum.

ORGANIC LAW: *Article 1.* A region wishing to become a province must (*a*) have a population of at least 700,000; (*b*) demonstrate economic resources that will allow it to meet budgetary demands. Nevertheless, if a region does not meet condition *a*, it may still become a province through the sole reason of political and social imperatives.

Article 2. The central government will receive the request for the transformation of a region into a province in the form of a petition signed by two-thirds of the national and provincial representatives of the region.

Article 4. The new province that after three years cannot function due to adverse circumstances will cease to exist, and will merge with another province after a referendum.

According to the organic law, the creation of new provinces could be justified not only by concrete criteria but also by recourse to "political imperatives" that had no legal definition. This vagueness produced frantic arguments between legislators and provincial delegations about what territories and ethnic groups should be allowed provincial status. The central government remained silent on this issue, maintaining that exact criteria for the establishment of new provinces should be reserved for the drafting of the Congo's permanent constitution. It therefore limited itself to coordinating the conflicting petitions that passed ceaselessly between the Ministry of the Interior and the Committee on Internal Affairs of each house of Parliament.

The events of this period illustrate the widespread confusion about procedural and legal matters among Congolese legislators. For instance, one report on the situation took the form of a bill submitted and discussed by the House Committee on Internal Affairs on March 23.[21] The bill was plainly unconstitutional for three reasons. First, neither the House nor the Senate had yet passed the organic law determining the validity of petitions for provincial status; second, the House took an initiative in preparing the bill that it had previously agreed to leave to the central government; third, the bill did not establish criteria for creating provinces, but rather indicated that the petitions received by the House Committee on Internal Affairs allowed their de facto creation. This bill caused such fierce debate that the congressmen finally returned to their study of the proposed organic law, charging "the executive with the task of delimiting the new [provincial] entities."[22]

Procedural confusion was also evident in the play of pressures, alliances, and agonizing reappraisals that characterized the negotiations for new provinces. For instance, representatives from Lomami and Maniéma agreed to merge their two districts into the province of Lomami-Maniéma.[23] Although their petition had not been signed by two-thirds of the provincial and national representatives as required by the organic law of April 27, it was declared valid by the House Committee on Internal Affairs "since the Department of the Interior has not prepared any bill regarding that region."[24] A few days later, however, Congressman Jules Milambo killed the bill, declaring that "some people have abused the good faith of my colleagues from Maniéma during my absence from Léopoldville."[25] Still more confusion was caused by those who signed several petitions at the same time, as did three national representatives from Kivu and twelve assemblymen from Kasai, all of whom withdrew their signatures from the petitions they had initially signed.[26] These men shifted their support quite willingly, either in return for recognition of their own provinces or for other political favors.

By July 30, the provinces of North Katanga, South Kasai, and Kongo Central had been created by acts of Parliament, and legislators began to press for rapid approval of other proposed provinces. As Table 6 shows, arguments in favor of new provinces were most commonly based on frequently distorted claims of ethnic homogeneity, or on a given delegate's assertion that he alone represented his people's interests and that failure to create a new province would place one tribal group at the mercy of another, unsympathetic one. Crude and grossly simplified racial stereotypes were of course presented in support of the latter argument. For instance, Congressman Lumanza from Ubangi regarded the Ngombe populations of Moyen

TABLE 6

Themes of Parliamentary Debates on New Provinces

Reason given for creating new provinces	Debates in House		Debates in Senate	
	Number	Percentage	Number	Percentage
Tribal homogeneity	31	49.2%	42	28.4%
Rational or legal criteria				
political	5	7.9	21	14.2
social or economic	5	7.9	21	14.2
Representativeness of regional leaders	22	34.9	64	43.2
TOTAL	63	99.9%	148	100%

SOURCES: CR, *Compte-Rendu*, 1962; *Annales Parlementaires*, Sénat de la République du Congo, Léopoldville, 1962.

Congo as "bureaucrats" who were afraid of manual labor, an old stereotype invented by colonists in the province of Equateur. In the same vein, Congressman Massa "refused to live" with the populations of the northern part of the Lac Léopold II district, since he considered them uneducated savages. Senators Mutshungu, Midiburo, and Ndudry, all from North Kivu, all saw their neighbors, the Banyarwanda, as "the true colonialists" of the Congo, illegally settled in Kivu and plotting to dominate and oppress other groups in the area. Some legislators relied on still less sophisticated arguments, asserting that their presence in Parliament with a petition bearing a number of signatures was in itself sufficient reason to create a new province.

The prolonged parliamentary debates saw the emergence of a number of regional leaders as influential figures in Congolese politics, and ended in the promulgation of sixteen new provinces by the chief of state in August 1962. The newly eminent leaders included Vital Moanda (Kongo Central), Alois Kabangi (Lomami), Gregoire Kamanga (Unité Kasaienne), Andre Diamasumbu (Sankuru), Andre Anekonzapa (Ubangi) and Jason Sendwe (North Katanga). Most of these men had attended the Round Tables of national reconciliation as prospective heads of state and in fact considered their respective provinces to be their own personal fiefs.

The new provinces resulted neither from ethnic imperatives nor from a rational political process. They were the product of arduous discussion between powerful individuals, and so did not necessarily exhibit tribal uniformity. As Table 7 shows, only ten provinces out of 21 were in fact marked by tribal homogeneity or by the hegemony of one ethnic group over others. Kongo Central, South Kasai, Luluabourg, and Cuvette Centrale were the only provinces to demonstrate real ethnic cohesion, while in Sankuru, Kwango, Lac Léopold II, and Maniéma latent political cleavages tended to polarize the two main tribal groups. Finally, in provinces that lacked any ethnic solidarity, such as Kwilu, Haut Congo, and Ituri, only disciplined regional parties like the MNC-Lumumba and the PSA-Gizenga could provide a degree of political homogeneity.

One of the chief factors offsetting tribal influences in the creation of new provinces was the example of previously existing colonial administrative districts. The borders of sixteen of the new provinces roughly followed those of the former districts. Further, a former district commissioner has assured the author that by independence, the

TABLE 7

Profile of the New Provinces at the Time of Their Creation

Province	Ethnic composition			Preindependence borders	Viable administrative infrastructure	Viable economic resources	Incipient fragmentation
	Total homogeneity	2 groups competing	1 group dominant				
Kongo Central	Yes	—	—	Partial	Partial	Yes	—
Kwango	—	Yes	—	Yes	—	—	Yes
Kwilu	—	—	—	Yes	Yes	Yes	Yes
Lac Léopold II	—	Yes	—	Yes	—	—	Yes
Cuvette Centrale	Yes	—	—	Partial	Yes	Partial	—
Moyen Congo	—	Yes	—	Yes	Partial	Partial	—
Ubangi	—	—	Yes	Yes	—	—	—
Haut Congo	—	—	—	Yes	Yes	Yes	Yes
Ituri	—	—	—	Yes	—	—	—
Uélé	—	—	Yes	Partial	Partial	Yes	—
Kivu Central	—	—	—	Yes	Yes	Yes	Yes
North Kivu	—	—	—	Yes	—	—	—
Maniéma	—	Yes	—	Yes	—	Partial	Yes
Katanga Oriental	—	—	Yes	Partial	Yes	Yes	—
Lualaba	—	—	Yes	Partial	Yes	Yes	—
North Katanga	—	—	Yes	—	Yes	Partial	—
Lomami	—	—	Yes	Partial	—	—	—
Luluabourg	Yes	—	—	—	Yes	—	Yes
Sankuru	—	Yes	—	Yes	—	Partial	Yes
South Kasai	Yes	—	—	—	Partial	Yes	Yes
Unité Kasaienne	—	—	—	—	—	Partial	—

SOURCES: Young, pp. 552–53; Benoit Verhaegen, "Présentation morphologique des nouvelles provinces," EC, 4 (Apr. 1963); Willame, Provinces.

district administrations had lost all autonomy and served only as communication channels between provincial authorities and the colonial administration.[27] This fact was to create nearly insurmountable obstacles to the installation of some provinces, for at least nine of the new entities had very inadequate administrative infrastructures. The reduction, by as much as two-thirds, of the area governed by former provincial capitals created further problems. As Verhaegen points out: "The weight of the administrative and economic infrastructures, the plurality of those ethnic groups that migrated from neighboring regions, the presence of a more politicized ruling class, and the material advantages that these towns offered the provincial elite all acted to prevent the provincial capitals from allowing any limitation of their functions."[28]

The economic survival of many new provinces was also uncertain. Seven of them, when isolated from their former capitals, had no real

The New Congolese Provinces

economic resources and were forced to rely upon government sub-
sidies, while some provincial capitals faced the loss of hinterland
areas necessary to their continued commercial and industrial development. In the northern border provinces of Uélé, Ituri, and
North Kivu, for instance, illicit trade relations with neighboring
Sudan and Uganda reached disturbing proportions in 1963, and led
to the economic isolation of these regions' former chief town, Stanleyville.[29] Again during February and March 1963, political leaders in
Kongo Central prevented local traders from selling their products in
Léopoldville's markets. The boycott was enforced in opposition to

the central government's decision to assign federal status to Léopoldville, long considered a Bakongo fief.[30]

By far the most disturbing result of the Congo's territorial reorganization was the increased likelihood of political feuds at the provincial and local levels. In at least ten cases, incipient conflicts had already existed between rival local leaders. From December 1962 until
the 1964 rebellions, in fact, rivalries between patrimonial leaders
(and relations between these leaders and their followers) were to
dominate the politics of the newly created provinces.

Patterns of Patrimonial Relationships

At the Tananarive and Coquilhatville Round Tables, the heads of
the regional delegations clearly acted and spoke as the potential chiefs
of state of their territories. It was widely believed at the time that
the Congo was moving toward a confederal system radically different
from the framework established by the Fundamental Law of 1960.
With the formation of the Adoula government in July 1961, most
regional leaders set aside the confederal formula and lent their support to Congolese national institutions as restored by the United
Nations under the direction of Dag Hammarskjold. Nevertheless, the
implementation of the new provincial organization allowed local
leaders to reinforce the network of pyramidal relationships existing
within their own territories. These men, though frustrated in their
efforts to head states of their own, fell easily into roles of patrimonial
rulership.

As Table 8 shows, relationships between patrimonial rulers and
their estates in the new provinces fell into four general categories.
The first of these was direct suzerainty, a type of relationship favored
by those leaders who acted in full accord with the Tananarive and
Coquilhatville resolutions and whose assertions of legitimacy as the
sole representative rulers of their regions went unchallenged in the
period following the two Round Tables.

The three most striking examples of direct suzerainty were found
in the provinces of North Katanga, Unité Kasaienne, and Sankuru.
In North Katanga, Jason Sendwe emerged as an outstanding leader
immediately after independence.[31] Elected congressman from Katanga with 20,282 preferential votes in 1960, he was the representative of the Baluba-Katanga ethnic group that had clashed violently

TABLE 8

Patrimonial and Cliental Relations in the Congo, 1962–65

Province	Type of relationship	Regional or patrimonial leader	Head of province or political opposition
Kongo Central	Direct suzerainty	—	*V. Moanda*
Kwilu	Indirect suzerainty	*C. Kamitatu*	N. Leta
Kwango	Indirect suzerainty	*A. Delvaux*	A. Pashi
			P. Masikita
			P. Kavunzu
	Direct suzerainty	(J. Kulumba)	*(J. Kulumba)*
Lac Léopold II	Direct suzerainty	V. Koumoriko	*V. Koumoriko*
	Indirect suzerainty	*(J. Massa)*	P. Zagambie
South Kasai	Factional comradeship	—	*J. Ngalula*
Luluabourg	Factional comradeship	—	F. Lwakabwanga
	Direct suzerainty	(A. Lubaya)	*A. Lubaya*
Unité Kasaienne	Direct suzerainty	G. Kamanga	*G. Kamanga*
	Direct suzerainty	(F. Mingabengele)	*(F. Mingabengele)*
Sankuru	Direct suzerainty	A. Diamasumbu	*A. Diamasumbu*
	Factional comradeship	—	*(P. Sumbu)*
Lomami	Indirect suzerainty	*A. Kabangi*	D. Manono
North Katanga	Direct suzerainty	J. Sendwe	*J. Sendwe*
Maniéma	Direct administration	Central government	Extraordinary commissioner
Kivu Central	Factional comradeship	—	*S. Malago*
North Kivu	Factional comradeship	—	*B. Moley*
Haut Congo	Direct administration	Central government	Extraordinary commissioner
Uélé	Indirect suzerainty	F. Kupa	*P. Mambaya*
Ituri	Factional comradeship	—	*J. F. Manzikala*
Cuvette Central	Indirect suzerainty	J. Bomboko	*L. Engulu*
	Indirect suzerainty	(P. Bolya)	—
Moyen Congo	Indirect suzerainty	*J. Bolikango*	L. Eketebi
	Indirect suzerainty	(J. Anany)	*(L. Eketebi)*
Ubangi	Factional comradeship	—	*A. Nzondomyo*

SOURCE: Willame, *Provinces.*

NOTE: Katanga Oriental and Lualaba excluded. Italics indicate that the main focus of political activity was at the provincial level. The opposition factions in parentheses have been mentioned only where their actions were significant.

with the secessionist regime in Elisabethville. Sendwe's position as a leader of the Baluba-Katanga was definitely established at the Coquilhatville Round Table, where he was recognized as "chief of state of Lualaba" (North Katanga) by his colleagues. However, he deliberately left the formation of North Katanga's first provincial government to his trusted lieutenant, Prosper Mwamba Ilunga.

By the end of 1962, Sendwe's prestige was at its peak. As president of Balubakat, the powerful coalition of Luba politicians, Sendwe could exert great influence in the affairs of the Baluba. At the same time, he combined the official functions of the extraordinary commissioner representing the central government in his province with the vice-presidency of the Adoula government. Yet his unexpected dismissal by the Senate in December 1962 compelled Sendwe to withdraw from national to local politics. Forcing Mwamba Ilunga to resign, he took his place as president of North Katanga in July 1963.

The suzerainties of Gregoire Kamanga in Unité Kasaienne and Andre Diamasumbu in Sankuru both followed strikingly similar patterns. Both men came into prominence relatively late, at the Coquilhatville Round Table. As representatives of the moderate political forces then in power, and as members of the central government since 1961, they exercised a much broader appeal in their constituencies than their rivals, Francois Mingabengele and Paul Sumbu, whose political resources were limited by the fact that they occupied no official positions. Unlike Jason Sendwe, neither Kamanga nor Diamasumbu displayed any great ambition in Congolese national politics. This could not prevent the undermining of both men's power and prestige, however, as they were drawn deeper and deeper into local and regional politics. There, neither man could escape intense pressures from the same factions that had brought them to prominence. Each patrimonial ruler's rise to power in his constituency coincided with the formation of a coalition of political allies and relatives that monopolized such key public offices in the province as the ministry of personnel, the ministry of the interior, and the vice-presidency. Thus in Sankuru, Diamasumbu relied exclusively on the so-called "Ekonda faction" composed of his fellow clan members. The rival Eswe, or Batetela, faction was expelled from the administration in Lodja, the capital of Sankuru, and forced to take refuge in the neighboring town of Lusambo. In North Katanga, Sendwe's autonomy was severely limited when the overzealous attitude of two close associates in his entourage, Ildephonse Masengo, the health minister, and Roger Kabulo, the cabinet director, reanimated an old conflict between Sendwe and followers of Mwamba Ilunga.[32]

It would be helpful at this point to clarify the dynamics of pressure groups and political factions. Unlike pressure groups, which operate within a pluralistic environment where the maintenance of the existing political system requires that conflicts be kept within manageable bounds, the raison d'être of political factions is open conflict, usually aimed at the elimination of all opposing groups. Also, members of a faction are most likely to be recruited directly by its leaders or by the patrimonial ruler and his lieutenants, and are likely to remain active in the faction only at the direct initiative of the leader himself. The patrimonial leader responsible for organizing a faction is generally a man with more political power than any of his followers. At the same time, the leader's relative lack of charismatic appeal may make him dependent on his followers. This fact might help account for the instability of direct suzerainty.

Ironically, feuds between local factions invited political intervention by such would-be patrimonial rulers as F. Kabange Numbi in North Katanga, Francois Mingabengele in Unité Kasaienne, and Paul Sumbu in Sankuru. All three men eventually emerged as the new patrimonial rulers of their provinces as some members of the factions previously in power shifted their support to the challengers.[33] One is reminded here of Machiavelli's warning that "it is easy to enter [kingdoms] by winning over some baron . . . ; there being always malcontents and those desiring innovations . . . ; but afterwards, if you wish to keep possession, infinite difficulties arise, both from those who have aided you and from those you have oppressed."[34]

Other patrimonial rulers chose to exercise their authority by means of indirect suzerainty. Such rulers usually operated through clients, political comrades, or other intermediaries whom they placed in positions of authority in a new province, and whom they held directly accountable to themselves. The best example of indirect suzerainty is provided by the province of Lomami (Kasai).[35] Until 1965, it was effectively ruled by Alois Kabangi, the central government's personnel minister and an outspoken representative of the Basonge in Léopoldville. Kabangi ruled with the aid of Dominique Manono and Sebastien Ngoie, both highly influential figures at the local level. Kabangi's presence in the capital proved quite valuable to Lomami province. The province's governmental program was elaborated in 1963 with the aid of the Institute for Economic and Social Research at Lovanium University, a group with which Kabangi had close ties. He was also influential in regularizing the status of Lomami's civil servants, providing the province with improved transportation, and appropriating funds for the provincial treasury.[36]

Dominique Manono, an old friend of Kabangi's from school days, served as president of the provincial government.[37] His administration was marked by a lack of political cohesion and by administrative incompetence. Perhaps this was inevitable, though, since Manono's prime task was to placate the dissident non-Basonge elite groups in the province. Though never directly challenged by these groups, Manono was at one point compelled to fire members of his own government who were accused of tribal favoritism. Also, he frequently acceded to exaggerated demands for non-Basonge representation in local institutions.

A measure of continuity and administrative efficiency was supplied by Provincial Secretary Sebastien Ngoie, Kabangi's most loyal supporter in Lomami.[38] In most provinces, the provincial secretary's functions had been undercut by a pervasive spirit of politicization and factionalism. However, in his instructions to the special commissioners in charge of Lomami's administrative apparatus, Kabangi specifically urged that the provincial secretary be maintained as the head of the local civil service, directly accountable to the president, in order to "ensure the continuity of the administrative apparatus in the face of political vicissitudes."[39]

In fact, Ngoie's office became the main channel for implementing presidential decisions. In addition to originating major administrative reforms, such as the creation of new communes, Ngoie controlled the employment and salaries of most civil servants, and was the only official regularly in touch with the lowest civil service ranks.[40] Ngoie's considerable power provoked opposition from the ministers of the interior and personnel. However, insulated as he was from local politics through his close association with Manono, Ngoie was able to maintain his favorable position in Lomami.

The stable arrangement that evolved in Lomami was unique in

Congolese politics. In most cases, relations between patrimonial rulers and their clients involved either outright confrontations between two powerful regional leaders or rebellions by clients against their suzerains, usually with the aid of other patrimonial chiefs.

The first pattern can be illustrated by the endless feuds between Congressman Albert Delvaux and Joseph Kulumba in Kwango, or between Minister Justin Bomboko and Senator Paul Bolya in Cuvette Centrale, from 1963 to 1965. Rebellions of clients against their patrons were particularly numerous on the eve of the legislative elections of 1965. For instance, President Norbert Leta of Kwilu province, traditionally considered the most loyal comrade of the interior minister, Cleophas Kamitatu, joined the opposition group led by Senator Yvon Kimpiobi at the end of 1964. In the province of Moyen Congo, Jean Bolikango, a leading representative of the Bangala and a figure of long-established prominence in Congolese politics, came into conflict with the man whom he had placed at the head of the provincial government, Laurent Eketebi.[41] At the end of 1963, Eketebi suddenly broke with his patron and endorsed the new Congolese Democratic Party (PDC) that Congressman Jerome Anany was promoting among the province's dissatisfied minority groups.[42]

In general, such revolts of followers against their patrons did not prove politically viable. After gaining power in the 1965 provincial elections, Leta's new allies repudiated him and sought new leadership to fill the Kwilu presidency. Also during the 1965 elections, Laurent Eketebi disappeared from the political arena when his suzerain, Jean Bolikango, received overwhelming electoral support from his native constituency. In fact, the 53,083 preferential votes that Bolikango received in Moyen Congo made him the most popular Congolese politician after Moise Tshombe, who received 86,009 preferential votes in his province.[43] Such events suggest that the system of indirect suzerainty, though offering no absolute guarantee of political stability, did allow patrimonial rulers to maintain control over their holdings with relative ease.

The provinces of Kivu Central, Ubangi, and, to some extent, North Kivu and Ituri illustrate a third type of political relationship in which no independent, influential patrimonial ruler emerged as an acknowledged leader. In such cases of factional comradeship, power struggles took place within a very intricate network of relationships and interactions centered almost entirely at the local level. The national representatives of these provinces, who elsewhere would have been patrimonial rulers, stayed relatively aloof from the politics of their regions; possibly they realized that their relative isolation from local groups severely limited the political resources at their disposal.

This lack of external interference from national representatives facilitated the emergence of a distinctively coherent, homogeneous, and sometimes autocratic rulership at the provincial level. In Kivu Central, for instance, a sort of triumvirate dominated the allocation of political power between 1963 and 1965. This group was composed of Dieudonné Boji, a representative of the politically dominant ethnic group in Bukavu, the Bashi from the Ngweshe region; Cyprien Rwakabuba, a leader of the Banyarwanda ethnic group; and Simon Malago, the president of the province. Rwakabuba and Boji had both held ministerial portfolios prior to 1962, and President Malago was a former congressman from Kivu. Together these three men monopolized the most important public posts in Bukavu, notably the presidency, the interior ministry, and the department of personnel.[44]

In the provinces of Ituri and North Kivu, Jean-Foster Manzikala and Benezeth Moley succeeded in establishing strongly authoritarian regimes that virtually eliminated all opposition groups from the time these provinces were created. The influence of both provinces' representatives in Léopoldville was negligible, as most of them either lost interest in their home territories or merely served as intermediaries between the provincial president and the central government. Local rulers maintained control of their provinces either by skillfully manipulating local politicians or by using local army garrisons as private militias.

In a few cases, a new province might be administered directly by an extraordinary commissioner, an appointee of the central government who held discretionary powers in the province. This type of rule, which cannot be strictly classified as a kind of patrimonialism, was maintained permanently in Maniéma and Haut Congo, the provinces that had produced the hard core of nationalist dissidence following independence. The extraordinary commissioner's official task was to arrange a temporary reconciliation between the contending factions in his province. In practice, any reconciliation tended to benefit such moderate, antinationalistic leaders as Tshomba Fariala in Maniéma and Paul Isombuma in Haut Congo.

No analysis of centrifugal movements in the Congo would be complete without taking into account the impact of tribal politics on the types of political relationship described above. One may assert, as do many social scientists and African leaders, that political leaders are motivated primarily by tribal and primordial identifications, and that this fact constitutes a fundamental problem in the formation of a modern civil state. In the words of Clifford Geertz:

> By generalizing and extending tribal, racial, linguistic or other principles of primordial solidarity, [ethnicity] permits the maintenance of a profoundly rooted "consciousness of kind" and relates that consciousness to the developing civil order.... But, on the other hand, it also simplifies and concentrates group antagonisms, raises the specter of separatism by superimposing a comprehensive political significance upon those antagonisms.... The integrative revolution does not do away with ethnocentrism; it merely modernizes it.[45]

It is now taken for granted that ethnicity and tribalism involve identifications significantly different from those of precolonial times, but this fact by itself says very little about the modernizing or integrative nature of those newly defined identifications. Moreover, despite its intellectual attractions, Geertz's argument does not precisely define the function of tribalism in Congolese politics. Though many political alliances in the Congo were dominated by ethnic affiliations, there are also many cases in which they did not affect the actions of the political elite at all. For instance, the ruling triumvirate in Kivu Central, composed of men from three different tribes, has already been mentioned. Similarly, Jason Sendwe's political ambitions were not limited to his own Luba constituency, but extended to embrace political suzerainty over all of Katanga province after the eviction of Moise Tshombe in 1963. Similarly, Jean Bolikango was motivated to seek the presidency of the ethnically mixed province of Equateur. In the face of mounting pressures for the territorial reorganization of the Congo, each of these leaders strove to keep his respective province from being partitioned, although both men's efforts in this direction were to prove as futile as their presidential campaigns.

Political cleavages and factional strife were also subject to complex tactical considerations that often took priority over ethnic or tribal issues. In the struggle against Jean Bolikango, Laurent Eketebi's faction unhesitatingly allied itself with a tribal minority in the provincial assembly, namely the Budja from the Bumba territory. This alliance destroyed the myth of a unified Bangala tribe that Bolikango had used to enhance his prestige and influence.[46] Similarly, Cleophas Kamitatu, a benefactor to Kwilu province and a leading representative of the Bambala, enjoyed a particularly close political relationship with Norbert Leta, a member of the rival Bapende tribe from the Gungu region.[47] The two men split about six months prior to the 1965 elections because Leta was dissatisfied with the dominant position of Kamitatu's Bambala tribal group in Kwilu politics. Prior to the split, however, Leta served as Kamitatu's righthand man, and Kamitatu in turn assisted a bid by Leta for the presidency of the province.[48]

Finally, the intense ethnic polarization that developed among such tribes as the Baluba of North Katanga or the Mongo of Equateur did not produce the lasting "consciousness of kind" that Geertz mentions. In many cases, emergent tribal nationalism, created and sustained by the presence of Belgian colonialists, could not resist corruption at the hands of political leaders who stood to profit by exacerbating parochial grievances and aggravating hostility against those in power.

 CHAPTER 4

Private Armies

IN HIS ANALYSIS of patrimonial authority, Max Weber gives special attention to the structure and social organization of military forces. In Weber's view, an army is one of the most efficient instruments for establishing and maintaining a ruler's influence. Weber distinguishes four basic types of military organization used by patrimonial rulers.[1]

The first type consists of peons, serfs, slaves, or other subordinates to whom the ruler has granted land in exchange for their services as personal bodyguards. This system of recruitment, Weber stresses, is highly unstable, for once such dependents are settled on the land, their involvement in agricultural work greatly lessens their effectiveness as fighters. Consequently, a ruler is more likely to organize a military force whose interests coincide with his own. Such a force might consist of former slaves who are not involved in agriculture, and who are entirely cut off from the local society. All armies that Weber cites as examples of this type were held together by adequate and regular pay to their troops and functioned as disciplined forces at the absolute disposal of their patrimonial rulers. Additionally, most such armies facilitated the emergence of large bureaucratic or praetorian empires.

A third practice common in patrimonial rule is the recruitment of mercenaries. Weber notes that such armies are especially dependable when composed of aliens having no real contacts with the subject population, a point that will be discussed in greater detail later in this chapter. Finally, a patrimonial ruler may form a personal military force from among his own subjects. To protect his own interests and undercut his political rivals, a ruler will often recruit from the less privileged social strata, and particularly from rural areas. He will often fill the need for a standing army by making the military service a full-time, well-trained profession. This last is the most important common form of patrimonial army.

Weber's typology provides a useful starting point for an analysis of Congolese military forces. While from the time of the Free State until the 1960 mutinies the Force Publique closely approximated Weber's second type, this colonial force subsequently disintegrated into several armies of the fourth, most typically patrimonial sort.

Also, independence has seen the use of mercenaries and auxiliary forces by both regional rulers and the central government. The presence of alien troops on Congolese soil has substantially shaped political events in the country, both during the Katangese secession, which could not have been maintained without outside support, and during the suppression of the 1964–65 rebellions.

Aside from the section dealing with the Force Publique, this chapter will examine only those military forces organized by public figures for the protection of their territorial or political interests. Though owing exclusive allegiance to individuals like Moise Tshombe, Godefroid Munongo, Patrice Lumumba, or Albert Kalonji, such forces were all organized in terms of the principles of discipline and chain of command that distinguish true armies from bands of armed followers.

The Force Publique: Instrument of Colonial Coercion

Weber identifies isolation from local society as the prime characteristic of the armies that were organized for the defense of large empires. In regard to isolation from society, there is a striking similarity between such imperial armies and the colonial Force Publique. As a 1961 student manifesto stated: "At the beginning of independence, there were two classes in the Congo, the basenji, or 'natives,' and the soldiers [first Hausa, then Congolese] of the Force Publique. The soldiers were responsible for the conquest of regions inhabited by the basenji and for the subjugation of the basenji to white rule."[2]

The Congolese Force Publique was founded by a decree from King Léopold on August 5, 1888. The first European penetration of the Congo Basin had been carried out almost exclusively by African auxiliaries recruited in Zanzibar for the conquest of the eastern Congo, or by Hausa from the Ivory Coast recruited for the exploration of the western part of the colony.[3] The decree of 1888 placed the entire Congo under a mixed civilian and military rule. In this system, the administrators of territorial districts were military officers immediately responsible to the governor-general, who was also the supreme commander of the Force Publique. By 1897, Congolese troops in the Force Publique numbered 12,000, and non-Congolese African troops numbered 2,000. Also by this year, the Force Publique had already distinguished itself by its performance in the antislavery campaigns of 1892–94.

Recruitment to the army rank and file was purely voluntary until 1891. After that year, conscription began to augment voluntary recruitment and soon came to supply the bulk of Force Publique troops. Officially, recruits were to be chosen by lottery, but most were simply culled from rural areas by the paramount and sector chiefs whom the Belgians had placed at the head of their smallest administrative units. The local chiefs usually conscripted slaves, prisoners taken in intertribal wars, criminals, the chronically ill, and other marginal elements in the community.[4] That the same practice still prevailed in the 1950's was noted in the colony's annual report for 1954: "Surveys suggest that many recruits from urban centers were assigned to the army because of their undesirable traits. The territorial administration has often recruited these men into the Force Publique rather than send them back to their villages."[5]

The rulers of the Congo Free State also sought a large proportion of recruits from the Bangala, Azande, and Batetela, because these were considered the most aggressive and warlike tribes in the Congo. The Belgians hoped to turn "to a loftier cause the enthusiasm these wild cannibals show in their domestic struggles."[6] Camille Coquilhat, a well-known pioneer and a founding father of the Force Publique, dealt with the Bangala of Moyen Congo in this way:

I have just succeeded in a long-term plan to enroll the Bangala in the service of other nations. To accomplish my plan, I first tried cooperating with the natives who were building my house. Next, I hired them for a week, then for a month. . . . This operation has been highly successful. Nine of my young bodyguards have embarked for Stanley Falls [Stanleyville] after ten months of service. To stimulate the enthusiasm of the local population, the enlisted men were immediately clothed and armed. They were then proud indeed as they pranced before their fellow citizens.[7]

Such recruitment practices produced an army dominated by a few tribal groups, and one whose troops were permanently separated from their tribal communities. Such an arrangement was to prove unworkable in the long run, however. In 1896, Batetela recruits mutinied at Luluabourg. Much evidence suggests that the rebellion was carefully planned, and that the mutineers intended to regroup in their native territories to the north.[8] To avoid a repetition of the mutiny, conscription and enlistment were spread out, at least in principle, among all Congolese tribes. The Force Publique would then be so fragmented ethnically that even units at the squad level would be free of domination by any one tribal group. In addition, troops were to be routinely stationed far from their tribal communities. Complete homogeneity was never achieved, however, as the investigation of the second Luluabourg mutiny in 1944 revealed.[9]

From the outset, then, the military organization of the colony rested upon the fragile basis of an army whose troops were alienated from Congolese society as a whole and its tribal origins in particular. Such isolation was strongly reinforced by the white officer corps, which sought to instill an esprit de corps based on loyalty to the Belgian crown and the person of King Léopold. White officers also took special care to emphasize the heroic deeds of the Force Publique during the antislavery campaigns. Finally, autonomous technical schools, specialized newspapers, journals, and radio broadcasts, veterans' associations, and the use of a common vernacular, the lingala, were all institutional devices that enhanced the troops' pride in belonging to a military elite. That such an elitist spirit survived in the postindependence ANC is shown by this excerpt from the army's *Bulletin Militaire*: "The best remedy for subversion and corruption in the army is the isolation of the troops by inculcating a positive zealotry toward their craft and the nobility of military ideals [and by teaching them] to despise the masses, who lack military discipline."[10] The material advantages and welfare benefits provided the Congolese soldier and his family further reinforced the caste spirit of the Force Publique. As one commander wrote:

The Force Publique is, after all, a professional army. It is normal and necessary that the comfort of the black soldier be of particular concern to the authorities. . . . Such has not always been the case. . . . It seems, however, that . . . substantial progress has been made in the housing of the units and, in a more general way, in all that concerns the material and moral welfare of our black troops.[11]

Despite frequent complaints about poor treatment, the soldiers of the Force Publique were the most privileged group of Africans in the Congo, particularly after independence. Indeed, the salaries of army troops increased three times at the end of 1960, making them the best-paid civil servants after members of Parliament.[12]

Still, privileged treatment, esprit de corps, and professionalism are features common to most modern armies. What made the Force Publique unique was the strictly colonial nature of its structures and activities, a characteristic that casts doubt on Lucian Pye's assertion that armies in developing nations (or at least those that were once colonies) may serve as modernizing agents for their societies.[13]

Though its leaders always denied this obvious fact, the real purpose of the Force Publique was not the defense of the Congo against external enemies but rather the suppression of any disorder on the part of the civilian population. The Force Publique was involved only twice in international conflicts: 12,000 troops participated in the East African campaigns against the German army in 1916 and 1917, and 10,000 troops fought in Nigeria and Egypt during World War II. Within the colony, by contrast, the Force Publique undertook major police operations against any populations that resisted European penetration, such as the Afro-Arab traders in the eastern Congo, and fought sporadically with the Mahdists of the northern Congo between 1893 and 1910. Additionally, the army routinely suppressed rebellious tribes and ambitious chiefs throughout the entire history of the Congo Free State.[14]

The Belgian government's take-over of the Congo in 1908 did not lessen the importance of internal security. In 1915, the annual report of the Belgian Congo noted that at least 30 police operations had taken place that year. The Force Publique was involved in a popular uprising that broke out in several districts of the Equateur and Kasai provinces between 1918 and 1921, and its suppression of strikes in Elisabethville and Matadi resulted in hundreds of civilian casualties. The army also took part in a variety of minor punitive actions, notably exaction of tax or compulsory labor payments from rural populations, return of fugitives to their home districts, and resettlement of populations in areas designated by the colonial administration. Repressive acts like these caused the army rank and file to behave as though it were occupying conquered territory. Indeed, the annals of the Force Publique bear no mention of the looting, rape, and indiscriminate killing that were a routine part of the various police operations it undertook.

It is not surprising that a professional army trained for repression should also be a bastion of racial discrimination. A year before independence all officers were Europeans, and no Congolese recruit could hope to advance beyond the rank of sergeant.[15] Though a military academy was opened in 1955, it was not expected to graduate Congolese lieutenants before 1968, and it was only in the intense climate of politicization just prior to independence that the Belgians nominated ten Congolese *adjudants,* or master sergeants.[16] The unchanged attitudes of racism and isolation that still prevailed at the end of Belgian rule are succinctly defined in the equation that the army's commanding officer, General Janssen, chalked on a blackboard a few days after June 30: "postindependence equals preindependence." Clearly, the Force Publique was not about to undergo any fundamental change.

Racial barriers in the Force Publique were strongly reinforced by its tradition of isolation from the metropolitan Belgian army, a tradition that James Coleman says is unique in the history of African colonial armies.[17] In French West Africa, for example, metropolitan troops are still stationed at permanent bases in Dakar and Brazzaville. In British Africa, black officers, though comprising only 10 and 25 percent of the Ghanaian and Nigerian officer corps respectively, were well steeped in the military ethics and traditions of Sandhurst.

The separation of the colonial and metropolitan armies was reinforced by the unbridled disdain of white officers in the Congo toward their counterparts in Belgium. The Belgian army's relative lack of experience in military operations and its defeat in two wars were widely contrasted with the many victorious campaigns of the Force Publique.[18] When a small contingent of metropolitan troops was sent to the Congo at the time of the Korean War, it was badly received by the high command of the Force Publique. The high command considered the presence of Belgian troops an unwarranted interference in the internal affairs of the colony.[19]

It was the total social and political isolation of the colonial army that laid the groundwork for the mutinies in the early days of Congolese independence. Though mutinies had occurred throughout the history of the Force Publique, such events as the Batetela-Bakusu uprisings in 1897 or the revolt of the Luluabourg garrison in 1944 may be viewed as specific reactions to insufficient pay or the racist attitudes of the white military hierarchy. The postindependence uprisings reflected all the contradictions inherent in the structure of the Force Publique and gave vent to long-suppressed grievances on the part of black soldiers.

In general, the mutineers expressed less hostility toward their white officers than they did toward the new class of Congolese évolués and political leaders. Several anonymous letters and editorials published in *Notre Kongo, Emancipation* and *Solidarité Africaine*, all nationalist newspapers in Léopoldville, echoed the troops' deep antipathy toward the new Congolese elite:

Independence will produce two classes. The first will be the mixed class of "great" Congolese leaders and their white advisors. These [men] will reap all the benefits of independence.... The other class will include those subordinates who shouted "Hooray for independence"... and who will remain the servants of the mixed class.... Prime Minister Lumumba has said that in spite of independence, no second-class soldier will become a general. How hurtful it is to tell the people such things. Mr. Lumumba considers us unable to do the jobs of our own officers, but with what rank, may we ask, did any general in the Force Publique begin his military career?[20]

As this statement suggests, the army rank and file fully expected promotions and material benefits to accrue from independence, but the new leaders utterly failed to fulfill the troops' expectations. Accordingly, the first incidents at the Léopoldville garrison were marked by attacks on the homes of Prime Minister Lumumba, Chief of State Kasavubu, and several members of Parliament. "Clearly, the hostility of the military was directed against Congolese ministers, who were accused of appropriating houses, luxury cars, and funds. . . . [The anger of the military] was directed specifically at Lumumba, who had promised many benefits that the military never received."[21]

In addition, frequent bloody clashes between the military and the civilian population had established a climate of mutual fear and hatred. The army was especially strained on the eve of independence because it was responsible for policing electoral campaigns throughout the Congo: "The personnel of the Force Publique was extremely weary from having to maintain public order after January of 1959, especially during the electoral campaigns. The participation of the Force in independence celebrations was exhausting as well. Several observers noted that the first mutinies occurred among those units that were most fatigued."[22] On June 30, the soldiers experienced their supreme frustration. While civilians danced in the streets, the troops spent the entire night confined to their barracks.

Violence against whites during the 1960 mutinies was quite mild in comparison to that of the preindependence uprisings; no Belgian officers were killed, and all were eventually evacuated with their families. However, there was a deep feeling of racial frustration in the Force Publique, as one group of African soldiers made clear:

Everybody knows that we, the army rank and file, are treated like slaves. We are punished arbitrarily...because we are niggers....We may read no newspapers published by black civilians.... There is no human contact between our officers and ourselves, but rather a relationship of [white] domination that turns us into racially inferior slaves. There is total paralysis in the Africanization of the [army] staff.[23]

With the actual outbreak of mutiny, however, the prevailing mood among Congolese troops became one of fear toward their white officers. According to Gérard-Libois and Verhaegen, both the mutinies and the European reaction to them assumed a general pattern as they spread through the various Congolese garrisons:

At the outset there was reciprocal fear in both the black and white communities. Among the Europeans, [this fear was caused by] memories of the Luluabourg mutiny of 1944 and the Léopoldville uprising of 1959. The African soldiers feared intervention from Belgian paratroops.... Thus Europeans armed and formed self-defense brigades.... Belgian officers attempted to cut off the Congolese troops' access to munitions and, in some cases, distributed weapons to Europeans.[24]

As Europeans panicked and attempted to flee, Congolese troops tried desperately to restrain them. The Congolese feared that once the Europeans had fled, Belgian paratroops would intervene. In spite of such mutual terror, anti-European incidents were far less tragic than might have been expected. It is likely that the complex nature of army grievances, as well as the widespread confusion at the time of the mutinies, kept the level of purely racial violence to a minimum.

The Emergence of Private Armies

The fragmentation of the Force Publique (called the Armée Nationale Congolaise [ANC] after independence) into various private militias was caused not only by its demoralization following the 1960

mutinies, but also by Congolese leaders' attempts to turn army grievances to their own political ends. During the 1960 electoral campaigns, the military became involved in tribal politics by attending
political rallies and by selling party memberships, especially in the
MNC-Lumumba, which was very active among the Batetela and related groups in the army. Also, the 1960 mutinies allowed several political leaders to establish close relations with tribal leaders in the
Force Publique. As Gérard-Libois and Verhaegen state: "Congolese
leaders, who hypothesized a colonial war as early as 1959, sought to
limit its . . . magnitude by destroying or paralyzing the institution
that could lead to such a war, the Force Publique. They did so by
establishing close contacts, on a tribal basis, with Congolese noncoms
and with some of the 'natural leaders' among the troops."[25] In the
panic and uncertainty prevailing at the time, such contacts protected
politicians from the anarchic behavior of angry and frightened
troops. Thus President Kasavubu himself was known to rely on the
protection of Adjudant Nkokolo, a Mukongo who later became commandant of the Léopoldville garrison. Similarly, Jean Bolikango,
who was nominated minister of national defense after the mutinies,
enjoyed great popularity among the Bangala rank and file.

Clearly, the politicization and tribalization of the ANC began during the 1960 mutinies. Such divisive tendencies reached their full
extent, however, during the secessions of South Kasai, South Katanga,
and Orientale provinces.

The South Kasai Army. In September 1960, Albert Kalonji proclaimed the independent state of South Kasai.[26] Quite naturally,
Kalonji's first concern was to secure his new state against a very real
threat of outside aggression. To this end he quickly rearmed the approximately 250 policemen and 200 Baluba soldiers who had fled
their Kasai and Katanga garrisons to join the secession. At its inception, the South Kasai army was organized into three companies of
120 men apiece, each headed by a Baluba officer. According to unofficial estimates, the army grew to 2,500 men by the middle of 1961.

As an irregular army, the South Kasai force armed and paid its
troops with aid from the government of South Katanga, technical
assistance from Belgium, and dividends that Kalonji received from
the South Kasai mining trust, MIBEKA. The majority of recruits
were Luba, though some came from the neighboring Bemba, Lenze,

and Basalampasu tribes. According to John Roberts, the British officer to whom Kalonji entrusted the army's recruitment and training, the enthusiasm of the Baluba volunteers was determined largely by a desire for rapid promotion. Kalonji solved this problem just as Patrice Lumumba had solved a similar one in Léopoldville:

> There was [one day] a formal parade of the men at which the Commander in Chief, Kalonji, conferred the ranks. A man would be called up one minute and made a Private; a few minutes later he would be called again and promoted to Corporal. In one instance a man was called up several times and promoted from Private to Sergeant-Major within half an hour.[27]

The fighting spirit of this improvised army was bolstered by magical charms. Each soldier wore a length of twine diagonally across his chest so that a juju of dried paste hung directly over the heart. Witch doctors gave the troops additional charms and drugs and led "curse dances" against Lumumba before battles.[28]

The South Kasai regime received military support from sources outside its own army. Some help came from the MNC-Jeunesse, a group of young men who emigrated spontaneously from Luluabourg and Elisabethville to South Kasai and there formed armed bands independent of the Kalonji government. Also from Elisabethville came a small group of Belgian, British, and French mercenaries led by a Frenchman, Colonel Gillet.

Kalonji's chief military resource outside the South Kasai army was the warriors of traditional chiefs, and particularly those of Mutombo Katshi, who represented himself as the chief of all the Baluba Kasai. The Luba chiefs enjoyed an especially close relationship with the Kalonji government, and their considerable influence was evident in the South Kasai capital of Bakwanga. There, Kalonji's residence was swamped daily by chiefs who came "to request jobs in the local administration, or merely to make sure that they were still recognized as the traditional rulers of their chieftaincies."[29] Kalonji's habitual generosity toward the Luba chiefs soon attracted chiefs from Songhe, Bakwa Mputu, and Bakuba regions. Kalonji openly welcomed these non-Luba chiefs, too, as potential sources of troops in case of emergency. In fact, Louis Tshibamba, Kalonji's chief advisor and the "great witch doctor" of the South Kasai army, was himself a Songhe chief who held considerable influence in Bakwanga.[30]

In early 1961 South Kasai troops undertook a campaign to expand

the borders of the new state, which then encompassed only the small
Bakwanga and Gandajika territories. In the district of Kabinda north
of Bakwanga, the South Kasai army fought Basonge warriors and
a small ANC garrison stationed at Kabinda. In the Mwene-Ditu area
south of Gandajika, the MNC-Jeunesse and the South Kasai army
together participated in bloody engagements against Kanyoka troops
who refused to submit to Kalonji's authority.[31] During these campaigns, South Kasai officers showed considerable ingenuity in coping
with a shortage of arms and ammunition. In Bakwanga, for example,
an enthusiastic crowd saw a demonstration of a homemade recoilless
machine gun.[32]

Political events in March 1961 produced significant changes in the
structure of the South Kasai army. Following his election as *mulopwe*
(Tshiluba for "emperor") of South Kasai, Kalonji and his Baluba
chiefs established an autocratic and semitheocratic regime at Bakwanga. One consequence of the change was the emergence of a palace army led by a twenty-year-old general, Floribert Dinanga, and devoted exclusively to the mulopwe himself. The hard core of this force
was the former MNC-Jeunesse, whose ranks had swelled with the
constant influx of unemployed Luba youths into South Kasai.[33]

As opposition to the new authoritarian regime mounted, regular
army recruits were increasingly drawn from Kalonji's tribal group,
the Bena Tshibanda, and particularly from his own Bakwa Disho
clan.[34] Older units of the armed forces remained intact, however,
effectively producing two separate armies by the end of 1961. Each of
the armies exhibited almost total ethnic homogeneity.* Not surprisingly, such a cleavage in the South Kasai army dangerously weakened
Kalonji's authority in the long run.

Opposition to Kalonji was led by the former prime minister of
South Kasai, Joseph Ngalula, whom the mulopwe had exiled to Léopoldville. In July 1962, Ngalula and his associates planned to foment
a mutiny among South Kasai troops. The execution of this plan was
delegated to one M. Kankolongo, himself a former Kalonji partisan
who had been a high general commissioner in South Kasai.[35] The

* In an interview in July 1968, Theodore Tshiswaka, former finance minister for
South Kasai, stated that some Bakongo and Bangala elements from the former
South Kasai constabulary did remain in the army after the declaration of inde-
pendence.

mutiny broke out as planned at the end of September. On October 5, a battalion of ANC troops was sent from Léopoldville to Bakwanga to support the mutineers. Eventually, all Baluba officers in the South Kasai army were taken prisoner, though officers who were not members of Kalonji's own ethnic group were soon released.

Some 2,000 soldiers from the former South Kasai army joined the ANC by the end of 1962. Yet despite the collapse of the South Kasai government and Kalonji's flight from the region, many soldiers remained convinced that their mulopwe would return to power and so fled to the northern part of the province. These rebels were led by a General Mwanzambala, previously a sergeant in the Force Publique. They undertook guerrilla operations against Joseph Ngalula's new provincial administration and the Léopoldville troops stationed in South Kasai. When General Mwanzambala surrendered at the end of 1963, he was able to stipulate that his partisans should be integrated into the ANC with the same ranks they had held in the South Kasai army.[36] About 1,200 of the rebels reenlisted in the regular army in 1964.

The South Katangese Army. The secession of South Katanga in July 1960 would have been impossible without a strong, well-equipped fighting force. Noteworthy for its stiff resistance to ANC offensives in Katanga and UN military operations in the province's urban centers, the South Katangese army was also outstanding in its utter devotion to the leader, Moise Tshombe.

The formation of an autonomous army in South Katanga began with the mutiny of the Force Publique garrison in Elisabethville in July 1960. The Katangese government reacted to the mutiny with dispatch, disarming and expelling all but 200 of the soldiers in the garrison on the grounds that they were politically unsafe. In their place, a brand new force was created, its recruits drawn mainly from the Balunda and Bayeke tribes of President Tshombe and his interior minister, Godefroid Munongo. The numerical strength of the Katangese Army has been estimated at 5,000 men, "well equipped, and trained by 400 non-Congolese officers and noncoms," in February 1961.[37] A UN report states that there were about 11,600 troops in mid-1961, though Young's estimates place the figure for that period at 19,000.[38]

The Katangese regime could not rely entirely on untrained troops who, despite their modern equipment, still depended on foreign military advisors whose presence was forbidden by UN resolutions. Therefore, certain paramount chiefs favorable to the Tshombe regime were allowed to maintain their own militias. Thus Kasongo Nyembo, chief of the Baluba Katanga, had 400 armed subjects at his direct command,[39] while a Muyeke chief, Antoine Mwenda Munongo, controlled a detachment of warriors armed with modern weapons.[40] These relatively small traditional armies proved instrumental in dealing with the Baluba rebellion in North Katanga. As a Belgian correspondent pointed out in December 1960:

Military repression will solve nothing at this stage. . . . [This is why] warriors have been recruited from loyal tribes in the rebel areas. Once armed and trained . . . , these warriors will provide valuable aid to the mobile units. Divided into squads of about 25 men, the warriors will be able to fight in depth from the bush along the roads. Moreover, since they will be defending their own territories they will fight with greater conviction than regular Katangese troops, who are fighting far from home.[41]

These irregular troops were later incorporated into the South Katangese army and placed under the command of one General Moke.

With the end of the secession and Tshombe's temporary exile in Spain, most South Katangese soldiers refused to be incorporated into the ANC on the grounds that their loyalty to the Katangese leaders might be penalized, or that they would lose their privileged status within a reunified national army. Some formed small armed bands in the countryside, where they survived by banditry and looting. About 15,000 others were hired by mining companies or emigrated with white mercenaries to the farms that Tshombe owned in Rhodesia. In September 1963, UN Secretary-General U Thant stated that former Katangese troops were "leaving jobs at Elisabethville in such great numbers and in such a pattern that they seem to be planning to regroup elsewhere in organized units."[42] Though the existence of any such overall plan was never finally determined, the mere suggestion that South Katangese units might be massing outside the Congo greatly accelerated Tshombe's return to Congolese politics. Tshombe's sudden designation as prime minister of the Congo on July 10, 1964, coincided with the reconstitution of the Katangese army, whose units nonetheless remained separate from the bulk of the ANC.

During the 1964 rebellions, the legend of an efficient, tough, and hard-fighting Katangese army spread throughout the Congo, particularly among Europeans. Once part of the ANC, however, the Katangese stood revealed as arrogant and undisciplined troops, far more eager to claim pay due them than to head into combat.[43] As during the secession, they obeyed only the direct orders of Prime Minister Tshombe or the white mercenaries who headed their units.

Agitation spread through Katangese ranks with Tshombe's dismissal in November 1965. In January 1966, there were unconfirmed rumors of a mutiny of the Katangese troops posted on the Congo's border with Uganda. In July, a mutiny broke out among Katangese soldiers in the eastern garrisons. The mutiny in the Bukavu garrison collapsed by July 16, but in Kisangani 2,000 paratroops under a Katangese officer, Colonel Tshipola, held the airport and the western part of the city for two months. The rebels demanded higher salaries and called for the resignation of the ANC commander in chief, General Bobozo. Negotiations between the mutineers and Prime Minister Mulamba failed after several weeks. According to some sources, the mutineers were receiving financial aid from Katangese politicians, and Moise Tshombe was communicating with Colonel Tshipola from Madrid.[44] On September 23, the ANC, together with a few mercenaries, captured the airport and the rebels there. Most of the captured troops were killed, and Colonel Tshipola was arrested and sentenced to death in October.

Katangese troops were involved in still another mutiny that broke out in Bukavu and Kisangani in July 1967. However, this revolt was initiated by white mercenaries rather than Katangese officers, since the Katangese army had ceased to exist as an autonomous unit after its defeat by the ANC.

The Stanleyville Nationalist Army. The Stanleyville nationalist army was something of an anomaly among the private armies of the Congo. This force consisted primarily of the ANC regiment stationed in Stanleyville, where it had long been exposed to nationalist and anticolonial propaganda from the MNC-Lumumba. The commandant of the regiment, General Victor Lundula, was named commander in chief of the ANC by Patrice Lumumba. It was Lundula's subsequent decision to join the Stanleyville secession that allowed this dissident regime at least partial control over the Stanleyville garrison, though the troops' pay was still coming from Léopoldville.

As Young describes the situation: "One of the most curious aspects of this period of schizophrenia in the ANC was that the composition of the troops remained mixed; many soldiers controlled by Léopold-ville served under General Lundula, and vice versa."[45]

However, General Lundula returned to Stanleyville from Léopold-ville in November 1960, and soon managed to bring the local troops under his command; a military parade on November 26, in which virtually all army units in Orientale province took part, made the general's control plain to all observers. During the following months, General Lundula set up a staff composed almost entirely of officers from Orientale and Kasai provinces. The three most important army officers at that time were Major Loso, who commanded the military police, Major Opepe, and Colonel Camille Yangara.[46] To strengthen the Stanleyville army against possible attack from Léopoldville, General Lundula and his staff intensified recruitment among the un-employed urban youth of Stanleyville and the MNC-Jeunesse loyal to Lumumba.

Unlike the South Kasai or South Katangese armies, the Stanley-ville army was not held together by loyalty to a patrimonial ruler. Though Antoine Gizenga was the titular head of the Stanleyville secession, he was a Mupende from Kwilu and so could claim power in Orientale only as the direct political heir to Patrice Lumumba. The Stanleyville army was given its political cohesion by the troops' respect and admiration for General Lundula, and by Patrice Lu-mumba's nationalist ideology and strong emotional appeal. In early 1961, when the news of Lumumba's death reached Stanleyville, three to four thousand soldiers gathered spontaneously to take revenge on the city's European residents, whom they held responsible for their hero's murder. Only General Lundula's nightlong appeals for calm pacified the soldiers and persuaded them to leave the European sec-tion of the city.[47]

From late 1960 on, the Gizenga regime sought to expand its in-fluence beyond the borders of Orientale province. However, the Stanleyville nationalist army proved clearly unequal to this task. In December, about 60 soldiers were sent to establish a link between the Stanleyville army and the garrison at Bukavu in Kivu province. However, a UN report states that "General Lundula's authority over the ANC troops stationed in Kivu was never fully established."[48]

In September 1961, General Lundula dispatched 200 troops to North Katanga to engage Katangese forces there. The expedition ended shamefully a month later with a troop mutiny at Albertville, in Kivu, and the massacre of thirteen Italian pilots at Kindu, in Katanga.[49]

Military setbacks, the political deterioration of the Stanleyville regime, and his own moderate views eventually persuaded General Lundula to align himself with the new Adoula government in Léopoldville.[50] In November 1961, Lundula was publicly reinstated as commander in chief of the ANC. The leaderless Stanleyville army wallowed in confusion, ignoring Antoine Gizenga's orders to arrest Lundula but also resisting the central government's moves to end the secession and jail Gizenga. UN forces eventually put an end to the dilemma in January 1962, when they occupied Stanleyville and arranged to transfer Gizenga to Léopoldville.

The Mercenaries

The role of foreign armies in the political development of new states is subject to two sharply contrasting interpretations. In Weber's view, mercenaries hired by patrimonial rulers constitute especially dependable armies, since they consist of foreigners who have no real contact with the subject population and therefore respond solely to the ruler's own commands. However, Weber's tendency to treat the mercenary force as a neutral instrument of rule while discounting the feelings of the mercenaries themselves somewhat lessens the value of his model. Machiavelli more closely approaches the political reality of most developing nations in holding that although arms may be needed to establish order in newly founded states, continued reliance on the use of force will weaken such states in the long run. While Weber's argument for the reliability of mercenaries is based on such objective factors as regular payment from the ruler, Machiavelli is much more concerned with those specific attitudes of mercenary armies that, in his view, are likely to corrupt the new state and stunt the development of its civic virtue. In fact, Machiavelli asserts that mercenaries can offer no real benefit to any ruler: "Mercenary captains are either capable men or not; if they are, you cannot rely upon them, for they will always aspire to their own greatness, either by oppressing you, their master, or by oppressing others against your intentions."[51]

Nowhere in modern times has this observation been more fully vindicated than in the Congo. Throughout the postindependence period, foreign adventurers have involved themselves deeply in the political intrigues and civil wars dividing the country and have clearly done their part to shape its political development. Accordingly, no study of Congolese politics can be complete without mention of these mercenary forces.

Mercenaries entered the Congo for the first time during the Katangese secession. Their involvement in Katanga was a direct result of Belgium's continued interest in her former colony. The consensus in Belgian governmental and financial circles was that the reintegration of the Congo should begin from Katanga, where the swift intervention of Belgian troops had preserved relative order and stability. Outside military aid was clearly esssential to the maintenance of Katangese autonomy, for Luba uprisings in the northern part of the province were taking their toll of the inexperienced Katangese troops. Since Belgium could not risk open defiance of the UN prohibition against foreign intervention in the Congo, the Katangese leaders and their Belgian advisors were forced to recruit foreign troops on an individual, contractual basis. The first recruitment missions, most of which were led by idealistic Belgian supporters of Moise Tshombe, left Katanga for Europe at the end of 1960:

[These missions] dealt with the recruitment of Katangese troops, as well as with problems related to their outfitting, financing, management, and training. [Such operations] were willfully concealed by Colonel G——, an employee at the Belgian office of military security who was in charge of investigating the mercenary candidates. An unofficial link also existed between the head of the mission and Major L——, personal advisor to the Belgian minister for African affairs.[52]

Unexpectedly strong resistance from Luba dissidents, coupled with Belgium's unwillingness to become too openly involved in the Katangese secession, prompted the Tshombe government itself to begin recruiting foreign mercenaries. An autonomous "International Company" composed of white South Africans and Rhodesians was established in early 1961.[53] At the same time, recruiters were sent to France to seek out rightwing military officers whose experience in

Indochina and Algeria had given them a valuable knowledge of guerrilla warfare. Thus in January 1961, Colonel Claude Trinquier, known for his role in the suppression of Algerian nationalists, was named the commander in chief of the Katangese armed forces.[54]

By the end of 1961, the Katangese government had hired 195 Belgian and 80 French mercenaries, organized either as autonomous fighting units like the International Company or as officer cadres in the regular Katangese army. In August and September 1961, the UN mission tried repeatedly to oust the foreign units but failed each time. Just prior to the final confrontation between Katangese and UN forces in December 1961 and January 1962, the mercenaries were still estimated at 150 to 200 men.[55] At that time, Robert Denard, a former French army sergeant and a veteran of the Indochina war, was the operational commander of the Katangese mobile units.

The mercenaries' exploits in combat were legendary throughout Katanga, especially among Europeans seeking military protection. As one Belgian journalist wrote:

The *affreux* ["frightful ones"] are outstanding in combat. They have been recruited from all over, and many of them have fought in Korea and Indochina before coming here. They look like pirates and toughs with their shaggy hair and droopy mustaches, and they make really frightening adversaries. [The mercenaries] have been the object of both high praise and harsh criticism, but they were at their best on Saturday, rushing courageously into combat to rescue a wounded comrade or to retrieve a machine gun left in rebel hands.[56]

The mercenaries enlisted for a variety of reasons, ranging from an idealistic urge to defend Western civilization against Communism to a simple desire to make easy money. Indeed, money, arms, women, and drink became the only motivations to these twentieth-century soldiers of fortune, and violence and killing became part of their daily routine. Most mercenaries were alienated from their own societies, and since they formed an assemblage of psychopathic individuals, no real solidarity could exist among them. Also, the international scope of the Tshombe government's recruitment drive gave rise to personal rivalries that increasingly undermined relations between French and Belgian officers.

Moise Tshombe's return to the political arena and the spectacular progress of the 1964 uprising caused the Léopoldville government to adopt a policy of mercenary recruitment on a far wider scale than that of the Katangese secession. By September 1964, some 800 mercenaries were stationed in military bases in Kamina. According to General Joseph Mobutu, this figure rose to 1,500 by August 1965. This second wave of mercenary recruitment was in many ways analogous to the earlier Belgo-Katangese employment of foreign troops. For instance, recruitment was not undertaken directly by the ANC, but by unofficial groups associated with the prime minister. As in South Katanga, the mercenary force was a highly international one in which South African, Rhodesian, German, and French recruits were preferred to Belgians. The troops were organized into small units with a high degree of mobility and firepower. Such units usually included some Katangese and regular ANC troops.[57] While the central government was hiring its foreign troops, European settlers were themselves organizing mobile units like the Kivu Volunteer Corps (CODOKI), and industrial enterprises were maintaining militias of their own.

Foreign military aid cost the Congolese central government 2,034 billion Congolese francs in 1965, or 3.5 percent of its total expenditures for that year.[58] At the same time, the virtual collapse of the 1964 uprisings made the mercenaries something of an embarrassment to Joseph Mobutu. In July 1966, President Mobutu stated in public: "The rebellions are over. I no longer need [the mercenaries], but I will not expel them. There is a human side to the problem that I cannot ignore: [the mercenaries] have been good friends to me. They will leave of themselves, as their contracts will not be renewed."[59]

In reality, the discipline and efficiency of the mercenary troops declined visibly about this time, and some mercenary units seemed unwilling to eliminate the remaining pockets of rebel resistance that justified their presence in the Congo. The period of uncertainty following the collapse of the rebellions aggravated conflicts that saw Katangese troops and mercenary units opposed to the rank and file of the ANC.

Machiavelli's prophecy that mercenaries, though useful in war, can only cause trouble in peacetime was fulfilled in July 1967. It was then that two mercenary officers, Robert Denard and Jean Schram, led the remaining foreign troops and some South Katangese units in an attempt to take over the Congolese government.[60] This attempted coup was probably supported by Moise Tshombe from his exile in Madrid. The mercenaries were far better soldiers than they were political strategists. Their attack strengthened rather than sapped the spirit of the ANC, and Congolese resistance, particularly in Kisangani and Bukavu, was far stiffer than anticipated. The attempted coup ended in failure, and the departure of the defeated mercenaries from the Congo left the ANC fully as self-confident and arrogant as it had been before the mercenaries' arrival.

CHAPTER 5

Conditions for Political Change

So far, this study has reviewed three patrimonial elements in Congolese politics: the appropriation of public offices as the prime motivation to the elite, the primacy of personal relationships, and the reliance on private armies to maintain patrimonial authority. Since the topic under discussion also includes change in Congolese politics, it is essential to consider the inherent propensities for change in patrimonial politics as influenced by a given socioeconomic setting.

Weber's ideal types will be of only limited use in this area, for a major weakness of Weberian analysis is its lack of dynamic perspective.[1] By applying Weber's models wherever possible, though, and approaching new material pragmatically, this chapter will isolate the elements that led to the breakdown of patrimonial politics in the Congo. It will also seek to determine whether such subsequent events as the 1964–65 rebellions or the emergence of a bureaucratic-Caesarist regime after late 1965 might have been predicted.

The Question of Resources

Eisenstadt says that access to resources has been a critical necessity of bureaucratic empires throughout history:

The historical bureaucratic policies were characterized by the coexistence of "free floating" resources (that is, manpower, economic resources, political support, and cultural identifications), and of political forces and orientations. This coexistence was the fundamental prerequisite for the functioning of those systems.[2]

Eisenstadt's statement about the bureaucracies of the past can be applied to any type of political system, so long as that system involves what Easton calls the authoritative allocation of values. Talcott Parsons comes even closer to the point when he defines the essential function of a political body as the "mobilization of societal resources and their commitments for the attainment of collective goals, for the formation and implementation of public policy."[3] Similarly, Gabriel Almond analyzes political systems in terms of their performance in the development, regulation, and distribution of resources.[4]

Not all political systems have had equal success in mobilizing human and material resources. In the bureaucratic empires of the past, rulers were usually able to maintain strong control over the allocation of favors and benefits by means of a powerful and impersonal administrative apparatus. In modern states, natural resources are usually developed and distributed by the entrepreneurial and analogous social classes, a fact that keeps resources from being wasted in competition for public office and political power. In patrimonial states, by contrast, constant competition for public office is especially destructive, for it is just such states that lack the moderating influence of a strong central bureaucracy or a modern social structure. Also, the patrimonial ruler's inclination to treat administrative offices as personal property, to be disposed of as he wishes, clearly hampers the rational allocation of resources and leaves the ruler vulnerable to other powerful individuals capable of mobilizing support on a personal basis. Such conditions promote unpredictable behavior on the part of politicians, the widespread abuse of personal power, and a political system that lacks any division of labor. As Weber stresses in his treatment of patrimonialism in France between the sixteenth and eighteenth centuries, the appropriation and trading of political favors creates a particularly inflexible administrative structure. Such a structure is incapable of undertaking new tasks and is impervious to any systematic regulation; it contrasts strongly with the purposive organization of modern bureaucracies.[5]

The first chapter of this study, which describes how a group of unimaginative petty bureaucrats came to dominate the social and political hierarchies of the Congo, clearly establishes patrimonialism's inability to channel social resources constructively. A similar characteristic of patrimonialism, and one that requires closer attention here, is its inherent tendency toward decentralism and instability.

The Instability of Patrimonialism

Since it is based on a ruler's personal resources, a patrimonial form of government cannot easily cope with problems that arise when large territories fall under the ruler's authority, and this inherent weakness is compounded by other limiting factors. Specifically, subjects in a patrimonial state are generally free to dispose of their lives and property as they see fit. In the patrimonial empires of the past, such freedom may have been given institutional expression by the subjects' inheritance rights, their right to marry without the ruler's consent, their right to a hearing before independent courts, or their right to own and bear arms. It was also generally true that the political duties of subjects, as opposed to members of the ruler's immediate entourage, were defined by a body of traditional obligations and restrictions.[6]

Subjects in modern patrimonial states also have certain established rights, including, of course, the right to choose their rulers by ballot and the right to shift their political allegiance between vying factions. Most important, modern patrimonialism appeals to the masses by presenting the ruler as the "father of his people." Since the ruler legitimizes his authority by looking after his subjects' welfare, he is to some extent dependent on their goodwill. It is worthwhile noting that such restraints on patrimonial authority are not usually derived from ancient traditions, as had been the case with classical patrimonialism.[7]

In general, areas under a patrimonial form of government possess neither sophisticated transport networks nor disciplined administrative personnel. This characteristic further complicates the extension of central authority to all parts of a patrimonial state, since the ruler may not always be in contact with his state's periphery. Thus any patrimonial ruler in a central position of power will be threatened both by the relative isolation of his supporters at the local level and by the power struggles that are likely to arise among them. As Weber says of the patrimonial regimes of the past:

With the extension and decentralization of a patrimonial regime the duties of the personal dependents may become attenuated as their actual independence from the master's control increases. And, conversely, in the case of political subjects, their rights diminish and their duties increase as their physical and political dependence upon the ruler is enhanced by circumstances or as the ruler increases his adherence to tradition.[8]

Patrimonial rulers and their governments have evolved various means to counteract such centrifugal tendencies. Some have relied on kinship groups, guilds, and other organizations held collectively responsible for certain public services and duties. Historians identify this form of social and political control with the rigid and sharply delineated status structures of preindustrial societies.[9] Other organizational checks were the appointment of circuit officials with regular tours of duty, periodic visits by the ruler to various parts of his domain, and the maintenance of a central court in which nobles could be kept under the watchful eye of the ruler himself.

None of the usual countermeasures to political fragmentation were ever applied systematically in the Congo. Only in those rare cases where traditional political structures remained relatively strong, as in Kwango, Uélé, Kivu, and parts of Katanga, did the central government or patrimonial leaders attempt to use local chiefs as intermediaries to the rural population, and even these attempts had only limited success.[10] Between 1962 and 1965, the central government had no direct contact with the countryside. Neither the prime minister nor the president ever toured the Congo, and governmental and parliamentary delegations visited the interior only in times of grave crisis. Finally, the Board of Special Commissioners and the Board of Extraordinary Commissioners, both intended to link Léopoldville with the provinces, functioned only intermittently.

Because of the inherent instability of the patrimonial form of political structure, it is essential that any patrimonial ruler organize a military force to maintain order among his subjects and dependents. Weber stresses, however, that the use of force to expand one's domain may be dangerous if it transforms patrimonialism into a kind of sultanism: "By the use of these instruments of force, the ruler tends to broaden the range of his arbitrary power which is free of traditional restrictions and to put himself in a position to grant gifts and favours at the expense of the traditional limitations typical of patriarchal structures."[11] Also, a ruler who relies solely on a private militia or army to maintain his authority is ultimately at the mercy of his troops and must often buy their loyalty with increased material benefits. In case of military defeat or civil disorder, angry troops may still rebel and overthrow their patron. Most important, excessive use of military force makes violence a fact of everyday life and will eventually undermine a nation's political cohesion.

Events in the Congo clearly demonstrate that military force is of limited use in maintaining governmental authority. Though never as well publicized as the spectacular conflicts in Kasai, Kivu, and Katanga, the army's outright violence against civilians in all parts of the Congo was enormously disruptive. As we have seen, the colonial Force Publique was a brutal coercive tool that underwent no fundamental change with independence. Further, the dispersion of the ANC throughout the countryside made the entire Congolese population painfully aware that its army was arrogant, undisciplined, and overpaid. Thus it is not surprising that during the rebellions in the early days of Congolese independence, the unpopularity of the ANC swelled rebel ranks and robbed the central government of considerable rural support.

Environmental Constraints

Most studies of African politics overlook the fact that to some degree political systems function and change in response to factors outside of themselves. Clearly, African countries are deeply affected both by their underlying social values and by fluctuations in international economics and politics. It is essential to take such influences into account if decolonization is to be understood as more than a simple transfer of power from one elite to another.

In general, the degree to which a political system can absorb and integrate outside influences directly determines the rulers' success in promoting autonomous and valid programs for change. It is in just such a capacity that patrimonialism is especially weak, according to Eisenstadt.[12] Here, however, we will be concerned less with the nature of patrimonialism in the abstract than with the interaction between patrimonial politics and the various outside influences affecting it. In the Congo, such influences include the political value system, which is extraneous in origin; the dominance of foreign capital investment in the national economy; and the frequent intrusion of international conflicts onto the domestic political scene.

The Extraneous Nature of the Political Culture. In their analysis of colonialism, sociologists and psychoanalysts both stress that the domination of any people by a foreign minority is very likely to produce structural imbalances and cultural frustrations to which the dominated people must inevitably react. In the past, reaction has taken such forms as rebellions, retreatist attitudes, syncretic movements, and the exaltation of the past through such pseudoscientific intellectual constructs as "negritude" or "Africanism." Decolonization, viewed as the transfer of political power to indigenous elites, has not provided the new African nations with more authentic national cultures. Instead, a new sociocultural synthesis has emerged. This new synthesis is often known euphemistically as the "transitional society," but Jean Poirier is more accurate when he calls it the "condominial situation." The outstanding feature of the condominial situation is its dualism, a dualism evident both in the relationship of African political elites to foreign economic cartels, and within modern African cultures themselves.

The sharp encounter between modern colonialism and traditional cultures has produced cleavages, contradictions, and tensions that still persist within newly independent states. Overt aggression and anxiety, the conspirational nature of politics, the alternation of long periods of dormancy with brief ones of frantic activity, and ambivalent feelings and attitudes toward the Western world are the most evident manifestations of the condominial situation.[13] As Poirier says:

The passage from the colonial to the condominial situation is, in large part, a passage from dependence to alienation. Despite its crises, its masked tensions, and its open conflicts, the colonial era brought a certain equilibrium. There was an order, a certainty, and a hierarchy there: one knew where authority lay, what was predominant and what subordinate, what was permitted and what forbidden. In a sense, paternalism was reassuring and balancing.... Conversely, independence, which produces the condominial situation, eliminates all possibility of evasion ... : the new nations are condemned to be themselves.... It is here that alienation appears, no longer within a narrow circle, but widespread among the masses.[14]

In the Congo, the lack of integration is demonstrated by the coexistence of colonial authoritarianism, paternalism, and bureaucratism with modern notions of democracy and majority rule. The new ruling elite, suddenly aware of its vested interest in the status quo, has maintained this mixed value system through constant reaffirmation of colonial welfare policies and the ritualization of western democratic forms.

The term "ritualization" implies a faith in the primacy and effectiveness of form over content in human activities. All social organizations exhibit some ritualistic traits, but Hobsbawm points out that modern associations lack deliberately contrived rituals and derive their validity from a shared belief in substance rather than in form: "The docker or doctor who takes out the card of his union or professional organization ... knows without special formalities that he is committing himself to certain activities and forms of behaviour. . . . But he does so with no greater ceremony than the taking of a piece of pasteboard of purely utilitarian design on which stamps are periodically stuck."[15]

In the Congo, parliamentary institutions have been the prime object of ritualization; at the same time, they have proved almost totally ineffective as decision-making bodies. Procedures in provincial assemblies after the creation of the new provinces provide a case in point:

After long and difficult negotiations, both inside and outside the assembly, a provincial government is finally set up. Of necessity, it includes representative sprinklings of various tribal and regional interest groups. Such extreme care is given to the question of representation that ethnic relationships take precedence over competence. Because the ministerial and administrative staffs are supposed to represent all the major political forces, they should be able to keep institutional crises within manageable bounds. As a matter of fact, ethnic arithmetic does not solve the problem of representation, which must be qualitative as well as quantitative. Thus in most provincial assemblies there emerges a small group of political activists whose representatives hold the principal offices (the presidential staff, the ministry of the interior, and the civil service). Soon, this faction is suspected of dominating the others; rather quickly, the initial cohesion begins to melt away. Alliances between minority groups are proposed, made, and constantly unmade, finally polarizing in an opposition movement that always wins in the long run, since it feeds on the government's chronic inability to cope with social and economic problems. After a period of violent agitation, a new political faction rises to the top, only to find itself caught up in the same vicious circle as its predecessors. It, too, must bow to a new and ephemeral majority.

In the face of such intense factional squabbling, only the strictest respect for matters of form has allowed any cohesion among provincial delegates. Speeches by delegates, motions of censure, votes, and parliamentary procedures in general have become ritual incantations that are thought to possess magical powers of their own. Such a ritualistic approach to parliamentary forms is derived in part from the knowledge that these forms have proved highly successful in Western democratic nations. Also, parliamentary institutions in the Congo have been held almost sacred as the guardians of the people's interests, or as the keystone of all other governmental institutions in the country.[16] In this sense, the democratic assembly functions as a substitute for the colonial administrator, who in a different way was the father and protector of his constituency. Indeed, the roles of high civil servants and other public officials in the Congo have been directly influenced by the old image of the colonial administrator. Like their predecessors, Congolese officials frequently express concern for the welfare of the "natives." Likewise, their conception of popular welfare is strongly reminiscent of Belgian paternalism in its emphasis on rural community development, law and order, compulsory labor, and the necessity of foreign investment in the Congo.[17]

The administrative structures of the colonial period have also been maintained and, to some extent, strengthened since independence, particularly at the local level. Sector chiefs, customary chiefs, and other petty bureaucrats in the territorial administration at first suffered verbal attacks as collaborators with white colonial rule; the oldest and least skilled of them were replaced by literate youths who had occupied marginal positions in rural society. Still, the rigid hierarchy and blind bureaucratism of the Congolese territorial service have not been eliminated since independence and have been aggravated in some cases by the relative inefficiency of the new appointees.

The heavy colonial heritage is also reflected in the geographical organization of the new nation. As we have seen, the provincial reorganization of 1962 did not really change territorial divisions in the Congo, since the new provinces followed the borders of former colonial districts. Also, territories, chieftaincies, and sectors, the basic units in colonial administrative hierarchy, have been retained without modification by the Congolese government.

During 1963 and 1964, many provincial governments implemented administrative reforms intended to foster local and regional autonomy. Specifically, the reforms were supposed to increase grassroots political participation and answer local demands for the creation of new territories and sectors. In fact, the reforms served less to revitalize local government than to thwart certain elements of political opposition and create jobs for the clients of regional patrons. Though the reforms did result in the creation of some prefectures and urban communes to replace territories and sectors, the new administrative units differed from the old in name only. Inevitably, they fell prey to the same hierarchical inertia that had necessitated the attempted reforms in the first place. As Monnier says of the province of Kongo Central: "These reforms by no means expressed or externalized a will to cultural or political autonomy. They merely indicated that the Congolese who now dominated the power system had adopted the goals and administrative structures of colonial authority."[18]

Economic Dependence on Foreign Capitalism. Any political entity must rely on some means of production to furnish the goods and services needed for the pursuit of its collective goals. It is probably in this area that developing nations have been most dependent on external factors, and scholars increasingly stress the need to relate political events to the variables of economic development. Henry Bienen expresses this need in regard to the study of African politics:

The comparative treatment of new states has often meant analyzing individual political systems so that a detailed knowledge of one country's politics is presented in a way that makes comparisons and generalization feasible and allows us to qualify one past treatment in the light of new data. Rarely will one scholar undertake concrete comparisons between systems— economic and political—in a single work.[19]

Bienen himself has contributed to the linkage of the political and economic spheres, but his conception of the economic environment is restricted to such static elements as natural resources or productivity. Thus it offers no real analysis of the fundamentally unbalanced economic situation of emerging nations. It must be stressed here that differences between the levels of economic development in African and Western countries arise not only from deficiencies of natural resources or from inefficient management, but also from the radically different ways in which the means of production have developed in the two areas. However great its impact upon the European nations in which it first took place, the industrial revolution was in fact an organic part of those nations' political, social, and economic development. In African countries, by contrast, modern production techniques (as well as the postindustrial concept of the welfare state) were introduced suddenly from without and fostered by a protective colonial regime.

Though they still lacked the tight interrelationship necessary to a modern industrial state, the political and economic sectors were left to coexist as best they could when colonial rule ended in Africa. Also, in contrast to a rising European bourgeoisie that was able to pursue many of its collective goals through parliamentary representation, the African national bourgeoisie has generally wasted its vital energy in internal political feuds. As a result, foreign economic interests have been left totally unaccountable to any political authority within the African states themselves.

The best example of the political unaccountability of foreign capitalism in the Congo is the Union Minière du Haut Katanga (UMHK), until recently the most powerful corporation in the country. UMHK's production of 280,000 to 300,000 tons of copper yearly equaled 5.5 percent of total world production in 1960 and 6.7 percent in 1965; the company is also a major world producer of cobalt and radium. UMHK is of vital importance to the Congolese economy, contributing 50 percent of total budgetary receipts in 1966 and providing the country with more than 70 percent of its hard currency reserves in that year.[20]

UMHK has long stood at the heart of a vast industrial complex with branches in Belgium and Katanga. In addition to its own prospecting, mining, and refining enterprises, UMHK holds major shares in such Belgian trusts as Métallurgie Hoboken, Société Belge pour l'Industrie Nucléaire, and the Compagnie Belge pour l'Industrie de l'Aluminium. In the Congo, it controls an impressive list of subsidiaries in the electrical, chemical, grain-processing, coal, and cement industries.[21]

Like any other giant corporation, UMHK is itself controlled by a complex of international cartels. For many years, the most important of these was the Katanga Special Committee, a board comprising four major shareholders designated by the Belgian crown and two others designated by UMHK itself. This association of state and private interests began in June 1900 in accordance with a convention between the Congo Free State and the chartered Katanga Company.[22] The fifth article of that convention put two-thirds of all UMHK assets in the hands of the Free State (and eventually the Belgian colony), while the remaining third was to be the property of the Katanga Company.[23] However, both partners' interests were actually managed by the General Society of Belgium, a trust that used its direct and indirect financial participation in the Katanga Special Committee to control UMHK and, by extension, the whole Katangese economy.[24] Thus the presidency of the board of UMHK was assigned at the outset to one of the governors of the General Society; British and American trusts, including Tanganyika Concessions and some subsidiaries of the Oppenheimer group, also had a hand in directing the company. The accompanying diagram illustrates the complex network of private interests controlling UMHK, as well as the peripheral position of the cartel's major shareholder, the colonial government. Table 9 shows the division of capital investment in UMHK as of early 1960.

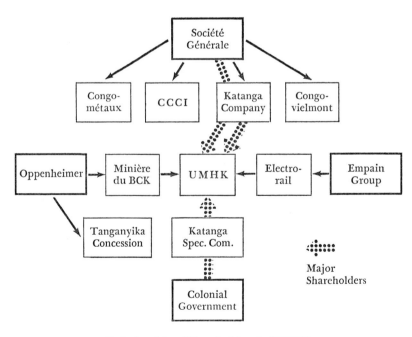

Relationship of Shareholders in UMHK
SOURCE: Gérard-Libois, *Secession*, p. 108.

TABLE 9

Distribution of Shares and Votes on the Board of UMHK

Shareholders	Number of shares	Number of votes
Katanga Special Committee	315,675	248,000
Tanganyika Concessions	179,760	134,016
General Society	57,685	31,584
Katanga Company	18,400	—
Congométaux	4,000	—
Electrorail	3,370	—
Congovielmont	3,000	—
Minière BCK	598	—
Others	1,394	—
TOTAL	583,882	413,600

SOURCE: Gérard-Libois, *Secession*, p. 110.

The predominance of private companies in the directorate of UMHK could continue only as long as the Congolese government refrained from using its options as the major shareholder. If the government did take an active role in the Katanga Special Committee, it would then have four representatives as opposed to only two from the Katanga Company. Further, the government's statutory right to designate the president of the Katanga Special Committee would give it an absolute majority within the Committee, and thus total control of UMHK. On the eve of independence, steps were taken to prevent what threatened to be an embarrassing situation for private interests. On June 17, 1960, the Belgian Parliament passed a law allowing Belgian corporations operating in the Congo to either install their head offices there or place themselves completely under Belgian jurisdiction. The boards of most major concerns, including UMHK, chose the second alternative. Michel Verwilgen comments on the law in this way: "It is most striking to see the boards of these private corporations invested with the kind of authority usually given to extraordinary assemblies.... One can't help noting how unacceptable such a system becomes when the major shareholder, the colonial government itself, chooses to exercise its legal prerogatives."[25]

The future of the Katanga Special Committee posed a more complex problem, since the Committee would involve direct cooperation between private interests and the new Congolese government. The topic was discussed for two days during the Economic Round

Table of April 1960. Following the discussions, it was announced that "the Congolese delegates have decided unanimously to put an end to the Katanga Special Committee."[26] This solution, though highly satisfactory to both parties at the time, demonstrates the shortsightedness and irrationality of Congolese nationalism. For the majority of Congolese, the dissolution of the Katanga Special Committee meant the end of yet another colonial institution with excessive holdings in land and mineral rights.[27] However, its dissolution really stood to consolidate private control of UMHK, since it would effectively increase the number of nongovernment votes to 248,403 out of a total of 414,000.[28] Private interests also benefited indirectly from debates between the Katangese and other Congolese delegations concerning the disposition of Katanga Special Committee holdings. The Katangese delegation proposed a three-way division of assets, one-third to belong to the province of Katanga, one-third to the Congolese government, and one-third to the Katanga Company. On the whole, the dissolution agreement that was signed on June 24, 1960, proved highly advantageous to the Katanga Company. By the terms of the agreement, the Congolese government relinquished its interest in the Katanga Company as well as paying it the sum of 40 million Congolese francs in return for all outstanding real estate and mineral rights.[29]

Clearly, Congolese leaders were ready to make enormous sacrifices in the name of independence and nationalism. However, the dissolution agreement, once signed, could not be implemented. Until 1964, no Congolese government either approved or rejected the agreement, thus leaving all previous colonial conventions in force.[30] The already difficult situation was made insoluble by the Katangese secession. European financial interests, though temporarily frustrated, took some comfort from the stability that the secession provided. Still, it would be erroneous to ascribe the rise of the Tshombe regime to the covert manipulations of foreign capitalists. Although the advantages of secession were probably discussed in British and Belgian financial circles,[31] the 1960 agreement concerning the Katanga Special Committee actually hampered the federalist plans of the Katangese tribal confederation, CONAKAT. Also, relations between Tshombe and Belgian financial interests in Elisabethville grew strained as the secession wore on. In September 1960, the Katangese government, dissatisfied with the lack of Belgian support, unilaterally transferred its mining concessions from the Katanga Special Committee to the South African trust, General Mining,[32] and threatened to nationalize UMHK.[33]

UMHK continued to pay mining fees and taxes to the secessionist government and openly expressed its sympathy toward Moise Tshombe, but it still failed to take steps to prevent the financial collapse of his government. Some disagreement seems to have existed between the directors of UMHK in Brussels and their Elisabethville representatives, the latter being increasingly unwilling to involve their company in the Katangese "adventure." Indeed, during the whole Katangese affair, European financial groups formulated no long-term policies and seemed very reluctant to become embroiled in Congolese political strife. Their passive stance was vindicated when the secession ended. Gérard-Libois points out that despite the unanimous hostility of the Tshombe regime, the UN, and the Congolese government, UMHK emerged as powerful and influential in the Congo as it had ever been: "Its status remained unchanged. Its resources in hard currency were guaranteed by a special convention with the Congo Monetary Council signed in January 1963. Its installations were untouched, and its personnel were at their posts."[34]

However, the argument that foreign industrial and financial interests profited excessively during a period of national bankruptcy is not entirely correct. After Congolese independence, UMHK policy decisions were all aimed at maintaining a relatively static productive capacity while avoiding Congolese state control of the company. According to the Institute of Economic and Social Research (IRES) at Lovanium University, UMHK attempted to stabilize production in the face of rising demand, as reflected by the fact that its copper production rose from 280,400 tons in 1959 to only 288,600 tons in 1965. This was an actual decrease of 1.4 percent relative to total world production.

At the same time, UMHK strove to maintain its reserve stocks of minerals and mineral products at a level far greater than necessary for its own use or for projected sales. On December 31, 1965, reserve stocks were valued at more than 4 million Belgian francs; in other terms, they represented more than 5 months' production and accounted for about 20 percent of the company's assets.[35] The IRES report makes it clear that such conservative UMHK policies reflected a conscious desire to extract wealth from the Congo and to convert it into hard currency for the protection of foreign shareholders.[36]

The next round of discussions concerning the dissolution of the Katanga Special Committee took place in January 1965, between the Katanga Company and the Congolese government under Moise Tshombe. Here again the European corporations were able to maintain control over their Congolese holdings. Prior to the talks, the central government had unilaterally abolished the Katanga Special Committee and openly denied the legal existence of the Katanga Company. Using an impressive array of logical, historical, and juridical arguments, President Kasavubu attempted to prove that the Katanga Company was not an ordinary commercial enterprise, since it had been granted expropriation rights by Léopold's Free State, itself more a commercial enterprise than a true national entity.[37] Whether inspired by a desire to prove Congolese independence from the forces of neocolonialism or by the influence of the French government, this presidential decree drew such strong protests from the Belgian government and foreign financial interests that the Congolese had no choice but to negotiate.

As discussions began, it seemed inevitable that the Katanga Company would lose many of the advantages incorporated in the 1960 dissolution agreement. In fact, the secret convention that was signed on February 6, 1965, left foreign shareholders in a stronger position than ever. UMHK and the Katanga Company each kept their one-third ownership of all financial assets previously held by the Katanga Special Committee. Furthermore, the Congolese government relinquished its 12 percent share in the Katanga Company in return for 12,500 shares of UMHK stock and the right to levy mining fees on UMHK and several of its subsidiaries.[38] Finally, Moise Tshombe agreed explicitly that the presidency of the board of UMHK should be entrusted to "a figure representing the interests of the General Society of Belgium,"[39] and that "the policy hitherto followed by the Company should not be modified."[40] Prime Minister Tshombe came away from the negotiations with a check for 92.4 million Belgian francs in payment for all dividends, fees, and interest accruing from Congolese participation in UMHK capital investment after 1960.

TABLE 10

Distribution of UMHK Shares and Votes in February 1965

Shareholders	Percentage of shares	Percentage of votes
Democratic Republic of the Congo	17.95%	24.49%
Tanganyika Concessions	14.47	20.21
Katanga Company	8.95	12.24
General Society	4.64	6.94
Others	53.99	36.12
TOTAL	100.00%	100.00%

SOURCE: *L'Echo de la Bourse*, Brussels, February 1965.

However, as Table 10 shows, Tshombe had still not gained effective control over the coalition of foreign economic interests operating in the Congo.

The case study of UMHK plainly shows that the Congo's economic dependence on foreign capitalism was not caused only by the extraneous origin of property rights or foreign ownership of the means of production. Other determining factors were the foreign companies' lack of legal responsibility toward the Congolese government and the Congolese leaders' ignorance of the complex forces underlying international capitalism. In sum, UMHK's drive to protect its stockholders' interests at the expense of production efficiency; the Congolese elite's haste to rid its country of all colonial institutions, even at the expense of its own long-term interests; and the Congolese government's failure to take advantage of its obvious strengths all demonstrate the Congo's lack of autonomy in the economic sphere.

The Irrationalities of the Cold War. Another kind of restraint on the autonomy of any modern political system is the influence of international tensions and conflicts. Just as they have done in regard to the economic environment, scholars today often stress the close relationship between domestic and international politics. As Wolfram Hanrieder says:

The traditional distinction between domestic and foreign politics, made by both decision-makers and analysts, is increasingly called into question by contemporary historical developments. The cold war conflict and the attending mobilization of military, socio-economic, and psychological resource by the super-powers and their allies; ventures of regional economic integration; the changing nature of the nation state; the close connection between the conditions prevailing in the international system and the attempts made by the new states to modernize . . .—these are just a few examples of how foreign and domestic policy projects have become overlapping and perhaps entirely inseparable.[41]

By linking the national and international political spheres, contemporary Marxian literature exercises a beneficial influence on the study of political science. However, as Erich Fromm points out, few Marxian analysts who treat the influence of major powers on developing nations can avoid a dogmatic, Leninist interpretation of imperialism as a form of capitalist economic expansion into backward societies.[42] Accordingly, unbiased, empirical research on the evolution and structures of all modern societies, whether capitalist or socialist, is still needed.

Moreover, the postwar relationship of Western powers to the Third World cannot be reduced to any simple economic formula, for it is governed by diverse political, military, and ideological considerations as well. Thus obsessive fear of Communism, concern for the preservation of the international status quo, and an almost messianic faith in the virtue of representative democracy are factors that distinguish modern imperialism from mere economic expansionism. They are also factors that will temper an international climate that affects even the smallest of states.

The Congo is a prime example of a nation helpless before the influence of international politics. As we shall see, successive foreign interventions in the Congo disrupted the emerging balance of political elites within the country and served ultimately to invalidate some of the myths underlying the international order itself. It should be noted at the outset that because of gaps in available information and the bias of many observers, the case study method that was valid elsewhere is inappropriate to the topic of foreign interventions in the Congo. Rather, a review of major historical trends is likely to be the most fruitful approach in this area.

It is widely agreed that the "internationalization"[43] of the Congolese problem was a chain reaction caused by wildly exaggerated reports of one specific event, the mutiny of the Force Publique. Thus Belgium became involved in the Congo out of concern for her nationals there; the USSR was drawn in because Patrice Lumumba claimed that "foreign aggression" was taking place, and the U.S. acted from a fear of Communist penetration in Africa. Eventually,

even various African and Asian leaders went to the Congo to ob-
serve the dire effects of radical nationalism on the politics of an
emerging nation.[44] This internationalization of the Congolese crisis
may be conveniently divided into two periods. The first period extended from July 1960 to June 1964 and was marked by extensive
UN operations in the Congo. The second began in July 1964 and
saw more direct intervention from Belgium and the U.S.

During the first period, the Western powers lent tacit support to
UN operations. Secretary-General Dag Hammarskjold took this opportunity to test his personal view of the UN as a peacekeeping
force abiding by the principle of nonintervention, and an organization specifically committed to the socioeconomic development of the
Third World.[45] Hammarskjold's lofty ambitions were soon thwarted,
however, and the Congolese affair dealt the UN a blow from which
it never fully recovered.

The UN failed in the Congo because of the basically contradictory
assumptions underlying its involvement there. In 1960, Hammarskjold wrote that the UN "should try to keep new conflicts isolated
from areas of disagreement between international blocs. When conflicts arise that do touch upon, or fall completely within, these areas,
the Organization should make every effort to limit them."[46] In fact,
both the secretary-general and the Security Council considered maintaining order within the Congo less important than preserving
world peace.[47] Such an attitude arose naturally from the assumption
that the Congolese crisis (and attendant conflicts between super-
powers) so endangered world peace that UN intervention was imperative. This assumption cannot now be absolutely proved or dis-
proved. Many scholars have since concluded that in spite of its short-
comings, the UN operation lessened international tensions by preventing the involvement of interested superpowers.[48] However, Hoskyns may be closer to the truth when she suggests that the UN operation was conceived as a convenient vehicle for the imposition of
Western concepts of peace and, in some cases, the protection of
Western interests:

One of the anomalies of the Congo story remains the extent to which public
attention was focused on a relatively minor Soviet intervention at a time
when a much more extensive Western intervention was taking place in
Léopoldville and in Elisabethville.[49]

Even granting a direct relationship between maintaining order within a country and keeping peace in the international arena, it is clear that the UN peacekeeping mission in the Congo did not assess the situation there in its total perspective. The Congolese crisis resulted not only from a disruption of governmental functions, but from the collapse of the country's entire socioeconomic structure following decolonization. Gendebien very correctly maintains that the problem at hand was far too complex to be solved by a simple police action.[50]

Also basic to the UN effort in the Congo was the great importance that Hammarskjold ascribed to the time-honored principle of nonintervention. The contradiction here is plain to see, since the mere presence of UN forces was bound to alter power relationships in the Congo. It is more significant that in most cases the UN presence benefited only the Western powers. One of the most flagrant instances of biased interference was the UN officials' vigorous opposition to Patrice Lumumba and overt support of President Joseph Kasavubu. As Hoskyns says: "There seems to be little doubt that much of the responsibility for the fact that Lumumba was deposed in September 1960 rests with the Western powers."[51] Other examples include the decisive influence of some UN officials in forming the compromise Adoula government at Lovanium University,[52] and the UN's role in ending the Stanleyville secession.[53] Though their efforts proved ineffective, UN officials also directed considerable diplomatic and military pressure against the Katangese secession between 1960 and 1962.

Such deep involvement in national politics prevented Dag Hammarskjold and his staff from finding original solutions to problems of modernization and development in the Congo. Despite the thousands of experts and millions of dollars it poured into the Congolese civil service, the UN was content to superimpose its own bureaucratic structures onto the vestiges of existing ones rather than draft new governmental programs. Moreover, most UN expenditures were devoted to military operations rather than to the civil service; thus at the end of 1963, the military budget reached $120 million, while technical assistance amounted to slightly more than $5 million.[54]

The UN began to lose its initiative in the Congo after Hammarskjold's death on September 18, 1961, and negotiations increasingly took place directly between the major powers concerned. Thus from late 1961 on, UN headquarters in New York became the site of private talks between the Belgian foreign minister, Paul-Henri Spaak, the U.S. representative to the UN, Adlai Stevenson, and the head of the British foreign office, Lord Home. In Léopoldville, U.S. Ambassador Edmund Gullion intervened directly and openly in private talks at Kitona between Moise Tshombe and UN officials concerning the reintegration of Katanga province. Gullion's intervention in fact marked the emergence of the U.S. as the leading outside influence in the Congo. According to Gendebien:

American influence became critical in December 1961. At the time American diplomats offered their services as mediators, the military situation still favored the UN. . . . It is for this reason that the American intervention in the Kitona meeting was not appreciated. . . . A major power had taken some of the initiative away from the UN.[55]

By June 1962, Belgium, Great Britain, and the U.S., together with Secretary-General U Thant, had agreed that it would be necessary to end the Katangese secession and the costly UN operation in the Congo. In July, the U.S. State Department formulated a plan of action that served as a basis for discussions between the three powers.[56] In their turn these discussions produced the Thant Plan and Course of Action, published in late 1962. On paper, this plan was a compromise. Neither Belgium nor Britain favored economic sanctions against Katanga or UMHK, whereas some U.S. officials took a hard line against Katanga, fearing that the secession there might open the door to Soviet influence in the Congo. Ultimately, Belgian and British efforts to protect Katanga were ignored. In January 1963, UN troops, aided by a U.S. military mission that had arrived in the Congo a month before, occupied all urban centers in the province.

With the collapse of the Katangese secession, it was widely believed that the UN had fulfilled its goal of establishing institutional legality and political order in the Congo. One year later, UN forces began to withdraw. Ironically, the last UN troops departed just when Moise Tshombe was returning to power in Léopoldville and just before the outbreak of the 1964 rebellions. The troops left so precipitately because the UN mission to the Congo was by this time utterly bankrupt.

The end of UN operations in the Congo marked the beginning

of the second phase in the internationalization of the Congolese crisis, that of bilateral interventions. Belgium began to exert intense diplomatic pressures with the outbreak of the 1964 rebellions. The abject inability of the Congolese Army to suppress the popular uprisings and the fear of "new Communist gains in Africa" led Belgian authorities to seek a general reconciliation between the central government and the various rebel leaders. In a letter to Congolese Prime Minister Adoula, Belgian Foreign Minister Spaak stated that Belgium strongly favored political negotiations over military intervention in pursuit of this goal. Spaak added that in his government's view the success of any reconciliation effort would depend in large part upon the return of Moise Tshombe, who was at that time in exile in Madrid.[57]

Though Tshombe was often considered a representative of neocolonial interests in Africa, his contacts in Belgian and British business circles, his underground corps of Belgian advisors, and his long experience in parliamentary negotiations made him a key figure in Congolese politics and the Belgians' logical first choice. Even with Tshombe's return to Léopoldville, however, exclusively political measures failed to contain the wave of new rebellions, and pressure from Washington and Léopoldville caused the Belgian government to undertake military action. Thus in September 1964 a mechanized unit, commanded by 300 Belgian officers and supported by a detachment of warplanes, was ordered to retake rebel-held areas "on behalf of the Congolese government."[58]

The U.S. response to the 1964 rebellions was guided at the strategic level by a commitment to the moderate forces of the political center (which caused some initial distrust of Tshombe as an enemy of order and stability), and to the establishment of a close triangular relationship between Washington, Brussels, and Léopoldville. At the tactical level, however, U.S. policy was far more rigid. In particular, an obsessive fear of Communism led U.S. policymakers to classify Congolese political leaders in overly simplistic terms. Thus President Kasavubu and Colonel Mobutu were favored because they had "curbed Soviet diplomats." Prime Minister Adoula was described as "a Catholic anticommunist trade unionist who helped end the communist-supported Stanleyville secession," and Moise Tshombe himself was considered "one among the many anticommunists in the

Congo."[59] In U.S. policy terms, then, "neutralizing" the Congo meant less insulating it from the irrational conflicts of the Cold War than purging it of any Soviet influence whatsoever: "Washington believed that a neutralized Congo ... would remain within the hegemony of the Free World, and that Western influence could eventually be introduced because this weak state would need substantial outside aid."[60] Even more significant was the State Department's obsession with the abstract concept of law and order. In the words of Mennen Williams:

> Until a viable political solution can be found, the rebellion must be contained and outside intervention halted. ... Only with the restoration of peace and order can that vast country in the heart of Africa get on with its task of building a strong and viable nation.[61]

Several facts suggest that the U.S. considered the possibility of a military operation involving more than the ANC alone. Between 1960 and 1964, the U.S. contributed $168 million to UN police operations, a sum equaling 42 percent of the Organization's total military budget for those years.[62] When it became evident that the UN would withdraw from the Congo, State Department officials were anxious to know if the ANC could maintain order in the face of growing agitation from Lumumbist politicians, who were then suspected of being Communists.[63] In March 1963, Undersecretary of State Averell Harriman led a special mission charged with investigating the situation. A few months later, a military mission was sent under U.S. Army Colonel Wrengen to coordinate delivery of war materiel to the ANC.[64] These activities culminated in a military agreement between the U.S. and the Congolese government in July 1963. Still, the U.S. avoided any direct military role in suppressing the rebellions. Instead, it increased its deliveries of trucks, mortars, and aircraft, and dispatched about 180 troops to protect and maintain this equipment. Aside from a handful of soldiers recruited by the CIA to fight in Kivu, no U.S. troops took part in the campaign against the rebellions.[65]

Another aspect of the bilateral interventions was the massive amount of economic assistance both powers poured into the Congo. In 1963, the U.S. enriched the Congolese economy by approximately $25 million in hard currency in return for preferential treatment of American imports. The U.S. also contributed about $117 million in agricultural assistance between 1960 and 1962, lent heavy financial backing to development plans, and gave military aid amounting to $15.3 million between 1964 and 1965.[66]

Belgian economic aid to its former colony was also impressive, with the cost of technical-assistance programs between 1960 and 1965 exceeding $500 million.[67] This sum does not include Belgian contributions to such specialized international institutions as the UN or the European Development Fund. Belgium also gave outright military assistance that amounted to $660,000 by 1965. Other nations contributing were the German Federal Republic, Italy, and Great Britain.[68] Characteristically, neither the USSR nor any other Communist country was given the opportunity to send financial or other aid to the Congo.[69] In fact, all Congolese diplomatic and trade relations with the Communist world ended with the death of Patrice Lumumba.

Though Western assistance to the Congo was massive, equaling 13 percent of the country's fiscal resources in 1965, the absence of any overall plan for economic development greatly reduced its effectiveness. Funds and technical experts were dispatched haphazardly, economic missions followed one another without rhyme or reason, and ambitious plans for development were outlined in the absence of any higher agency that could implement them. In the light of such arrant disorganization, it is difficult to view Western aid to the Congolese as anything but a convenient public relations service. As Baldwin says: "Using technical language to divert attention from controversial issues is an old tactic, one that has worked well in the case of technical assistance."[70] At the same time, the Western experience in the Congo calls into question the usefulness of any form of external aid to a nation where such basic social and political problems as the formation of a modern class structure and the creation of legitimate public institutions remain unsolved.

The progressive internationalization of the Congolese crisis serves to illustrate two political myths considered crucial in our time. The first of these is the abstract principle of nonintervention in the internal affairs of sovereign states. As we have seen, those Western nations that most strongly advanced the principle of nonintervention were the first to intervene in the Congo. One may conclude, as Hoskyns does, that the principle of noninterference should be reasserted as a fundamental requisite of the international order.[71] However, this principle, like those of territorial integrity and democratic freedom, belongs to a tradition that was evolved by a group of equal and independent nations in nineteenth-century Europe. That tradition must undergo a thorough reinterpretation if it is to apply to developing nations short on resources, managerial skills, and functioning political institutions.

A second myth is the automatic assumption that all political instability or popular unrest results from Communist agitation. Blinded by this assumption, the Western powers supported political leaders who were not the most appropriate ones to the evolving Congolese political situation, but who knew how to capitalize on Western fears of Communism. By supporting such leaders the Western powers often thwarted the spontaneous expression of political tensions in the Congo. Thus a short-term concern for peace and order seriously hampered the Congo's overall chances of achieving real political stability.

The Direction of Change

So far, this study has dealt extensively with the propensities for change inherent in patrimonial politics, and with some of the environmental elements that may cause change within a political system. Still, nothing has yet been said of the alternative political forms that instability and change may produce. In this regard, it is relevant to ask whether events like the 1964–65 rebellions and the emergence of a bureaucratic-Caesarist regime in the Congo (both of which will be treated in succeeding chapters) might not have been predicted. Stated in broader terms, the question concerns the extent to which patrimonial politics and its environmental constraints contain clear predispositions toward popular rebellion or bureaucratic Caesarism.

In theory, the inherent instability of patrimonialism predisposes it to one of two likely patterns of change. Either the patrimonial structure will collapse under popular pressure, or a leader or faction holding a key position in society will take the system over. The first possibility is enhanced by the rising expectations of most populations under patrimonial rule. After all, patrimonialism differs from other political systems in the relative liberty granted its subjects, and in the ruler's implicit responsibility for his people's welfare. The second alternative is facilitated by the absence of established political traditions and the relative arbitrariness of patrimonialism. Aside from routine changes in administrative and ministerial personnel, then, either a popular uprising or a coup d'etat by one group in the political arena would appear to be the logical outcome of patrimonialism.[72]

Environmental constraints may serve to reinforce either alternative. The exclusively technocratic and bureaucratic ideology of a new regime may reflect a return to colonial, hence external, values and institutions after the failure of newer ones tailored exclusively to patrimonialism.[73] Such a shift also meets the standards of rational and efficient planning universal in the international environment. The impact of external factors on change through popular uprisings is also clear. Foreign support of a weakly legitimized patrimonial ruler may suppress the dynamic elements within a society; often, popular reaction to such suppression will be sudden and violent. Verhaegen makes this point in regard to the UN operation in the Congo:

The fundamental ambiguity in the UN operation ... lay in its failure to allow new political forms to emerge, even though it held the chief instruments of control [finances, administration, army] for three years. By preventing violent clashes between political forces in the Congo, it protected a ruling group that neither represented nor enjoyed the support of the Congolese population. The UN also stifled the expression of social tensions by means of military pressure and technical assistance to urban centers. The UN action was less a cure than an anesthetic that worsened political strife by postponing it. The objective causes of conflict persisted and tensions deepened in the absence of any overt expression.[74]

 CHAPTER 6

The Breakdown of Patrimonialism

As we have seen, the inherent weaknesses of patrimonial-ism, together with certain outside influences, set the stage for the popular insurgencies of 1964–65. More immediately, though, the rebellions stemmed from a temporary alliance between various peripheral social forces that were to prove mutually antagonistic in the long run. The first section of this chapter will analyze the immediate setting of the rebellions and the various social groups involved in them. The second section will demonstrate why the rebellions could present no meaningful political alternative for the Congo.

The Immediate Context of the Rebellions

In their origins and orientation, the 1964 uprisings recalled the banditry, peasant rebellions, preindustrial urban mobs, and labor sects that preceded the great modern revolutionary movements in Western Europe and elsewhere.[1] Like them, the rebellions belonged to a world long accustomed to the oppressive state apparatus of policemen, soldiers, prisons, tax collectors, and corrupt civil servants:

[They also] belong to the world of people who neither write nor read many books—often because they are illiterate—who are rarely known by name to anybody except their friends, and then often only by nickname, who are normally inarticulate and rarely understood even when they express themselves. Moreover, they are prepolitical people who have not yet found, or have only begun to find, a specific language in which to express their aspirations about the world.[2]

The 1964 rebellions were striking in their extreme heterogeneity. Among those taking part in the rebellions were politicians, soldiers, and peasants. These social groups were largely isolated from one another, and their grievances against the governmental elite varied widely. Clearly, a close look at the origins and motivations of these groups is called for here.

Sources of Popular Discontent. Recent studies of economic development in postcolonial Africa frequently stress the growing split between the rural and urban milieux. Such a split usually brings a partial collapse of the rural cash economy and a return to subsistence farming in some areas. At the same time, the inflationary economic policies of the new political elite foster an urban lumpenproletariat of small retailers and wholesalers. As Giovanni Arrighi and John Saul put it:

> The higher wages and salaries foster the stabilization of the better paid section of the labour force whose high incomes justify the severance of ties with the traditional economy. Stabilization, in turn, promotes . . . greater bargaining power, and further increases in the incomes of this small section of the labour force which represents the proletariat proper to tropical Africa. These workers enjoy incomes three or more times higher than those of unskilled labourers and, together with the elites and sub-elites in bureaucratic employment in the civil service and expatriate concerns, constitute what we call the labour aristocracy of tropical Africa. It is the discretionary consumption of this class which absorbs a significant proportion of the surplus produced in the money economy.[3]

Though the rural-urban split must not be exaggerated, Saul and Arrighi's observations are, on the whole, accurate in regard to the postcolonial Congo.

As Table 11 shows, some socioeconomic groups benefited more substantially from independence than others, though all were to some degree victims of an inflationary trend that they helped create. Rather than politicians or high civil servants, the three most favored groups were, surprisingly, nonqualified administrative workers, teachers without diplomas, and army sergeants. A fourth category, that of wage earners in large agricultural or industrial enterprises, was afforded some protection against inflation by the company stores that employers organized to stimulate labor productivity. Urban workers were hit hardest by inflation, though some workers, particularly teachers, gained a measure of bargaining power through their affiliation with trade unions.

Not appearing in Table 11 is the social group that derived the

TABLE 11

Increase in Wages and Salaries by Socioeconomic Category, 1960–65
(1960 = 100%)

Category	Nominal increase	Real increase[a]
Public administration		
Auxiliary agents	498%	102%
Clerk	678–1,073	139–219
Bureau chief	241	49
Secretary general	153	31
Army		
Army rank and file	414	85
Sergeants	571	117
Teachers		
Auxiliary teachers	333	68
Teachers without diplomas	566	116
Wage earners in the private sector		
Minimum wage (bachelor)	306	63
Minimum wage (married with		
3 children)	255	52

SOURCE: Gérard Dupriez, "Le Marché du Travail au Congo," in *Evolution économique du Congo: 1960–65* (Kinshasa: CRE-IRES, Université Lovanium, forthcoming).

[a] Nominal wages divided by the index of prices on Léopoldville markets (489 in December 1965).

greatest benefit from Congolese inflation, that of middlemen and speculators in consumer goods. According to Lacroix:

Variations between wholesale and retail prices in stores and markets, between the official hard currency rate and that current on the black market, between prices in the cities and those in rural areas—all of these are potential sources of profit that encourage speculation at the expense of production. That heterogeneous social group whose boundaries are vague and undefined, and where nationals and foreigners, major traffickers and small dealers coexist, is the only true beneficiary of monetary inflation.[4]

By contrast, those who suffered most from the economic crisis were those independent peasants whose incomes depended exclusively on agricultural exports and those whose access to urban produce markets was cut off by the deterioration of transport and communication networks. Here, the urban-rural split that Saul and Arrighi emphasize must be examined more closely. Such rural areas as the Bakongo region largely escaped the effects of the inflationary spiral because the rise in urban incomes and the rapid growth of such major cities as Léopoldville, Bukavu, and Elisabethville greatly increased the demand for basic food products.[5] Also, peasants who remained in contact with centers of consumption could adjust the prices of agricultural products to match those of manufactured goods. However, rural areas of Kasai, Equateur, and Orientale provinces were almost entirely cut off from urban centers, especially during periods of political tension. Table 12 illustrates the disastrous effects of inflation on Congolese agricultural production, which had provided the country with 40 percent of its income in hard currency and employed 78 percent of its total population prior to independence.

Though no statistics on agricultural production are available for the period after 1960, the volume of exports and domestic turnover of goods gives a sufficient indication of inflationary damage to the rural economy. The sale of manioc, a staple food of both villagers and urban dwellers, dropped from 50,000 tons in 1959 to 3,000 tons in 1964; similarly, the trade in bananas, another staple food sold by peasants in local markets, went from 30,000 tons in 1959 to 13,000 tons in 1964. Peasant exporters, especially those who harvested cotton for European factories, composed one of the worst-hurt socioeconomic groups. In their isolation from major industrial centers, such peasants were especially vulnerable to inflation and were frequently reduced to subsistence farming. For example, a grower who produced the same amount of cotton in 1963 as he had in 1960 could expect to see his real income for 1963 drop by at least 66 percent.[6]

It is likely that independent agricultural producers were not completely indifferent to their forced withdrawal into self-sufficiency. It is now widely acknowledged that in general African peasants are highly responsive to marketing opportunities arising through contacts with European business institutions.[7] At the same time, it

TABLE 12

Combined Volume of Congolese Exports and Domestic Turnover
of Goods, 1958–64

Type of goods	Volume in thousands of tons					
	1958	1959	1961	1962	1963	1964
Animal products	0.8	0.7	0.3	0.2	0.2	0.2
Vegetable products	739.9	819.9	552.4	512.0	466.5	457.8
Mineral products	749.4	752.3	757.8	767.4	598.0	706.6
Manufactured goods	9.2	8.3	11.1	14.1	35.3	26.3
Others	0.2	0.1	—	—	—	—
TOTAL	1,499.5	1,581.3	1,321.6	1,293.7	1,100.0	1,190.9

SOURCE: CES, 4, no. 2 (1965). No reliable figures are available for 1960.

should be noted that the concept of a cash economy, though known throughout rural areas, has not yet been fully integrated into the peasant way of life. As Coméliau says of Uélé province:

Basic needs are still satisfied without using monetary resources. Understandably, then, these resources are used in nonessential transactions, such as expenditures to maintain prestige and customary relations. . . . Since the circulation of money does play only a marginal role, irrational attitudes still prevail. Among these are the predominance of barter, the widespread use of credit, and an inability to undertake budgetary planning. On the whole, though, it seems that the idea of a cash economy has been sufficiently accepted to start an irreversible transformation that rests on a fragile basis but still proceeds without outside prompting.[8]

The Congolese peasants' responsiveness to modern economic conditions was demonstrated both by their decreasing agricultural productivity in reaction to a diminishing cash income and their open expression of discontent with the emerging bourgeoisie in major cities. Such discontent was most commonly aired during the infrequent public encounters between Congolese politicians and articulate representatives of the independent peasant class, usually local administrators and paramount chiefs. A mythic theme came to underlie all such peasant complaints, a theme by which the colonial era was reinterpreted as a kind of golden age. As early as 1961, for instance, traditional authorities in rural Orientale province told one of their assemblymen that

since independence, people have stopped working, for political propagandists have spoiled everything by making foolish promises to [their constituencies]. [Politicians] said that after independence, it will no longer be necessary to work, to till the soil, or to aid the chiefs and notables. They said, too, that machines would come to labor in the place of men. . . . When is independence going to end? When are the Belgians going to return?[9]

Since they were closest to their rural constituencies, it was naturally the provincial assemblymen who were most aware of peasant discontent. The interassembly conference at Boma in October 1963 clearly reflected rural unrest. The opening speech by Joseph Yumba-Lemba, president of the assembly of Kongo Central, summarized the problem in this way:

Those whom we allegedly represent have noted a dangerous situation to which we should put an end. The danger lies in growing unemployment, widespread social discrimination, and, above all, in the increase of favoritism reflected in popular speech by ironic jokes about [our legislative work].

... This is the people's way of warning their leaders of the popular dissatisfaction to which every conscientious politician should give his special attention.[10]

Again it must be stressed that economic grievances were not limited to the mass of independent peasants, though it was clearly this group that felt the worst effects of Congolese economic disintegration. During this period, another underprivileged and dissatisfied social group was appearing in large cities and small urban centers. This group consisted chiefly of young people who had rejected the traditional constraints of rural life, but who could adapt only marginally to the system of patronage prevailing in the cities.

The political relevance of Congolese youth was totally ignored until the outbreak of the 1964 rebellions, though the fact that an estimated 50 percent of the country's population was under fifteen years of age in 1960 gave clear warning of the problem to come. Before independence, much youthful energy was absorbed by lengthy compulsory schooling and by youth groups attached to Catholic missions. After independence, Congolese young people fell victim to their own high expectations and to the belief, shared by their parents, that a diploma would automatically ensure desirable employment. In consequence, student enrollments increased dramatically just after June 30, 1960: from 28,951 in 1959 the number of secondary school students rose to 38,000 in 1961, 68,350 in 1963, and 88,987 in 1964.[11] Such a rapid upsurge in enrollments caused a shortage of teachers, undermined educational standards, and produced a flow of secondary school graduates that neither the universities nor the labor market could absorb. The disenchanted young people quickly gravitated to the criminal populations of large and small urban centers. The young people's frustration was even more intense than that of Congolese peasants because they drifted in a no-man's-land between Western and traditional life styles. In his study of Uélé province, Coméliau accurately describes the problems of the young in and around Congolese cities:

For youth, the feeling of suffocation in the rural environment increases whenever school and other outside contacts offer new perspectives, new concepts of social relationships, and alternative value systems. In rebelling against the vexations of a gerontocratic rule and a social structure in which they count for nothing, these youngsters are at the same time giving up their share of the chieftaincy's meager economic activities and are cut off from the benefits of family and clan solidarity. Excluded . . . from their customary environment, these young people look elsewhere—especially in urban centers —for the place that has been denied them at home. Yet the modern sector is not large enough to absorb this influx.[12]

The uneven pattern of popular discontent resulted, too, from the fact that not all Congolese cities were equally affected by socioeconomic dislocations. In contrast to Léopoldville and Elisabethville, both centers of diverse economic activities, the Congo's third major city, Stanleyville, lost the industrial base that it had acquired before independence. Before 1960, it seemed likely that Stanleyville would soon reach a level of development equal to that of Léopoldville; by that year, Stanleyville already possessed two important breweries, a cigarette factory, and a cement works, as well as the commercial, financial, and administrative infrastructure indispensable to its economic takeoff. But the takeoff was never attained in Stanleyville, as Lacroix explains:

The trend toward industrial concentration in Léopoldville grew even stronger after 1960. Business enterprises could benefit from Léopoldville's relative political stability, its independence from the already deteriorating transport network, and its rapid increase in population. Consequently, the cement works at Stanleyville closed its doors and the directors of the cigarette factory chose to establish a new branch at Léopoldville rather than expand the Stanleyville plant.[13]

Stanleyville's economic stagnation resulted in large part from the political strife that gripped the city after independence, notably the 1960–61 Gizenga secession and the street fighting by Lumumba's MNC-Jeunesse between 1962 and 1964. A few weeks before secessionists took over Stanleyville, a Congolese press correspondent, Clement Vidibio-Mabiala, offered this gloomy picture of the city:

Stanleyville, doomed to a tragic notoriety, has been painted in the darkest colors; journalists, tourists, and politicians have expressed only profound antipathy toward the city. They have referred constantly to the reign of terror and to the idealism or Machiavellianism of the MNC-Jeunesse, for whom only the end was important, and who would stop at nothing to realize their dreams.[14]

Once again, it was the social stratum that was least integrated into the existing political institutions—here, the politicized youth of the MNC—that became the focus of discontent: "When the youths were excluded from the party [because of their radicalism], they wished

to avenge a cause that, rightly or wrongly, they believed to be worthwhile. The youths refused to disarm and fought mercilessly against
disparagers of the party. Eventually, they took the path of open revolt."[15]

Further expression of discontent transcending the urban-rural
dichotomy came from certain ethnic minorities distinguished by
their militant nationalism and opposition to colonial rule. It was
such tribal groups (notably the Bapende-Bambunda in Kwilu, the
Batetela-Bakusu in Sankuru and Maniéma, and, to some extent, the
Baluba in Katanga) that provided the hard core of resistance during
the 1964 popular uprising.

The Bapende-Bambunda's tradition of political and cultural resistance to colonization goes back to the early 1930's. In 1931 the
Bapende broke into full-scale revolt against the coercive attempts of
commercial companies and the colonial administration to recruit
Pende workers (who were known as the best fruit pickers in the region), and to make them increase their output.[16] In the following
years, discontent spread through the northern part of the district.
One messianic anticolonial movement, the "Speaking Snake" sect,
was highly successful in persuading the Bambunda to stop paying
taxes and performing other legal duties. Around 1945, Kimbanguism,
the most powerful messianic movement in the Congo, began to expand throughout the same area under the name of "Nzambi-Malembe." Still another sect, known as "Dieudonné," appeared in
Kwilu in 1950. Before being crushed by the Force Publique in the
following year, this last sect carried out several assassinations in Bapende territories.[17]

Such diverse manifestations of discontent took a more openly political form with the formation of the African Solidarity Party (PSA)
and the rise of mass radicalism in Kwilu. However, the postindependence era was also marked by a growing tribal cleavage within
the Kwilu political elite. Both the national executive and the local
branches of the PSA were progressively taken over by moderates
whose leaders all belonged to the Bambala and Bangongo tribal
groups. Meanwhile, Kwilu district was being acknowledged as the
personal estate of its avowed leader, Cleophas Kamitatu. When the
province of Kwilu was created in September 1962, most of its provincial ministers were chosen from the Bambala-Kamitatu group.

Accordingly, the Bapende-Bambunda became the victims of whole-sale discrimination. Their leaders were jailed or forced into the political opposition, their local elite was banned from public office, the economies of their territories were disrupted, and entire Bapende-Bambunda populations were harassed by the military or held suspect of political agitation.

The Batetela-Bakusu of Sankuru-Maniéma suffered from similar discrimination. Like the neighboring Baluba-Kasai, this group embarked very early on a path of social and economic assimilation. According to de Heusch, assimilation was stimulated by dynamic tension within the traditional Tetela-Kusu value system, which accorded prestige both on the basis of age and on that of wealth.[18] The Afro-Arab conquest in the late nineteenth century allowed the first outlet for this tension. Led by the slave traders Tippu-Tib and Gongo Lutete, the Batetela-Bakusu set off on a course of aggressive expansion. This event marked the eclipse of traditional tribal values by a sustained drive for power and wealth through contact with other cultures.

During the colonial era, the Batetela-Bakusu were drawn to the educational and economic opportunities available in Kasai and Kivu.[19] But because it was located in an economically poor region of the Congo and was subject to widespread distrust owing to its part in the slave trade, this tribal group failed to derive the same benefits from Belgian rule as did, for instance, the Bakongo and the Baluba. Initially, decolonization offered an end to this isolation, while the nationalistic MNC-Lumumba provided a fresh channel for the Batetela-Bakusu's expansionist drive. However, Lumumba's assassination and the victory of the moderate faction in Léopoldville left the group politically isolated once again. Finally, the Batetela-Bakusu's involvement in political violence during the 1960 election campaign left them ostracized by their neighbors, who resented their "domineering attitude" and "colonialist designs."[20]

A third group that was deeply involved in the rebellions, the Baluba of North Katanga, also has a long tradition of rebellion, civil war, and political opposition. From 1925 until after independence, strikes, such mass phenomena as the xenophobic Kitawala movement, and various other forms of resistance to authority followed one another without interruption. They culminated in the Baluba's bloody opposition to the Katangese secession between 1960 and 1962.[21] Verhaegen draws meaningful parallels between this conflict and the 1964 rebellion in North Katanga. In both cases, the rural population involved itself directly and spontaneously in guerrilla warfare, with political cohesion effected less by a common ideology or modern organization than by magical rites and feelings of tribal solidarity. Also, the violence of both rebellions was directed primarily against the local administration and paramount chiefs.[22]

Formation of a Counterelite. In the literature on African politics, the classical concepts of the one-party system and the one-party state generally refer to countries where political power has been appropriated and monopolized by a group of founding fathers and leaders of independence movements acting together within the framework of a single mass organization. Supposedly, it is such an organization (invariably a political party) that provides the new state with its ideological identification and structural cohesion. However, it can now be asserted that the one-party system in Africa has never been a functioning organizational tool, or at least that it is no longer the instrument of popular mobilization envisioned by its creators. As Wallerstein puts it:

The curious phenomenon . . . was not the emergence of a one-party system. It was rather its rapid loss of meaning. As soon as the one-party system reached its peak and thus performed its function of securing at least initial allegiance to the new state, as soon as it became an essential channel of both recruitment and participation, it seemed immediately to become little more than a formal framework despite all the talk about it.[23]

In fact, almost every new African state has seen the monopolization of political power by a single ethnic or other group, together with a decline in formal political organization, a purge of government-run auxiliary groups, and the suppression of all political opposition. Whatever their espoused political views, new rulers in Africa have seldom tolerated any independent centers of power; in most cases, potential opposition groups have been left the choice of being absorbed into the official institutional framework or going entirely underground.

Indeed, such has been the general pattern of events in the Congo. Except for constitutional issues, the greatest source of national and local political conflict has been the rift between one group that held all political power in the country and another that held none. In power, of course, were the moderates, including those regional leaders who backed Adoula's compromise government in return for control over their own provincial estates. In opposition were the supporters of Patrice Lumumba and Antoine Gizenga, both outspoken anticolonialists who were often suspected of Communist sympathies. It was the generally nationalistic Lumumba-Gizenga group that most strongly opposed the "balkanization" of the Congo into 21 new provinces.

The progressive isolation of the nationalist group began in January 1961 with the assassination of Patrice Lumumba, whose name remained a rallying cry for various social and political protest movements until the 1964 rebellions. The execution in February 1961 of several other nationalist leaders, notably Senator Gilbert Fataki, Jean-Pierre Finant, president of Orientale province, and District Commissioner Camille Yangara, reinforced the belief of all MNC-Lumumba supporters that their political enemies were about to liquidate them.

Undoubtedly, the killing of the opposition leaders was related to Antoine Gizenga's proclamation of the Stanleyville secession, and to the PSA and MNC partisans' subsequent emigration from Katanga, Kivu, and Léopoldville to the capital of Orientale province. However, the threat of continued persecution and the prospect of a national reconciliation eventually led some nationalists to support the new Adoula government. Thus on July 16, 1961, Christophe Gbenye and Anicet Kashamura, both high-ranking members of the Gizenga government, arrived at Léopoldville to participate in the second parliamentary session at Lovanium University. During the following weeks, a new nationalist caucus was formed among members of the Senate and House of Representatives; it soon captured the presidency, vice-presidency, secretariat, and other leading posts in Parliament.[24] At the same time, Adoula included several former ministers from the Gizenga government in his new cabinet.[25]

However, the alliance between the nationalist opposition and the central government soon disintegrated, and reciprocal fear and distrust led to renewed friction between the two groups. The government accused the nationalists of using their parliamentary majority to undermine the Congo's political stability, and of using the streets of Léopoldville for revolutionary agitation.[26] The opposition in turn accused Prime Minister Adoula, Colonel Mobutu, and the security chief, Victor Nendaka, of curtailing democratic liberties and harassing opposition figures. The most prominent focus of contention was Antoine Gizenga, who had been imprisoned on Bula-Bemba island since early 1962 despite MNC and PSA leaders' efforts to free him.

Though never really threatened by the nationalists' disorganized maneuvers in Parliament, the central government felt compelled to take extreme measures against them. In July 1962, Prime Minister Adoula reshuffled his cabinet to exclude all representatives of the nationalist opposition and expelled all nationalist leaders from provincial administrations.[27] Strong parliamentary protests against these acts drew further repressive measures. In August 1962, the Adoula government suspended Parliament; in October it arrested six opposition leaders in connection with an alleged secession plot in Kivu, Katanga, and Orientale provinces.[28] Finally, the government established a military regime in Léopoldville under the influential and powerful national security chief, Victor Nendaka.[29]

The following year, the Adoula government faced a new coalition of trade unions and nationalist caucuses, though the latter were now a minority in Parliament. Again, the central executives' informal ruling clique, the Binza group (comprising the prime minister, the chief of security, the secretary of the interior, Colonel Mobutu, and the minister of justice) felt strongly threatened and overreacted. In May, Nendaka "prohibited all political activities not specifically approved by governmental authorities."[30] In September, during a demonstration organized by the MNC-Lumumba and the PSA-Gizenga to demand that Gizenga be freed, seven congressmen were arrested, and Parliament was suspended once again.

Meanwhile, the central government was making every effort to prevent a resurgence of nationalist strength in the provinces. In Stanleyville, the provincial assembly summarily dismissed Georges Grenfell, the MNC-affiliated president of the newly created province of Haut Congo. Grenfell was dismissed at Nendaka's personal request. In Maniéma, a state of extreme emergency existed from September 1963 to June 1964, and members of the MNC-Lumumba were barred from the region. Stripped of their parliamentary immunity and subject to the constant surveillance of Nendaka's secret police, those opposition figures who had not yet been jailed fled Léopoldville for Brazzaville. There, they formed the Committee of National Liberation (CNL), aimed at overthrowing the Léopoldville government by violent and nonparliamentary means.[31]

Until forced underground, the opposition leaders posed no serious threat to the central government. Their programs and activities were limited by a fear of exclusion from public office and were therefore broadly similar to those of other coalitions and parliamentary caucuses. Most opposition leaders devoted their energies to such symbolic and rhetorical issues as "Lumumbism" and the freeing of Antoine Gizenga; to such common issues in Congolese politics as the South Katangese secession, governmental corruption, and ministerial shake-ups; or simply to the "protection of public and democratic liberties"—meaning, of course, the preservation of their own lives and liberty.[32] Even during their exile in Brazzaville, the CNL leaders' attitudes remained ambivalent. While calling for revolutionary action and armed struggle in the Congo, they were also negotiating a return to Léopoldville under a government of national reconciliation to be headed by Moise Tshombe.[33]

Several factors contributed to the relative ineffectiveness of the nationalist opposition in the Congo. First, the creation of the 21 new provinces dealt a heavy blow to the parliamentary opposition by dividing its ranks between those who favored the territorial reorganization and those who opposed it. The latter, who were widely considered as "not having any provincial estates of their own," were ostracized both by their former political allies and by members of the government. Also, the reorganization depleted the strength of the opposition by causing some leaders to withdraw to the regional and local levels rather than face an uncertain future in national politics.[34] Those opposition figures who did remain in Parliament were able to use personal conflicts between ministers and congressmen to push through a few motions of censure against the Adoula government. On the whole, however, they failed to capitalize on the latent anti-government feelings of most Congolese legislators. Finally, even the staunchest opposition groups fell victim to internal frictions and personal feuds. Thus conflict arose between the Kamitatu and Gizenga wings of the PSA, and the MNC-Lumumba split into four factions after April 1963.[35] After January 1964, a similar factionalism seized those opposition leaders who had taken refuge in Brazzaville. One faction of the CNL was led by Egide Bocheley Davidson (MNC-Lumumba), who supported Pierre Mulele's revolutionary movement in Kwilu. The other was led by Christophe Gbenye, formerly the minister of the interior in the Adoula government, who wished to duplicate Antoine Gizenga's Stanleyville secession of 1960–61.[36]

In sum, political opposition in the Congo was marked by the emergence of a counterelite,[37] a shifting political stratum that was lent temporary unity by its exclusion from the ruling elite, and by its members' failure to establish patrimonial relationships in their own territories. At the same time, the ambivalent position of the counterelite is evidenced by its actual policies, which did not differ radically from those of other coalitions of the time. Clearly, the counterelite aspired to the very role of national leadership that it had been denied. This attitude was to prove unacceptable to other participants in the 1964–65 rebellions, since those groups sought to destroy totally the existing structure of patrimonial authority.

The Rebellions and the Reasons for Their Failure

Organized violence first erupted in Kwilu province in January 1964 as Pierre Mulele led his armed bands in a series of attacks on government outposts, mission stations, commercial enterprises, and anything else even distantly connected with the formal administrative and political apparatus. The Kwilu revolt was followed four months later by a general uprising in the eastern portion of the Congo; in less than six months, two-thirds of the country was in open revolt, as the accompanying map shows. Rebel ranks swelled with the capture of Stanleyville in September 1964. Thousands of young recruits were then baptized as *simba* (Swahili for "lion") and attached to the Army of Popular Liberation (APL), which had been created hastily several months before by "General" Nicolas Olenga. The rebels also confiscated hundreds of vehicles from companies, traders, and expatriates, and seized large reserves of arms and ammunition from ANC supply depots. According to Young:

The six months which followed the capture of Stanleyville were the highwater marks of the rebellion. APL columns spread out in all directions. Within the next three weeks, all central government authority had vanished in the rest of former Orientale province. Rebel forces captured Boende and reached Ingende, only 75 miles from Coquilhatville; captured Lisala, on the Congo River; reached almost to Banzyville in the northwest; captured most of Sankuru province; and came to within 100 miles of Luluabourg. On the one hand, a large-scale attack on Bukavu with approximately 6,000 simbas from August 15 to 22 was repulsed as were rebel attacks on North Kivu province.[38]

Nothing seemed capable of stopping the rebels. At Léopoldville, foreign embassies made plans to evacuate their nationals, while a squad of U.S. marines disembarked at Njili airport to prevent anti-American incidents. However, with the exception of a few mercenary officers from the former Katangese army, none of the rebel groups had the potential to press home their attack on the crumbling

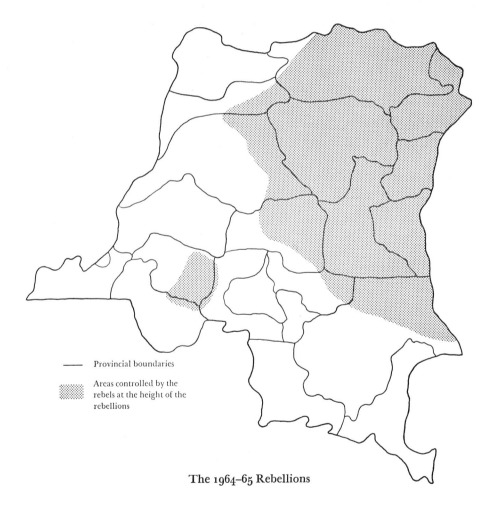

Provincial boundaries

Areas controlled by the
rebels at the height of the
rebellions

The 1964–65 Rebellions

central government, since they failed to consolidate their initial gains or even define the overall goals of their uprising. In fact, aside from the contrast between the radical nature of mass protest and the political views of the counterelite, the major factors contributing to the overall collapse of the 1964 insurgencies were the lack of class polarization and coordination within the rebel movement, the absence of any coherent ideology or disciplined revolutionary organization, and the persistence of power struggles and bureaucratic confusion among rebel leaders and cadres.

Tribal versus Class Polarization. A sharp polarization between rulers and ruled, masters and servants, oppressors and oppressed is essential to the success of any revolution or insurgency. Marx and Engels' classic formula is strikingly relevant in this regard:

Free man and slave, patrician and plebeian, lord and serf, guild master and journeyman, in a word, oppressors and oppressed, stood in constant opposition to one another, carried on an uninterrupted, now hidden, now open fight, a fight that each time ended either in a revolutionary reconstitution of society at large, or in the common ruin of the contending classes.[39]

In the Congo, the polarization of classes, and thus class antagonism, never developed fully. It is true that the Congolese patrimonial elite arrogated unto itself all of the prerogatives and benefits of national leadership. However, the elite's lack of overall strategy, its many internal conflicts, and the fluid, shifting nature of its alliances prevented it from ever becoming a united and autonomous class of oppressors. Also, it would seem that not all oppressed classes are politically conscious to the same degree. Specifically, the course of the Congolese rebellions suggests that the rebels' anger and sense of frustration were channeled into various tribal or regional conflicts. Thus the uprisings did not constitute a coordinated revolutionary movement, but rather a series of popular outbursts determined by purely local circumstances.

The initial rebellion in Kwilu province was engineered by Pierre Mulele, previously the Gizenga government's ambassador to Cairo, upon his return from a stay in Communist China. Mulele's first objective was to establish several guerrilla training camps in his own Idiofa territory. Verhaegen describes his recruitment techniques:

After his arrival in the beginning of August 1963, he [Mulele] proceeded as follows: using ethnic and clanic affinities and playing on the fact that he had been Gizenga's lieutenant, he gathered several Bambunda chiefs of clan, who agreed to send him a few youngsters from each village so that he might give them rudimentary political instruction in his training camps. In exchange, he promised to bring material prosperity to the Mbunda clans. He even convinced the chiefs that he knew how to make money, and he would teach the young people so that the entire clan or village could benefit from this knowledge.[40]

From the outset, then, the basis of the Kwilu uprisings was exclusively rural; the rebels operated solely from forest camps, and never captured any urban center. The movement in Kwilu was also distinguished—and hampered—by powerful conflicts between various tribes and clans. Although the Mbunda clans of the Idiofa territory gave full support to the rebellion, Mulele, a Mumbunda himself, met considerable difficulties in penetrating the neighboring Bapende tribe.[41] Thus in March 1965, after a brief collaboration between the Mumbunda and the Pende, bloody incidents occurred between troops from the two tribes. Specifically, the Pende accused the Mumbunda of killing several of their traditional chiefs and tribalizing the movement by relying entirely on Bambunda leaders.[42] Such internal tribal rivalries were to prove relatively minor, though, compared to the hostility of the nearby Bambala, Basuku, and Bayanzi ethnic groups to both the Pende and the Mumbunda. Such neighboring tribes were openly hostile to Mulele's enterprise largely because their local paramount chiefs, Catholic missionaries,[43] and politicians opposed it. Upon meeting resistance from these tribes, Mulele's partisans were largely inclined to the use of force and terror, thus jeopardizing the rebellion in its earliest stages.

The leaders of the eastern rebellions made frequent use of Mulele's name in such slogans as "Lumumbism is a doctrine; Mulelism is a force." However, there is no evidence of any political liaison between the Kwilu uprising and the eastern rebellions. Gaston Soumialot's revolutionary activities in North Katanga and Kivu, for instance, were initiated by the Gbenye faction of the CNL in Brazzaville, a group with which Mulele had no contact. The Kivu uprising began in January 1965, while the Kwilu revolt was in its third (and declining) phase. As elsewhere, violence in Kivu arose from strictly local circumstances, notably the bitter feud between Assemblyman Mussa Marandura and the provincial president, Simon Malago. As Verhaegen says: "Marandura and Bidalira, the civilian and military chiefs of [the Kivu rebellion]...did not follow the progress of the movement once it had gone beyond their constituencies. Their objective was to overthrow the provincial government and establish a rebel administration in their own region."[44] Moreover, the rebellion was limited exclusively to the Bafulero and Babembe tribes, with its expansion to the north curbed by the Bashi of Bukavu and the Warega of the Mwenga territory.

The uprising that developed in portions of North Katanga was also local in origin, resulting from complex political relationships between local members of the CNL, the Balubakat youth, and some dissatisfied political leaders in Albertville, the provincial capital. Specifically, an abortive coup d'etat in Albertville in May 1964 created a power vacuum; it was filled three weeks later by Babembe and Bafulero rebels arriving from Kivu. While these events transpired in Albertville, the rural Luba population of North Katanga remained aloof from the rebellion, for it viewed the rebel tribal groups as alien intruders.

In July 1964, Gaston Soumialot and other CNL leaders opened a third front in the provinces of Maniéma, Sankuru, Haut Congo, and Uélé. Between July and August, the cities of Kindu, Stanleyville, Paulis, Lodja, and Bunia all fell to the APL. In each case, the rebels' easy victory was due less to their own military prowess than to the general rout of the ANC and the collapse of provincial institutions. As Verhaegen notes: "The APL has met no real opposition in the course of its advance. Very often, a simple warning to the ANC is sufficient; the troops leave their garrison without fighting."[45]

At no time was there a real war of liberation in the Congo. Ethnic considerations and local politics played an increasingly large role in the emergence and spread of the rebellions, while popular involvement diminished accordingly. Thus in Orientale province, the cadres and the leaders of the APL were recruited almost entirely from among the Bakusu and Batetela of the Maniéma-Sankuru cluster; indeed, several reports from APL officers, including Gaston Soumialot and Christophe Gbenye themselves, brought attention to complaints about the preferential treatment given these two ethnic groups.[46] In the province of Sankuru, an armed band, estimated by some at as little as 100 rebels, met no difficulty in taking various other urban centers in the province, including Lodja, its capital. This band was eventually halted after it had killed civil and military authorities in Lodja and continued, for a time, its westward amble through

Sankuru. However, the rebels' experience in the small urban center of Kole clearly illustrates the lack of revolutionary involvement among local populations, as well as the insurmountable tribal barriers the rebels faced:

The rebels arrived at Kole on September 3 and occupied the ANC camp immediately. The rebels killed two soldiers. . . . The first sergeant attempted to flee with the others, but he fell down drunk and could not rise. An eleven-year-old boy finished him off with a spear. A second soldier, after making good his escape, returned to collaborate with the rebels, but he was killed also. The next day, the lieutenant of the garrison, the territorial administrator, and a small army squad recaptured Kole; the remaining soldiers then emerged from their hiding places in the forest. . . . Thereafter, the soldiers began to oppose the Batetela [rebels] to [their tribal foes] the Basongomeno, saying that the Batetela had called upon their brothers to exterminate all Basongomeno. The ANC troops and the Basongomeno then left together, setting fire to the city of Kole and to neighboring villages still in rebel hands.[47]

The Ideology of the Rebellions. A second prerequisite to any revolutionary movement is the development of a new and coherent ideology that offers a meaningful substitute for the myths of the old ruling class. Such an ideology must do more than name the "friends and the enemies of the revolution"; it must advance a view of reality qualitatively different from any previous one and outline a specific course of action well suited to existing conditions. The Kwilu rebellion was unique among the 1964 uprisings in its articulate ideology and its emphasis on the remodeling of Congolese society. As Verhaegen states:

The fundamental difference between the Kwilu rebellion and those of the eastern part of the country lay in its revolutionary radicalism. . . . The Mulelist leaders were ready to destroy the existing social, economic, and political fabric and build a brand-new society. It is without doubt the only case in which the term "revolution" could have any meaning.[48]

A striking paradox in the Kwilu uprising was the coexistence of a modernist ideology, clearly borrowed from Chinese Marxism, with primitive beliefs and rituals typical of all millenarian movements. Still, such a paradox is open to explanation. Hobsbawm emphasizes that millenarian movements can be revolutionary if they are modernized or absorbed into modern social movements. The essential question, then, is how, and to what degree, such modernization takes place. According to Hobsbawm, "it does not take place, or takes place only very slowly and incompletely, if the matter is left to the peasants themselves. It takes place most completely and successfully if the millenarian movement is fitted into a framework of . . . theory and program which comes to the peasants from the outside."[49] Though the Kwilu uprising received its ideological impetus from the outside, there was never any attempt to implement a revolutionary program of nationalization or land reform in rebel-held areas. Moreover, the uprising remained localized within the peasantry or the rural milieu in general. These two factors account for the failure of the movement to expand and "revolutionize" surrounding populations.

According to rare documents uncovered during and after the Kwilu rebellion, the ideological instruction given the partisans in their forest training camps stressed two modernist themes.[50] The first was that of Marxian struggle between antagonistic classes. In this interpretation, the people of the Congo were divided into three classes. One class consisted of capitalistic and imperialistic foreigners who exploited the country's natural resources. The foreigners in turn were aided by those Congolese who served the corrupt national government. Subgroups of merchants, teachers, and missionaries were said to occupy the fringes of this exploitive class of native Congolese. Supporting the other classes, of course, were the masses of the poor, consisting primarily of workers and peasants. The rebels' second main theme stressed the distinction between reformist and revolutionary struggle. Reformism might alleviate the people's sufferings, it was said, but it would never be far-reaching enough to produce real change. Revolutionary struggle, on the other hand, was presented as a sign that the people were taking the initiative in solving problems of national development.

Such relatively simple and easily assimilated principles, often presented in the form of proverbs, were augmented by a vague and idealized vision of the future. China and the USSR were frequently depicted as "countries of happiness" that would teach the Congolese to make bicycles, automobiles, and other machinery. Most significant was the emphasis on the rural way of life, which was described in the most idyllic terms:

Not only is this doctrine addressed primarily to villagers in the countryside . . . but it also asserts that their attitudes and way of life are superior to those of city dwellers, who have abandoned their land, their roots, and their traditions. . . . The new society is presented as one huge village, composed of thousands of smaller villages in which people will find the satisfaction of all their material needs, [as well as] creative endeavor, justice, happiness, and a meaningful existence.[51]

Radical ideology was used only in the Kwilu rebellion. Elsewhere, the leaders of the CNL, APL, and revolutionary governments were little concerned with teaching and educating the rural masses. Therefore, they fell back on the prosaic themes of prosperity, civil liberties, new national elections, and Congolese reunification that the nationalist opposition had long stressed. Shortly after the capture of Uvira by the rebels, Gaston Soumialot declared:

The CNL aims to establish peace within the country, to revitalize the economy, and to restore respect for democracy and the liberty of Congolese citizens and foreigners. Though both are nationalistic and share similar aspirations, one must not confuse the Mulelist movement in Kwilu with the CNL. . . . [the latter] is opposed to colonialism and imperialism. If Mr. Adoula and Mr. Kasavubu are ready to resign, conflict will cease, and Parliament will be free to deliberate again.[52]

In fact, public statements from the leaders of the eastern rebellions offered no revolutionary analysis of the Congolese situation as a whole. The only accepted credential of a "true revolutionary" was the MNC-Lumumba membership card, a card that eventually became indispensable to all officials in rebel-held territories. For instance, when the simba arrived in Lodja, they slaughtered all politicians or civil servants who had no MNC card but invited several local officials who had once been party members to join the new rebel administration.[53]

In sum, the ideological content of the uprisings in the eastern Congo differed sharply from that of the Kwilu uprisings. The eastern rebellions lacked any coherent body of revolutionary doctrine, and their leaders concentrated on expanding their influence rapidly without using mass education to consolidate their gains. In Kwilu, rebellion was sparked by a modernist ideology introduced from outside the Congo. However, that ideology was almost immediately diluted by the primitive beliefs of the prepolitical society to which it was transferred.

The Revolutionary Core: Armies of Popular Liberation. All modern revolutionary movements include some organization on the order of Trotsky's Red Army or, more recently, Mao's Red Guard. Political parties may become entrenched bureaucracies, as in the USSR or China, but popular armies of this sort will supply the impetus to overthrow the old regime and preserve the ideological purity of the new one.

Rebel leaders in Kwilu and the eastern provinces made extensive use of partisan bands and popular armies. In both regions, the armies were organized in modern chains of command like that of the ANC, but adapted to guerrilla warfare conditions. At the same time, they relied heavily on traditional and magical elements to reinforce their troops' esprit de corps and fighting ability. In Kwilu, partisans received intense ideological and physical training from a hierarchical organization extending to every village in rebel hands. The organization's basic unit was the "quipe," a term derived from the French *équipe* ("team"):

Each quipe is headed by a president, a kind of military chief who has had to undergo eight months of training and distinguish himself in carrying out an actual mission. The president is assisted by a corporal, a squad chief, and a section chief. Other members of the quipe include political commissioners and their assistants, a secretary to prepare regular reports . . . , a chief of camp, a man and woman to see to domestic chores around the camp . . . and a chief of the posts.[54]

In addition to military activities, each quipe was responsible for the villagers' ideological education: "Twice weekly, the Mulelists organize meetings that last from morning till night. Attendance at these meetings is compulsory for all villagers, women and children included. These initiation sessions are conducted in the question-and-answer style that Catholic missionaries use in catechism class."[55] Above the quipes were subdirectorates and directorates headed by high-ranking noncoms responsible for liaison between the various quipes, and liaison between each quipe and levels above it in the chain of command. At the head of the hierarchy, of course, stood Mulele and his central headquarters. The location of the headquarters was secret and shifted often, while Mulele himself was surrounded by bodyguards at all times.[56]

This modern hierarchy was shot through with magic, ritual, and taboo. Partisans were forbidden to eat certain foods, use (or even touch) things that had belonged to Europeans, turn their backs to the enemy, or utter Mulele's name. Each quipe had a witch doctor who administered European medicines, usually stolen from Catholic missions. Magical powers were ascribed to Mulele himself; as a savior-chief, he was thought to be impervious to bullets and capable of transforming himself into a bird or snake at will:

Some rebels and locals seem to think that Mulele's magical powers are such that if people do not follow him, they will be unable to bear children, or their children will fall prey to disease and death.... It is striking how similar the beliefs attached to Mulele are to those associated with various messianic movements appearing in Kwilu before and after independence. The leaders of these movements ... were also reputed to have magical powers of invulnerability, invincibility, and metamorphosis.... Like Mulele, they were considered both religious prophets and liberators.[57]

It would be erroneous to confuse Mulele's appeal with that of the ordinary charismatic leader. If one follows Weber's definition of charismatic leadership as a phenomenon derived from interpersonal relations rather than a quality inherent in a given individual,[58] Mulele's appeal was not charismatic, but chiliastic and messianic. This distinction implies a great deal about the revolutionary and modernist aspects of Mulelism, for it would seem that the messianic element of the Kwilu rebellion hampered its transition from primitivism to modernity. Weber points out that charisma, particularly institutional or depersonalized charisma, "can be transformed starting from the inside ... and may cause a change in the central tendencies of belief and action."[59] Prophecy of the millenarian sort, he notes, may also be a force for change, but it is generally unable to institutionalize itself, break its ties with traditional folk beliefs, or end its association with magical rites. Thus Mulele and his followers promised a total transformation of Congolese society but grew extremely vague when it came to actually implementing their modern social programs.

The development of the rebel army in the eastern provinces took a quite different course from that in Kwilu, though there were basic organizational defects in the eastern army, too. The armed bands that were to become the APL began as groups of peasants under leaders from rural areas, very much like the partisan bands in Kwilu. E. Lejeune, who observed the eastern rebellions, noted that "each band consisted of people from the same village who chose their leader from among themselves. This leader in turn chose his own rank. Only the highest ranks had any real meaning, for these were borne only by men who commanded large numbers of troops."[60]

Before their first victories, the rebel bands were relatively well integrated into the civilian population, with whom they shared common tribal and clanic origins. In a relatively short time, however, the partisan bands became an army whose uniform and general organization resembled those of the ANC. At the same time, recruitment was extended to a new social stratum, notably the young people of Balubakat, MNC-Lumumba, and other former urban political parties. This group was to constitute the most poorly disciplined, least integrated element in the APL.[61] During its expansion, the APL also attracted new tribal groups. Two such groups, the Batetela and the Bakusu, managed to take over all major positions of leadership in the army.

When the revolutionary government was finally formed at Stanleyville, the problems of discipline and tribal rivalry became increasingly acute. A mutiny broke out at Paulis in September 1964; at the same time, strong signs of discontent appeared among troops engaged in guerrilla operations near Kindu.[62] Living far from home and subject to growing tribal hostility, the recruits and cadres of the APL began to lose their revolutionary fervor and adopted an increasingly elitist mentality. The revolutionary army's isolation from local populations, as well as from such other rebel organizations as the revolutionary government and the CNL, became evident after the fall of Stanleyville. In September 1964, Gaston Soumialot, the leader of the CNL in the eastern Congo, stated that "it is strictly forbidden, especially in this phase of the popular revolution, for any politician or public administrator to take part in the affairs of the APL, or to have any contact with its members. This prohibition extends to all Congolese citizens and inhabitants of the People's Republic of the Congo, whatever their position or social status."[63]

The APL did not exhibit the messianic leadership or the visionary promises that typified the Kwilu uprising. However, it did somewhat resemble its sister rebellion in its use of magic. The APL relied on a specialized body of witch doctors, the *munganga*, which the leaders of the rebellion controlled as tightly as they might have an association of physicians or technicians. Also, APL rituals and taboos were far more rigidly codified than those of the Kwilu guerrillas. Among the most important of them were the initiation ceremonies, the ban on sexual intercourse before going into battle,[64] and the rituals surrounding the public execution of former politicians and high civil servants. Public executions grew more frequent after the rebel capture of Stanleyville and sometimes reached an extraordinary level of cruelty. Execution ceremonies usually took place before a statue of Patrice Lumumba and demanded the participation of all local residents, including white foreigners, in flower-bedecked processions and wild singing.

As far as can be determined, the various taboos and rituals were meant to reinforce the internal cohesion of the APL, offset its deficiencies in modern arms, and provide its troops with a sort of psychological weapon capable of terrorizing the ANC and striking fear and awe into the civilian population. Eventually, however, the magical devices used by the APL lost their effectiveness. Public executions degenerated into an unending round of needless violence that many politicians used to settle personal grudges.[65] Also, ritual and taboo lost their effectiveness as psychological weapons when small guerrilla units of foreign mercenaries began their counterattack on rebel-held areas.

Reactivation of Political Struggle. The fourth weakness of the Congolese rebellions lay in the revival of bureaucratism and power struggles as rebel administrations settled into such "liberated" urban centers as Albertville, Kindu, and Stanleyville. Having no clear revolutionary goals or programs, most rebel leaders in the eastern provinces carried on the same policies that their predecessors had followed. Thus activists and cadres were entrusted with police functions, while a petty bureaucratic mentality came to dominate all levels of the revolutionary government. In Albertville, Gaston Soumialot became a kind of "superadministrator":

The scope of his responsibility is extremely vast. The smallest dispute between two individuals requires his personal intervention, and a great deal of his time and effort is devoted to the reception of visitors, or to individual contacts. We found no sign of any liaison with department heads, military chiefs, or his [Soumialot's] own advisors.[66]

A similar trend emerged in Orientale province, particularly with the official proclamation of the People's Republic of the Congo at Stanleyville in September 1964. At that time, Christophe Gbenye assumed leadership of a cabinet consisting of no less than seventeen ministers. Gbenye then designated one extraordinary commissioner, with four to six assistants, to each of the former provincial districts of Haut Congo, Uélé, and Ituri. A sort of mixed civilian and military dictatorship arose throughout rebel-held areas as "national security agents" were appointed (or, in many cases, appointed themselves) "to each airport, to all harbors, to all railway stations, and to all liberated zones."[67] Efforts by Gbenye and his Stanleyville associates to build a functioning governmental bureaucracy merely created an island of order in a sea of violence, terror, and assassination. Gbenye's personal archives, which this writer had the opportunity to consult,[68] probably offer the best illustration of this dramatic contrast. The archives show the strong hold of bureaucratic ritual on the political elite and reveal President Gbenye as a very scrupulous civil servant. Indeed, he personally took charge of such administrative details as nominations, dismissals, settlement of private quarrels, and investigation of personal grievances; he even established office hours during which he received personnel from his own administration. There was no evidence of any ideological commitment or explicit policy in regard to economic, social, or administrative matters.

Gbenye's revolutionary goals were, in fact, prosaic. He wished to restore previously existing institutional structures, mostly in the hope of international recognition, and to end the disruption that the rebellions had produced. In fact, Gbenye's desire for political stability led to differences between his government and such other revolutionary groups as the APL, the MNC-Lumumba, and the CNL. Several relatively minor but significant disputes arose between Gbenye and Soumialot over the possible elimination of the MNC-Lumumba and the CNL. For Gbenye, "the voice of the revolutionary government should be the only one to be heard at all echelons, national as well as international."[69]

In fact, the dispute between Gbenye and Soumialot was never decisively settled. New conflicts and manifestations of mutual distrust constantly arose within the various local sections of the MNC-Lumumba, between the MNC-Lumumba and the APL, and between these groups and the so-called Council of Elders. This last was a local institution that had emerged spontaneously in Kindu in July 1964 and that aimed to control governmental activities "in the name of the people."[70] Meanwhile, a wave of petty opportunists was invading all rebel political organizations and thus aggravating institutional confusion. The newcomers' behavior differed little from that of the politicians who had previously been executed. In a letter to the extraordinary commissioners of Haut Congo, Uélé, and Ituri, Soumialot summarized the situation as follows:

More than one of our activists now in power engages in activities that contradict our [revolutionary principles]. . . . Thus some of our burgomasters have simply expelled humble families and taken over their homes. Others, in order to mask their abuses, have mingled their private affairs with party business. There is much to be said about arbitrary arrests arising from petty personal feuds. Often, urban authorities have used political means to settle familial or other matters.[71]

In sum, the recapture of Stanleyville and the other urban centers occupied by the rebels was due not so much to the successful counterattack of the ANC and the mercenaries, but to the bureaucratic inertia of the counterelite and the corruption of its lowest ranks.

CHAPTER 7

Toward a Caesarist Bureaucracy

THE POPULAR rebellions of 1964–65 ended the domination of Congolese politics by decentralized patrimonialism. Though they offered no meaningful alternatives to patrimonialism, these rebellions did improve the relative position of new groups in the political arena. At the same time, those groups that might have been able to provide an alternative to patrimonial politics were weak, and it took a coup d'etat to bring about an actual change in the form of government.

On November 24, 1965, after a period of political vacuum, General Joseph Mobutu and the ANC High Command summarily dismissed the two current contenders to the presidency, Moise Tshombe and Joseph Kasavubu, and proclaimed a state of extreme emergency. Mobutu has remained in power since then, and we can now see that his regime is not the military dictatorship it first appeared to be. Rather, it is a Caesarist bureaucracy, a type of rule characterized by a single authority figure at the head of a bureaucratic governmental structure. The bureaucratic structure is usually manned by diverse social groups that have come into existence during a preceding era of patrimonial politics.

The use of the term "bureaucracy" presents major conceptual difficulties, for like many other terms in the social sciences, bureaucracy is widely applied to a variety of phenomena in modern industrial societies, both socialist and capitalist. We must therefore distinguish pure bureaucracy or bureaucratism—a complex of attitudes affecting human relationships and decision-making in all sectors of social, political, and economic life—from the specific historical bureaucracies in which this complex occurs.[1]

Though they differ on some particulars, Marx, Weber, and Michels all define bureaucratism in broadly similar terms.[2] According to them, it implies an ensemble of hierarchical structures and relations involving the pursuit of rationality. Thus bureaucratism is characterized by a fixed jurisdictional system based on abstract and formal laws that ensure the continuous fulfillment of duties; the centralization and concentration of managerial authority; the elimination of uncertainties arising from the emotional element in human relationships; the recruitment of experts through co-optation, designation from the top, or examination; the separation of executive offices from the ruler's household; and the systematic use of secrecy and concealment both within the organization and in relations with outsiders. Obviously, these characteristics are very broadly defined and can be applied to a great variety of historical situations. However, one way of classifying historical bureaucracies is to note the degree to which bureaucratic elements are present in societies, and to examine the relationship between these elements and the class structures that surround them. It is this approach that we shall use in analyzing the Mobutu regime.

The Emergence of Bureaucratic Trends in the Congo

Since Mobutu's take-over in 1965, his regime has been marked by numerous clearly bureaucratic elements. These are the pursuit of an apolitical economic rationality, an emphasis on expertise in governmental functions, centralization of power, an attempt to minimize uncertainty caused by tribal or personal loyalties, and an emphasis on secrecy.

The Decline of Patrimonial Politics. A clear trend toward apolitical economic rationality appeared relatively soon after Mobutu's coup. In speeches given during December 1965, President Mobutu made clear the catastrophic price of patrimonial politics. His language was simple, and for the first time he told the Congolese people how much their incomes had declined after independence:

Before 1960, the Congo produced 120,000 tons of corn; today, she produces 50,000 tons. Before 1960, she produced 100,000 tons of rice; today, she produces 20,000 tons. Before 1960, she produced 15 million tons of manioc; today, she produces 900,000 tons. . . . In this country, we are producing 80 percent of what we did in 1960, but we are spending six times as much. Much money is spent, but there are fewer goods to buy. Such is the actual situation caused by the deficit in public finances. . . . To sum up, the price of merchandise has increased almost 500 percent since 1960.[3]

Accordingly, the objectives that Mobutu enunciated in his first speeches were economic ones. They included the reduction of state expenditures, some industrial construction (e.g. a dam, a hydraulic iron-smelting plant at Inga), and a "return to the land" in an attempt to reach 1960 production levels. This was a simple and dramatic appeal in which Mobutu asked Congolese society to reverse its fundamental priorities: "From 1966 to 1970, we are going to produce. We are not going to work in a disorderly manner, but in the context of a master plan that I will work out with my government in early 1967."[4]

The new regime sought to foster a high level of emotional involvement, especially in its early days. In his attempt to mobilize the people, Mobutu relied on a number of simple but effective symbolic appeals, including Operation Roll-Up-Your-Sleeves,[5] in which politicians, military officers, and cadres were widely exhorted to clean up the streets of their cities, cut weeds, and burn sweepings; and an order that all civil servants and high officials cultivate a field of at least 2.5 acres. Less symbolic was the establishment of a civil service compelling university students to work in secondary schools[6] and a four-year military draft for medical doctors.[7] The Mobutu regime also established numerous public and semipublic agencies headed by young technocrats and former politicians concerned with the Congo's social and economic development. Such organizations included the High Planning Commission for National Reconstruction; the Congolese Bank for Equipment and Industrial Development (BCDI), an organization providing new Congolese industries with capital investment and credit; the People's Cooperative, aimed at undercutting the black market by selling staple foods at low cost to the economically disadvantaged populations; the National Office for the Management of Real Estate (ONAGI); and the National Office for Agricultural Cooperatives (ONACA).

Mobutu's emphasis on economic and technical rationalization was paralleled by a deep distrust for politics. Unlike the army, which was presented as embodying the highest moral virtues of the nation,[8] the political sphere was portrayed as basically corrupt, unstable, and irrational:

Whereas the military situation [of the Congo] was satisfactory, the failure was complete in the realm of politics. . . . Political leaders indulged in a series of sterile struggles for public office without considering the welfare of the citizens of this country of ours.[9]

The ANC has won victory after victory, but the politicians of our dear Congo have ruined the country.[10]

What could the army high command do? Only what it has done: sweep the politicians out. . . . Nothing counted for them but power . . . and what the exercise of power could bring them. Filling their pockets, exploiting the Congo and its inhabitants seemed to be their only purpose.[11]

Even the word "political" itself began to disappear from official terminology. In the province of South Kivu, for instance, assemblymen were seemingly afraid to describe their parliamentary committees as political groups.[12] Indeed, party politics was banned throughout the Congo for a period of five years, and Mobutu consistently denied that his own Popular Revolutionary Movement (MPR) was really a political party. Rather, the MPR was described as a nationalist movement aimed at affirming "the uniqueness of the Congolese personality," and "mobilizing the popular masses for their education, information, and edification."[13] As such, it could not tolerate the existence of rival political organizations.

   The apolitical stand of the Mobutu regime is probably best illustrated by its creation of a new constitutional framework designed to promote continuity and permanence. Under the 1967 constitution, the president of the Congolese Republic is elected for a period of seven years and holds a position of supreme authority in the country. He governs strictly by ordinance and decree through an administration composed of apolitical ministers or high civil servants. Unlike its patrimonial predecessors, this government represents no tribal constituency and cannot exist independently of the Congolese people as a whole. Moreover, since General Mulamba's dismissal in 1966, the central government is no longer headed by a prime minister. It is now accountable only to the president, who nominates and dismisses its members at will.[14]

   Of course, such an authoritarian system strictly limits the traditional function of parliamentary institutions as centers of political debate.[15] Although the Senate and the House of Representatives were retained during 1966 and 1967, they, like all other political institutions, were restricted by the state of emergency proclaimed at the beginning of the regime. Mobutu used the Parliament to present a democratic facade to the outside world, as a means of reinforcing his legitimacy, and as a tool for controlling ministers and civil servants who wished to indulge in political activities. But members of Parliament were not pleased with this interpretation of their role, and in June 1967, after a violent antiparliamentary campaign in the press, Mobutu put an end to all controversies and complaints by dissolving both houses of Parliament.[16]

Thus the ideological and institutional priorities of the Mobutu regime differ sharply from those of previous Congolese governments. Of prime importance now are permanence, stability, continuity, and efficient regulatory mechanisms; the extreme spontaneity and institutional anarchy of patrimonialism have given way to predictable attitudes and behavior. When orders are given they are obeyed, even if they are still discussed in private.

The Mobutu regime's emphasis on economic rationality has produced positive results. Since the enactment of the 1967 plan for monetary stabilization, the Congo seems to have entered a period of unprecedented prosperity; as Table 13 shows, the country's GNP for 1968 exceeded for the first time the level it had reached just before independence.

The GNP was estimated at 720 million Zaires in 1968, an increase of 16 percent over 1958. According to the annual report of the Con-

TABLE 13

Congolese GNP, 1958–68, in Millions of Zaires

(1 Zaire = $2)

Year	Estimated GNP relative to current prices	Estimated GNP relative to 1966 prices	Estimated GNP relative to 1958 prices
1958	63.4	—	63.4
1959	65.1	—	64.1
1964	226.3	—	61.2
1966	304.1	304.1	68.2
1967	460.0	301.1	68.1
1968	720.4	324.6	73.4

SOURCE: Banque Nationale du Congo, *Rapport Annuel 1968–1969* (Kinshasa).

golese National Bank, this increase was mostly due to continuous
expansion of agricultural production (from 17.65 percent of the GNP
in 1966 to 24.30 percent in 1968) and not, as is sometimes asserted,
to rising copper production. However, the benefits of this improve-
ment have been partly offset by a constant population growth, estimated by some at 22 percent since 1958.

Production increases have sufficiently raised the state's income to
augment its hard-currency reserves dramatically, from 61 million
Zaires in 1967 to 100 million Zaires in 1969. Yet, had it not been
for the rising price of copper and other minerals for that period,
says the Congolese Bank report, there would have been a net deficit.
Moreover, growing public expenditures seem likely to limit further
increases in the GNP. The increase in expenditures between 1967
and 1969 (79.9 million to 222.4 million Zaires) was deemed "excessive" by the Congolese Bank report; it came largely from increases
in administrative salaries, which rose by some 30 percent from 1966
to 1969.

As Table 14 shows, economic prosperity has primarily benefited
the upper echelons of the administrative, political, and military hierarchy. Between 1966 and 1969, "substantial modifications have taken
place in the income distribution of various social groups."[17] In terms
of real income, the gap seems to be widening between skilled and un-
skilled workers on the one hand and high civil servants on the other.

Centralization. The trend toward bureaucratic centralization of
power is best illustrated by the political and administrative reorganization that eventually led to the elimination of the 21 new provinces.

TABLE 14

Real Income of Selected Occupational Groups

(1966 = 100%)

Occupation	1967	1968	1969
Private sector:			
Unskilled worker	80.4%	77.6%	77.4%
Skilled worker	96.3	93.2	92.8
Public sector:			
Assistant clerk	78.3	65.9	105.9
Clerk	89.3	75.2	84.7
Bureau chief	87.6	73.7	119.9
Secretary-general	86.2	72.6	188.2

SOURCE: Banque Nationale du Congo, *Rapport Annuel 1968–1969.*

This reorganization was initiated and executed in a manner typical of the Mobutu regime. At first, President Mobutu seemed little concerned with provincial institutions. In his speeches shortly after his coup, Mobutu said that the provinces would provide the geographical basis for national unity; and as in the past, the first cabinet was assembled with provincial origins in mind. Still, tight control over the Congo's central government logically demanded checks on political activity at the local level; this in turn required undercutting the power bases of influential regional leaders. Also, during his various tours of Congolese rural areas, Mobutu was frequently importuned by local factions who wanted him to arbitrate their petty conflicts.

Mobutu's first action on the provincial question was to substitute military officers for civilian authorities in politically unstable areas. Thus Colonel Bangala was sent to Kinshasa; Colonel Tshatshi to Uélé, Ituri, and Haut Congo; Major Falu to Sankuru; Major Kasongo to Lomami; and Major Ngaie to Luluabourg. These appointments were only temporary, though, since Mobutu was quite reluctant to involve the army in civilian affairs.

The first hints of an impending territorial reorganization appeared in February 1966 in the newspaper *Actualités Africaines*, which was said to be an organ of the presidency.[18] On March 22, President Mobutu sent a memorandum on reorganization to both houses of Parliament, which he characterized as "not a directive, but a proposal to be discussed."[19] Though dissatisfaction was not expressed openly, Kinshasa became the site of feverish maneuvering and short-lived alliances on the part of provincial delegates. However, Mobutu took the initiative again on April 6, when he unilaterally issued an ordinance reducing the number of Congolese provinces from 21 to 12.[20] The ordinance was followed in a few days by a ministerial decree summoning twelve new provincial assemblies so that they might elect governors and vice-governors.[21] Electoral procedures were fixed minutely, and to prevent candidates from contesting the offices, all elections were to be completed by midnight of April 25. The government forbade all discussion and debate while the assemblies were in session, and army officers supervised the voting in the provinces of Ituri, Kivu Central, and Kwilu.

The central executive clearly intended to control all political activities in the Congo, and to eliminate any political institutions

with other ideas. Local executives were allowed less and less autonomy of decision until, on October 31, 1966, Mobutu issued an ordinance investing the president with ultimate authority over the acts
of provincial administration.[22]

Eliminating Primordial Political Relationships. Mobutu's provincial reorganization was still not sufficient to ensure political stability in the Congo. Expressions of unrest by minority groups in
provincial legislatures threatened the new governors of Bandundu,
South Katanga, North Katanga, and Kasai Oriental. Also, continued
restlessness in the capital cities of many provinces impeded local
civil servants in the role Mobutu had assigned them, that of "high
state commissioners" engaged in "economic and social reconstruction."[23] Finally, several provincial governors were suspected of involvement in the Kisangani mutiny of 1967, a fact that further
strained relations between the national and provincial authorities.[24]

On November 25, 1966, General Mobutu announced that there
would be a new reduction in the number of provinces; and on
December 24, addressing the combined houses of Parliament at their
annual closing session, he said that this reduction would be from
twelve to eight. Except for the new province of Kongo Central and
the division of former Kasai Province into two entities, Kasai Occidental and Kasai Oriental, the new provinces were identical with
the colonial ones. However, the presidential decree involved much
more than a simple change in the number of provinces; it also removed provincial offices from the political realm and left them only
administrative functions. Governors and their appointees, the provincial commissioners and provincial secretaries, were transferred to
provinces outside their native regions and became high officials
directly accountable to the president. Provincial assemblies were replaced with purely advisory bodies, and the posts of provincial minister and vice-governor were eliminated.[25] As Etienne Tshisekedi, the
interior minister, pointed out in a report to Mobutu: "Thus we
paradoxically return to the administrative structure that existed
before June 30, 1960: a strong central authority relies on decentralized provincial administrations that carry out, through the district
commissioners and territorial administrators, all major social and
economic decisions [made by the central government]."[26]

At the highest administrative levels, at least, this structure eliminated the costly uncertainties that had resulted from the shifting loyalties of patrimonialism. There remained very little room for manipulation or maneuvering, since governors were completely foreign to the areas they governed. Still, the new reform did not bring total administrative stability. In 1967, a number of personnel changes were made in the highest provincial offices (see Table 15), for reasons ranging from "irresponsible attitude and negligence" during the Kisangani mutiny to reassignment to posts in the central government.

In early 1968 the policy of shifting provincial administrators away from their native regions was extended to district commissioners and territorial administrators. However, this reform was not completed without difficulty, since the central government's administrative apparatus was not yet functioning at maximum efficiency. Also, many local officials were reluctant to leave their own regions for areas

TABLE 15

Assignments of Governors and Provincial Commissioners During 1967

Province and office	January 1967	August 1967	October 1967
Bandundu:			
Governor	F. Lwakabwanga	F. Kupa	F. Kupa
Provincial commissioner	L. Kitanta	D. Boji	L. Kitanta
Equateur:			
Governor	J. Mukamba	J. Mukamba	J. Mukamba
Provincial commissioner	F. Kupa	D. Monguya	D. Monguya
Kasai Occidental:			
Governor	P. Muhona	P. Muhona	P. Muhona
Provincial commissioner	P. Masikita	P. Masikita	P. Masikita
Kasai Oriental:			
Governor	H. D. Takizala	H. D. Takizala	H. D. Takizala
Provincial commissioner	D. Boji	L. Kitanta	A. Sita
Katanga:			
Governor	J. F. Manzikala	D. Paluku	D. Paluku
Provincial commissioner	E. Kihuyu	E. Kihuyu	E. Kihuyu
Kivu:			
Governor	L. Engulu	L. Engulu	L. Engulu
Provincial commissioner	R. Bombo	R. Bombo	R. Bombo
Kongo Central:			
Governor	D. Paluku	F. Lwakabwanga	F. Lwakabwanga
Provincial commissioner	D. Sakombi	D. Sakombi	E. Ndjoku
Orientale:			
Governor	V. F. Moanda	M. Denge	M. Denge
Provincial commissioner	M. Denge	D. Diur	D. Boji

SOURCE: CRISP, *Congo 1967.*

where they could expect a hostile reception; most district commissioners and territorial administrators in Kwilu, for example, where I spent some time in the summer of 1968, remained there, hoping to escape the notice of the ministry of the interior rather than taking up the new posts to which they had been assigned several months earlier. One official of that ministry made a concession to this sentiment by announcing that all such appointments were temporary and made on a trial basis only.[27]

In addition to isolating the provincial civil service from local populations these transfers had another important effect. They allowed the provincial secretaries, who now held effective control in routine matters, to restore order and efficiency in their provinces. The secretaries fired corrupt financial officers, temporarily or permanently dismissed hundreds of contractual agents and cut the salaries of hundreds more, eliminated superfluous municipal administrations, and so on. They were impeded in their efforts by strikes and petitions from local trade unions, which forced a number of concessions, and by the absence of statistical and other information.[28] In particular, since most contractual agents had been hired on a personal basis, it was often impossible to find out how many were under contract and what they were doing.

Expertise. A third feature of Mobutu's regime is its growing reliance on the talent and expertise of such social groups as university and technical school students and former civil servants. During his first coup in September 1960, Colonel Mobutu had appealed to university students and graduates to serve in his College of Commissioners; he made a similar appeal after his 1965 coup.[29] In November 1966, Mobutu created the General Secretariat to the Presidency, naming as its head Gerard Kamanda, former president of AGEL (General Association of Lovanium Students), and as its other members three university students, Jacques Bongoma, Jean Umba-di-Lutete, and Barthelemy Bisengimana. A year later, this secretariat was expanded and renamed the Presidential Advisory Board. It now had fifteen members, all of them former graduate students, organized into four committees, as well as a new director, Evariste Loliki. The presidential advisory board was officially responsible for "studies, technical coordination, and liaison between public institutions."[30]

In practice it served President Mobutu as a brain trust, and as such it enjoyed considerable prestige and influence.

There are important differences between the styles of student involvement in 1960 and 1967. The "student government" of 1960 was strictly provisional and in theory, at least, it was apolitical. Its successor of 1967 appears to be permanent, and with its emphasis on radical symbols it has strong ideological coloration. Despite the relative secrecy surrounding activities of the Presidential Advisory Board, there are some indications that it was partly responsible for the hard-line policy that Mobutu followed in his dealings with foreign corporations in the Congo.[31]

The importance of university students has increased within official governmental and administrative agencies as well. In October 1967, ten university graduates and three holders of graduate degrees were included in the 21-member cabinet. And most of the degree-holders held important portfolios, notably interior (Tshisekedi); economic affairs (Nsinga); foreign affairs (Bomboko); finances (Mushiete and Lwango); information (Kande); and personnel and civil service (Emungania).[32] Former students of such technical schools as the National College of Law and Administration also joined the territorial and provincial civil service as administrators or district commissioners.[33] Finally, the Commission for Administrative Reform that Mobutu created in October 1966 included thirteen former University students among its seventeen members.

Secrecy and Elitism. General Mobutu's rise to power brought a new style of leadership to the Congo. The decentralized form of rule characteristic of previous regimes left no room for concealment or secrecy. Frequent conflicts, unstable alliances, and the use of parliamentary institutions as arenas for maneuvers by the opposition had made political life unpredictable, spontaneous, and open. As a former civil servant stressed to this writer: "During the first legislature, politicians made a lot of errors. Sure, the political system was bankrupt and corrupt, but politics had at least one virtue that it lacks today: it was a sort of game, a living theater in which people acted spontaneously and, to some extent, found a kind of fulfillment."[34]

In such a climate, politicians had been inclined to talk freely and take others into their confidence. This tendency made secrets hard to

keep, but it did allow the researcher easy access to firsthand information. Since Mobutu's take-over, political behavior has become more
predictable, but also more secret and less spontaneous. The researcher
now encounters considerable difficulty in his search for facts and
learns little from his conversations with insiders and political figures.
This is due not only to the general suspiciousness and insecurity of
many civil servants and high officials, but also to the fact that most
intermediary officials in the administration, such as the minister of
the interior, governors, and provincial commissioners, are now allowed much less initiative and responsibility.[35]

Another element in the style of the new regime is the increased
importance of the National Security Department (secret police),
which in 1966 was transferred from the jurisdiction of the ministry
of the interior to that of the president and entrusted to two influential members of Mobutu's personal entourage, Colonel A. Singa
(Kinshasa) and Captain S. Mika (Lubumbashi).[36] Also characteristic
of the new regime is the importance of the presidential entourage.
Its ministerial members, notably Etienne Tshisekedi, Justin Bomboko, Jean-Jacques Kande, and Victor Nendaka, have more direct
access to Mobutu than other ministers.[37] Other members, among
them Marcel Lengema and Bernardin Mungul-Diaka, have been used
as Mobutu's personal envoys to foreign countries or as military at-
tachés reporting directly to him.[38]

The secrecy surrounding public affairs in the Congo is justified by
a complex and elitist conception of political authority. The most
significant official document in this respect is an essay entitled *From
Legality to Legitimacy*, published by the Congolese information ministry and signed by President Mobutu himself. According to this
essay, any decision-making process involves two kinds of judgments,
one value-oriented, the other technical. Value-oriented judgments
at the mass level are "formulations of common aspirations"; they are
an amalgam of individual value judgments, of which anyone who
has reached the age of reason is capable, and are expressed through
elections and referendums. At the same time, there are "other categories of judgment, less perceptible to the masses but evident to the
elite, that are not dependent for their expression on elections or de-
liberating bodies."[39] The elite most qualified to make these technical
judgments and transform them into political actions (the word "po-

litical" is understood here in its technocratic sense) is not the political class, which is "immoral, incapable, and undisciplined," but the appropriate military, bureaucratic, or other experts attached to the central government.

Black Caesarism

The bureaucratic tendencies that have appeared in Congolese political life by no means presage the kind of impersonal, dehumanized bureaucracy typical of modern industrial societies. Several things give the Congolese bureaucracy a special character of its own. Among these are a heavy concentration of power in the hands of one person rather than in an office, a political machine, or an institution; the exaltation of the state; a reliance on direct popular appeals; and the formulation of a nationalist ideology. Thus unlike highly sophisticated bureaucracies, in which utopian, nonutilitarian values tend to disappear, the Congolese bureaucracy operates in a climate of political dramatization. Such a climate was typical of past Caesarist regimes that combined civil and military authority (e.g. Bonapartism and Nasserism).

It was in the name of the military high command that General Mobutu staged his coup of November 1965, and it seemed certain at that time that the Congo would follow the usual road to military dictatorship. However, public references to the army high command grew much less frequent after early 1966. Also, the army's brief actions against provincial disorder and civilian corruption and its involvement in Operation Roll-Up-Your-Sleeves were followed by a trend toward "recivilianization" and a "return to the barracks."[40] Mobutu himself appeared less often in uniform, for he clearly meant to stand above all factions in the Congo, including the ANC.

Mobutu's emergence as a dominant figure in both army and civilian politics is due to fortunate circumstances as well as to his political skills. Mobutu had two vital advantages over all his elders and commanding officers: "In his seven years' service in the Force Publique, from 1950 through 1956, he had developed a wide set of acquaintances among the noncommissioned officers. . . . Second, Colonel Mobutu was a resident of Léopoldville, . . . [where] as a journalist and active supporter of the MNC-Lumumba he was well connected in political circles."[41]

TABLE 16
Ministerial Reshuffles, 1965–70

Post	November 1965	September 1966	December 1966	October 1967	August 1968	March 1969	August 1969	September 1970
Prime minister	Mulamba	Mulamba	—	—	—	—	—	—
Defense	Mulamba	Mulamba	(Mobutu)	(Mobutu)	(Mobutu)	(Mobutu)	(Mobutu)	(Mobutu)
Foreign affairs	Bomboko	Bomboko	Bomboko	Bomboko	Bomboko	Adoula	Adoula	Adoula
Vice-minister	—	—	—	Umba-di-Lutete	Umba-di-Lutete	Loliki	Loliki	Loliki
Commerce	Mulelenu	Kashale	Kititwa	Bomboko	Bomboko	—	Adoula	Loango
Vice-minister	—	—	Mungul-Diaka	Umba-di-Lutete	Umba-di-Lutete	—	Bahizi	Ndongala
Resident in Belgium	—	Mungul-Diaka	—	—	—	Umba-di-Lutete	Umba-di-Lutete	Umba-di-Lutete
Delegate to UN	—	—	—	—	—	Umba-di-Lutete	Umba-di-Lutete	Nsinga
Justice	Madudu	Nsinga	Nsinga	Nsinga	Tshisekedi	Loango	Ndala	Tshibangu
Interior	Tshisekedi	Tshisekedi	Tshisekedi	Tshisekedi	Nsinga	Nsinga	Nsinga	Sakombi
Vice-minister	—	—	Sakombi	—	—	—	—	—
Finances	Litho	Litho	Litho	Mushiete	Nendaka	Nendaka	Namwizi	Ndele
Economic affairs	Kashale	Kahamba	Mushiete	Nzeza	Tumba	Namwizi	Loango	Namwizi
Plan and coordination	Kititwa	—	—	—	—	Tshisekedi	—	—
Public works	Bolikango	Apindia	Kahamba	Zamundu	Ilunga	Ilunga	Kazadi	Kazadi
Transportation	Nendaka	Nendaka	Nendaka	Nendaka	Nzeza	Nzeza	Alves	Alves
Agriculture	Zamundu	Zamundu	Zamundu	Litho	Litho	Litho	Litho	Litho
Labor	Kande, V.	Kande, V.	Kimvay	Kithima	Matobo	Lihau-Kanza	Lihau-Kanza	Lihau-Kanza
Middle class	Mungul-Diaka	Madudu	—	—	—	—	—	—
Health	—	Tshishimbi	Kashale	Tshamu	Tshibangu	Tumba	Kalonda	Kalonda
Mines	Kishiba	Kishiba	Tumba	Tumba	Okuka	Tshibangu	Tshibangu	Umba-di-Lutete
Real estate	—	Kititwa	—	—	—	Okuka	Kahamba	Kahamba
Social Affairs	Kidisho	Mulelenu	Lihau-Kanza	Lihau-Kanza	Lihau-Kanza	Lihau-Kanza	Lihau-Kanza	Lihau-Kanza
Education	Njadi	Njadi	Njadi	Mungul-Diaka	Kithima	Cardoso	Cardoso	Cardoso
Information	Kande, J. J.	Kande, J. J.	Kande, J. J.	Kande, J. J.	Kande, J. J.	Kande, J. J.	Kande, J. J.	Kande, J. J.
Cultural affairs	—	Isia-Amundala	Ndjoli	Ndjoli	Mushiete	Mushiete	Mushiete	Mushiete
Personnel	Colin	Colin	Colin	Emunngania	Ndjoli	Ndjoli	Iloo	Iloo
Post	Mwamba	Mwamba	Kikangala	Tshibangu	Zamundu	Zamundu	Agoyo	Zamundu
Portfolio	—	Kulumba	—	—	—	Nendaka	—	—
Customary affairs	Tshisekedi	—	—	Tshisekedi	—	—	—	—
Youth	Ngwenza	Ngwenza	Mwamba	Kibassa-Maliba	Kibassa-Maliba	Muhona	Muhona	Ndala
Community development	—	Mayala	Kishiba	Kibassa-Maliba	Kibassa-Maliba	Namwizi	Loango	Namwizi

SOURCE: CEP-IRES, *Archives.*

During the troubles following independence, Mobutu, then the ANC chief of staff, slowly increased his control over the military. Since he was tolerated by the old guard of the ANC, he was able to obtain key command positions for officers whom he trusted, notably Leonard Mulamba, Major Tshatshi, and his former drill sergeant, Louis Bobozo. Mobutu also had a sort of praetorian guard of about 800 parachute troops stationed permanently around his residence. Still, it was not until the end of 1963 that he was able to eliminate all his potential opponents in the ANC, either by relieving them of their commands or by assigning them to honorific posts.

Mobutu also exerted considerable influence in civilian politics. His first effort in this realm, the creation of the College of Commissioners following his 1960 coup, was a dismal failure, but it did gain him a measure of political influence. From 1962 to 1964, Mobutu was an influential member of the Binza group, the informal, semisecret caucus of high officials that controlled key political institutions in the capital.[42] As is sometimes suggested, the 1965 coup was a logical consequence of the de facto power and influence that Mobutu had exercised in previous governments.

After taking power, as we have seen, Mobutu moved to consolidate his personal control over the entire governmental apparatus. Once again, he seemed most concerned with possible threats to his position from people who by reason of ethnic or political appeal might have summoned a large following. In the years 1965–70, Mobutu reshuffled his cabinet eight times, as against nine comparable changes for the tense years 1960–65, each time for reasons that remain largely obscure. Thus in Kinshasa, promotion to minister is increasingly viewed as a passport to exile.[43]

As Table 16 shows, some sixty people have held posts in a cabinet that usually has only twenty members at any given time. Forty-six have retained their posts for as much as two years; in other words, they have survived an average of three ministerial reshuffles. Only one minister has been allowed to return to his post, and that only after three years' exclusion. The characteristic fate of Mobutu's ministers is best revealed by a brief look at the careers of some who managed to hold their posts longer than three years.

The first of these was Justin Bomboko, who had occupied the foreign affairs department since independence, except for one interruption during the Tshombe regime. Bomboko's fall occurred suddenly in March 1969. His colleague Victor Nendaka, whose political influence derived from his longtime control of the secret police, followed a similar path, although the president first assigned him such low-ranking portfolios as public transportation and finance. Similarly, Joseph Nsinga, who had been minister of justice from 1966 to 1968, was elevated to the key ministry of the interior in August 1968; he was then abruptly dismissed from office in September 1970, probably for having made too many acquaintances in the army and secret police.

For other ministers, the path to oblivion was more gradual. Etienne Tshisekedi, minister of the interior from 1965 to 1967, was successively demoted to the politically less important ministry of justice, and then to the ministry of plan and coordination prior to his dismissal in September 1969. Bernardin Mungul-Diaka, who in 1966 had been designated resident minister in Belgium, a post usually entrusted to a member of Mobutu's immediate entourage, was demoted to the ministry of education a year later and dismissed in August 1968. Only three ministers survived all the personnel changes. These were Mrs. Sophie Lihau-Kanza, whose influence lay more in her association with Mobutu's entourage than in her ministerial positions; Jean-Jacques Kande, who held the key ministry of information; and Jean-Joseph Litho, who is a relative of Mobutu's.

Another characteristic of Caesarism is its exaltation of the prestige and grandeur of the state. President Mobutu has been eager from the first to rehabilitate the Congo in the eyes of the world and to place his country in the first rank of African states. As Crispin Mulumba and Pierre Kasongo point out: "A formal stance that will lead to increased prestige thus appears to be a basic tenet of the new regime's foreign policy toward the rest of Africa. . . . This policy seeks first and foremost to assert a 'Congolese presence' whenever possible."[44] President Mobutu's success in the realm of international relations during 1966 was hailed by the Kinshasa press as the outstanding achievement of the new regime.[45] Congolese national pride has been expressed in other ways as well. The Congolese government built a second luxurious presidential palace 30 miles from Kinshasa, as well as an expensive residential complex for foreign guests. It also created special titles and decorations for ministers, lawyers, high civil servants, and foreign businessmen who had proved themselves loyal servants of the regime. Finally, the government organized yearly public ceremonies to commemorate Independence Day and Mobutu's coup.

Caesarist dictators characteristically keep their lines open to the masses on whom they depend for support: thus the bread and circuses of imperial Rome, Napoleon's appeals to the French peasantry, and Nasser's impassioned propaganda broadcasts during crises with Israel and the European powers. President Mobutu followed the same path with the help of his close friend Jean-Jacques Kande, who lent the full support of his ministry of information to Mobutu's campaigns against mercenaries, Belgian industrial trusts, politicians, and other supposed internal enemies of the regime. Moreover, President Mobutu has toured the countryside more frequently than his predecessors and has even announced important decisions during such tours, notably the provincial reorganization of 1966. One effect of the tours has been to divert attention from Mobutu's title of commander-in-chief of the ANC, the Congo's most hated institution.

Mobutu's direct appeal to the people has employed another device characteristic of Caesarist regimes, the plebiscite. Thus the constitutional referendum of June 1967 was more a means of reinforcing Mobutu's personal authority than a popular vote on constitutional issues. Though 97.8 percent of the Congolese people approved the new constitution, the government viewed the insignificant negative return as evidence of "sabotage" aimed at Mobutu and his regime. As expected, officials and representatives of constituencies returning a high percentage of negative votes were summarily arrested or fired.[46]

Finally, Caesarism more than any other political system involves the ruler's intense commitment to patriotic and nationalist values that he presents as the only alternative to ideological conflict: plebeianism vs. patricianism in ancient Rome, Girondism vs. Jacobinism in revolutionary France, Islam vs. Communism in contemporary Egypt. The Mobutu regime, too, has produced its own nationalistic ideology. According to the MPR manifesto, the Congolese revolution was essentially nationalistic and pragmatic; it had nothing to learn from "borrowed ideologies and theories such as capitalism, scientific socialism, or Communism."[47] In accordance with these sentiments, the MPR Presidium substituted the term *citoyen* ("citizen") for such forms of address as *monsieur, camarade,* or *frère.* In September 1967, the Congolese information ministry published a booklet entitled *Le Bréviaire du patriote* (*The Patriot's Breviary*) that developed the theme of the MPR manifesto. Using a question-and-answer format, the booklet emphasized the highly specific nature of the "Congolese personality" and the "Congolese revolution," and identified Congolese politicians and foreign trusts as the chief enemies of the revolution.[48]

The Regime's Supporting Groups

As we have seen, the political elite that emerged immediately after Congolese independence derived its status from the petty bureaucratic functions it had exercised during the colonial era. Mobutu's rise to power brought a significant change in the social stratification of the Congo. Besides the military, a traditional pillar of Caesarist regimes, the Mobutu regime is supported by social groups that could find no place for themselves under patrimonialism, notably urban youth, university students, and the nascent bourgeoisie of the big cities. The tacit alliance between these social groups, whose interests may not necessarily coincide in the long run, gives a special character to the bureaucratic Caesarism that has emerged in the Congo.

The Army. As we have seen, the 1965 coup did not produce a military regime in the Congo for two reasons. First, the Congolese military had a long tradition of noninvolvement in civilian affairs. Second, high-ranking officers in the ANC feared that involvement in politics would undermine the army's painfully acquired discipline. Yet the ANC's withdrawal from the political arena has been anything but total, as the three incidents described below make clear.

The army's first overt intervention in civilian affairs took place during the so-called Pentecost Conspiracy. On the night of May 30, 1966, four politicians were arrested and charged with conspiring to overthrow General Mobutu and his new regime. The men arrested were Evariste Kimba, whom Joseph Kasavubu had made his prime minister a few weeks prior to the 1965 coup; Jerome Anany, a former minister of defense in the Adoula government; Alexandre Mahamba, a former minister of real estate in the Lumumba and Adoula governments; and Emmanuel Bamba, a leader of the Kimbanguist church and a former minister of finance. According to the official report, the conspiracy was thwarted by "the vigilance and loyalty of the ANC."[49]

The full story behind the plot remains secret. However, it seems probable that the conspiracy involved more than an attempted coup by four civilians who, after all, were not influential in politics and did not have large followings either in Léopoldville or their native regions. During the trial (the official transcript of which was never made public), the defendants conceded that they had participated in illegal political gatherings but argued that the plans they were charged with harboring were in fact the work of army officers acting as agents provocateurs. In their own words: "None of us ever spoke of physically eliminating the chief of state, General Bobozo, or General Mulamba. . . . It was the officers who proposed this. . . . We were asked only to prepare a list of the people who would be in the provisional government."[50] President Mobutu explained the officers' participation in the plot as follows: "This conspiracy began in March. These four politicians sent officers and noncoms to some cities [with instructions to] stir up army opposition to the established authorities. We knew of their actions. We did not want to hurry; we let them go on with the conspiracy in order to find out exactly what their intentions were."[51]

If we assume that the officers were playing the role of agents provocateurs in the conspiracy it is easy to explain their eagerness to convince the civilian plotters that members of the ANC High Command should be killed. It is surprising, though, that only four people should have been involved in the conspiracy, and that they were tried so rapidly and in such secrecy. In fact, it seems more likely either that a rebellion was developing within the ANC itself, in which case the officers involved were being shielded by their superiors, or that the military overreacted to mere verbal expressions of discontent from unemployed politicians.

The military stepped in a second time to expel President Mobutu's prime minister, General Leonard Mulamba. Mulamba had been a heroic figure in the Congo since the 1964 rebellions, when he and a handful of soldiers repulsed a rebel attack during the battle of Bukavu. Mulamba's designation as prime minister after the 1965 coup therefore came as no surprise, but his high position and his growing popularity made his fellow army officers critical and jealous of him. In September 1966, the High Command openly attacked Mulamba for having negotiated with the Kisangani mutineers. The High Command held an extraordinary session on October 20, and three days later an Agence France-Presse dispatch stated that Mulamba's dismissal was imminent.[52] The following day, President Mobutu expressed indignation over this and similar rumors concerning Mulamba: "The High Command is neither a pressure group nor a political assembly, as some would like to believe. Rather, it is . . . a body of high-ranking officers of the ANC that meets four times a year. If the High Command discussed the Kisangani affair during its recent meeting, it did so in a strictly military context."[53]

Events soon shattered this myth. Two days later, on October 26, Mulamba was suddenly relieved of his post as prime minister and made minister of national defense. The same day, the ANC's chief of staff, Lieutenant Colonel Ferdinand Malila, publicly declared that the army would refuse this compromise and would demand stronger measures against Mulamba.[54] Willingly or unwillingly, President Mobutu acceded, and General Mulamba left the army to become president of an insurance company owned by the state. Several months later he was named ambassador to India.

A third military intervention in civilian affairs involved the Kwilu rebel leader Pierre Mulele. Sometime in 1968, after the breakdown of negotiations with provincial administrators in Kwilu,[55] Mulele fled to Brazzaville. In August 1968, the Congolese government announced a general political amnesty, and new negotiations began between Mulele and Justin Bomboko, Mobutu's minister of foreign affairs. On September 29 it was officially announced that Mulele and Bomboko had returned to Kinshasa together: "On his arrival, the former leader of the Kwilu rebellion said . . . that he had returned because he believed President Mobutu was restoring the policies of former Prime Minister Patrice Lumumba."[56] Yet on October 2 President Mobutu, probably under pressure from the High Command, announced that Mulele could not benefit from the August amnesty and would face prosecution as a war criminal. Mulele was tried by a military tribunal of three senior officers (whose names were kept secret) and shot by a firing squad on October 8. According to *Le Monde*, several high-ranking army officers denounced Bomboko for having given Mulele a formal assurance of amnesty during the negotiations. The officers also called for the resignation of the ANC's chief of staff, Major General Louis Bobozo, who had allegedly entertained Mulele in his home shortly after the latter's return to Kinshasa.[57]

In each of these three instances, the ANC stood revealed as an influential political group with a clear view of its own interests and no disposition to compromise. Two major reforms had helped to increase its influence. One was the creation in 1965 of a new system of military justice, which was promptly followed by the trial and conviction of hundreds of officers and men on charges of corruption, indiscipline, and incompetence.[58] Having cleaned its own house, as Verhaegen remarks, the ANC was readier to take a hard line with the politicians to whom it attributed all the Congo's miseries.[59]

The other reform was a series of decrees in 1965–67 that had the effect of sharply increasing the number of officers of senior rank and decreasing the number of junior officers and noncoms. These decrees essentially restored the hierarchy and discipline characteristic of the Force Publique before the events of 1960–61, and reversed the effects of the democratic practices of 1960–65, notably the election of officers by their men.[60]

To be sure, not all of the ANC's internal difficulties were cleared up by the reforms of 1965–67. According to Young:

Within the officer ranks, new alignments were beginning to replace the old . . . divergences. Two basic groups could be seen emerging:

(1) The old noncoms who had been promoted in 1960 to the top command posts. In some cases, typified by General Bobozo, they were little-educated men who qualified mainly on the basis of their long service (in Bobozo's case, more than 30 years). . . .

(2) The young officers, markedly more educated and endowed with the prestige and self-confidence of overseas training. These were viewed with some reserve by the old noncoms, who expressed the characteristic veteran's distaste for the greenhorn and felt they needed a number of years' experience as small unit leaders before they could be entrusted with important responsibilities.[61]

It is still too soon to know what effect, if any, these generational tensions will have on the army's political position.

Urban Youth. The mid-1960's saw a massive politicization of young people in the Congo's cities, especially Kinshasa. The earliest national organization of Congolese youth, the National Youth Council, supported the Tshombe government of 1964–65. It gave way under the subsequent Kasavubu-Kimba coalition to a new, semisecret youth organization called the League of Young Vigilantes, which vowed to fight imperialism, corruption, tribalism, and all other forms of neocolonialism in the Congo.[62]

At the time President Mobutu took power, he received an impressive amount of support from youth movements and organizations in Kinshasa. By January 1966, all such groups had consolidated themselves into the Volunteer Corps of the Republic (CVR). Despite its oft-asserted determination "to promote national consciousness among the masses and participate in the country's reconstruction,"[63] the CVR in its early years served primarily as a rudimentary intelligence agency, devoting much of its time and energy to the surveillance of foreigners and politicians whom the regime distrusted. In the provinces, its intelligence activities overlapped and sometimes conflicted with those of the national secret police, local police, or local army headquarters,[64] to the occasional annoyance of these agencies.[65] The popular mobilization aspect of the CVR was limited to its participation in the massive rallies and meetings that the central government organized on such occasions as Independence Day and the anniversary of Mobutu's coup.

Three factors seem to be largely responsible for the consolidation of a number of loosely structured youth organizations into a single national organization. The first factor, discussed at length above, is the growing sociological and demographic importance of young people in the Congo.[66] The second is the apolitical and Caesarist nature of the present regime. Prior to Mobutu's coup, each local and national political party had its own youth section, generally headed by a patron to whom the members felt personally beholden for jobs, loans, or favors. When President Mobutu banned party politics and made the Congolese politician a symbol of corruption and inefficiency, there was a natural tendency for unemployed youths to form a single centralized youth organization.

The third is the influence of prior examples, notably the simba of the APL in 1964–65 and the Youth of the National Revolutionary Movement in the Congo-Brazzaville. The latter was an important force in President Massamba-Deba's revolutionary government from 1964 on.

University Students. As we have seen, university students became involved in Congolese politics relatively early. The Economic Round Table that convened in Belgium in April 1960 marked the first appearance of a university-trained Congolese intelligentsia. The Belgian minister for Congolese economic affairs, Raymond Scheyven, initiated this conference as a sequel to the earlier Political Round Table that had set Congolese independence for June 30, 1960. Specifically, the Belgians were worried about the future of their investment in the Congo and hoped that the second conference would give reassuring information about the new state's financial policies. Unlike the Political Round Table, the Economic Round Table allocated seats to a number of Congolese university students and recent graduates. These "technical experts," as they were called, were representatives of the General Executive College that was serving as the traditional administration in Léopoldville.

The Executive College was well known for its inefficiency and lack of cohesion, and it was further hampered by the wholesale politicization of the Congo as independence approached. Its delegates to the conference fared no better, for these young experts found themselves torn between conflicting roles. On the one hand, they were expected to advance Congolese interests in matters where the politicians found themselves on unsure ground. On the other hand, the Belgian trusts expected them to be compliant enough to soften the politicians' more radical demands. During the course of the Round Table the student experts came to favor the Belgians both on points of procedure and in matters of principle. Many politicians, sensitive to the effect the conference would have on Congolese public opinion, withdrew because of the experts' deference to Belgian views. Patrice Lumumba and Joseph Kasavubu were among those absent from the closing session.

Students participated in Congolese politics again at the time of Mobutu's first coup in September 1960. Seeking to end the chaos that Congolese politicians had caused, Mobutu undertook a unique political experiment: he handed control of the state over to university students. To this end, he created a College of Commissioners staffed with university students and recent graduates and assigned it the awesome task of governing the Congo. Each commissioner received a ministerial portfolio related, whenever possible, to his academic major.

On the whole, Mobutu's experiment was a failure. Pressure from students caused the College to grow rapidly from 24 to 39 members, making it highly unwieldy. Its deliberations were often disrupted by newcomers fresh from the university who lacked political and administrative experience. Furthermore, the commissioners' functions were never clearly defined, and despite their public statements that they were technical experts who did not seek political power, many of the commissioners began to act like politicians in cabinet posts. In fact, three distinct groups emerged within the College. The technicians who had interrupted their studies to answer Mobutu's call formed the most numerous and politically least effective group. The second consisted of the supporters of Colonel Mobutu who had previously clashed with the politicians at the Economic Round Table. The third consisted of those commissioners who engaged openly in politics, either as individuals or as members of a partisan faction.

In a sense, the student commissioners appeared on the political scene both too early and too late to be really effective: they had not come forward during the period of electoral politics following independence, and their expertise was irrelevant to the tribal antagonisms that still colored the politicization of the Congo. Also, the skills of the student and the politician differ greatly. No matter how expert a student becomes in his area of formal study, he cannot match the politician's ability to communicate with the people and mold public opinion. Indeed, one may assert that the politician's visionary language and symbolic appeal are essential to maintaining cohesion in a changing society.

The collapse of the College of Commissioners and the politicians' return to power threw the university students into opposition. Year after year, annual student congresses denounced the corruption and inefficiency of the political elite, but students never became a real political force. During 1963 and 1964, student movements allied themselves with the parliamentary opposition to the Adoula government. This alliance reached its high point during the second congress of the General Union of Congolese Students, held in Léopoldville August 4–11, 1963. The importance of the meeting was underscored by the presence of such opposition leaders as Christophe Gbenye and Egide Bocheley Davidson, and of several well-known trade union leaders and Eastern European diplomats.

During their years in opposition, the students' original image of technical expertise gave way to one of political activism. The students' radical utopianism and the extravagant way they expressed it reflected their quest for a meaningful place in the Congo and a role in her salvation. On the whole, though, the students lacked corporate identity, unity, and sense of purpose. This fact became clear with Moise Tshombe's return to power in 1964, when endless arguments broke out between those students who opposed Tshombe and those who favored a government of national reconciliation. Ideologically torn, its leaders jailed or under constant surveillance in the Congo or abroad, the student movement fell into sharp decline.

Mobutu's rise to power greatly improved the position of Congolese students. The new regime responded positively to a crucial student demand by reintegrating the university-educated elite into national and regional administrations. Also, it paralleled the students' ideological stance in its use of radical nationalist symbols. In short, the Mobutu government accomplished what none of its predecessors were able to do: it combined the potent symbols of Lumumbism with concrete reform measures to harness the loyalty and energy of Congolese students.

Of course, the students still take issue with the government on certain points. They are bitter, for instance, about the poor material conditions they are forced to endure while attending the university, and the government has not yet paid attention to complaints on this score. Moreover, former graduate students entering the civil service often face hostility from older public officials who feel threatened by the newcomers' advanced degrees. On the whole, though, the university students have accepted the emphasis on expertise, economic rationality, and political stability that is one of the salient features of the Mobutu regime.

Economic Nationalism, Petty Businessmen, and Middlemen. In his analysis of rationalization, Weber makes some relevant observations on the economic consequences of bureaucratization. One of his chief assumptions in that respect is that a positive relationship exists between the development of capitalism and that of bureaucracy:

In modern times, bureaucratization and social leveling within political, and particularly within state organizations in connection with the destruction of . . . local privileges, have very frequently benefited the interests of capitalism. Often bureaucratization has been carried out in direct alliance with capitalist interests, for example the great historical alliance of the power of the absolute prince with capitalist interests. In general a legal leveling and destruction of firmly established local structures ruled by notables has usually made for a wider range of capitalist activity.[67]

Weber emphasizes that the mere fact of bureaucratic organization cannot indicate precisely what form its economic effects will take. In the Congolese case, however, the growth of bureaucratic trends in the political system has seen the development of indigenous business and commercial enterprises. The Congolese government has aided these enterprises in the name of "economic nationalism." It is such state involvement in the economic sphere that is likely to produce a new stratum of Congolese petty businessmen and middlemen.

The Congolese government became involved in economic affairs in two related areas. First, it took measures to increase its control over the foreign corporations operating in the Congo. Second, it gave generous aid to some Congolese economic enterprises that it organized along cooperative lines in an effort to foster "national" commercial activities, to fight the black market, and to halt the constant inflationary trend in the cities. The three major beneficiaries of such aid were the National Association of Tradeswomen (ANAFCO),[68] the People's Cooperative, and the Congo-Lux store.

ANAFCO was formed in 1966 with the support of President Mobutu. It was intended to remedy food shortages in Kinshasa and, consequently, to fight inflation. In April 1967, President Mobutu awarded ANAFCO 10 million Congolese francs to be used in buying food, clothing, and other basic consumer goods for resale at low prices.[69] In fact, ANAFCO's commercial activities remained very limited and never justified the financial help the organization received. ANAFCO's president, Mrs. Mboyo, complained that import firms refused to deal with her organization or its subsidiaries.[70]

The People's Cooperative also failed in its commercial undertakings. Created by ordinance in October 1967 and headed by a former congressman, Felicien Kimvay, the People's Cooperative had aims similar to those of ANAFCO. However, it covered a much broader territory, since it functioned as a national cooperative supplying low-cost consumer goods to economically disadvantaged groups. The People's Cooperative employed a system of membership cards that was supposed to protect the poor against inflation. In practice, the activities of the cooperative drew strong criticism. Many people, particularly in rural areas, complained that the cost of living was still rising, and that membership cards were being given or sold to members of such political organizations as the MPR, the army, or the provincial administrations.[71]

The creation of stores for the sale of luxury goods in major cities provides a clear example of a small commercial class developing under the protection of a state bureaucracy. For instance, the Congo-Lux store, of which President Mobutu is said to be the chief owner, resulted from the merger of two small Congolese import firms, MEBECO and Congo Radio, both of which had received government aid before their merger. MEBECO had been awarded a government contract to equip the international village that was built in Kinshasa for the fourth conference of the Organization of African Unity. Congo Radio had been granted a tax-free status and the sum of 150 million Congolese francs in order to import luxury goods for delegates to the conference.[72] Many people reacted unfavorably to Congo-Lux, feeling that it was merely a showpiece of Congolese capitalism and would cause prices to rise in Kinshasa. President Mobutu answered these criticisms personally by arguing that it was indispensable to aid dynamic enterprises rather than "some dishonest merchants who . . . prefer to invest in tissues rather than expand."[73] Moreover, President Mobutu stressed that

in any city, whether Brussels or New York, there are luxury stores reserved exclusively for ministers, members of Parliament, judges, and so forth. . . . Because of the OAU conference . . . it was necessary to create something of the sort in Kinshasa, and one may say that Congo-Lux has really bolstered our beautiful capital's reputation in the eyes of the African chiefs of state. Nevertheless . . . this store is not for everybody, and one must accept this fact.[74]

As noted above, the Mobutu regime's emphasis on economic nationalism led it to seek increased control over foreign capitalist corporations, though it was largely the foreign companies themselves that first prompted Congolese involvement in their affairs. Five months after Mobutu's coup, UMHK decided unilaterally to increase the price of its copper to match the price then current on the world market. This decision, made in Brussels with no prior consultation with the Congolese government, greatly irritated President Mobutu: "In Zambia and Chile, the local governments have decided by themselves, without external pressure, to increase the price of copper, while here it is UMHK, a private foreign concern, that makes the decision."[75]

Within 48 hours after Mobutu's bitter statement, his cabinet had passed three resolutions. The resolutions required all foreign companies to transfer their head offices to the Congo by January 1, 1967; increased Congolese export duties from 17 to 30 percent; and called upon all mining firms in the Congo to transfer 10 percent of their metal and alloy reserves to the national treasury. Both in Brussels and Kinshasa, long, hard negotiations ensued between President Mobutu's staff and UMHK representatives; by November 1966 an agreement seemed imminent. This agreement would have divided UMHK into two new companies. One of the companies would have been registered in Kinshasa, and the Congolese government would have held 50 percent of its stock. The second company, Union Minière Métallurgique, would have been registered at Brussels and would have held and managed all former UMHK assets located outside the Congo. The Congolese government would also have retained a 17.95 percent interest in Union Minière Métallurgique.

However, the talks came to an abrupt halt when UMHK representatives demanded that their company be given all the key positions on the board of the projected Congolese corporation. UMHK also sought control over the sale of copper and 6 percent of all revenue from mineral sales in payment for the technical assistance its personnel would provide the Congolese company. Also, the two delegations could not agree on the exact extent of UMHK assets outside the Congo. For the Belgian delegation, these assets included all mineral stocks located outside the Congo, as well as copper not yet delivered to customers. The Congolese government in turn asserted that UMHK had stockpiled minerals to a value of ten million Belgian francs in anticipation of the talks.[76] The conflict was further aggravated by the UMHK's refusal to comply with Congolese monetary exchange rates.[77]

In sum, UMHK entered the talks with two aims firmly in mind. It wished to maintain as much control as possible over decisions regarding mining in the Congo, and it sought to build up its hard-currency reserves outside the Congo in order to satisfy its shareholders.

Amidst intense hostility between the Congo and Belgium and a boycott on copper exports by UMHK and Tanganyika Concessions, President Mobutu announced the creation of the Société Générale Congolaise des Minerais (GECOMIN). The Congolese government held 60 percent of this company's stock and the remainder was offered for sale to private buyers.[78] For the Congolese government, then, UMHK ceased to exist. However, in February 1967, a technical aid agreement was signed between GECOMIN and the UMHK's Belgian marketing subsidiary, the Société Générale des Minerais. According to the agreement, the Société Générale des Minerais would carry out all industrial and commercial operations ordered by the directors of GECOMIN.[79] Though it saved face for everybody concerned, this agreement left some fundamental questions unanswered; the monthly report of the Institute of Economic and Social Research pointed out that "the crisis that the Congo has endured must be considered a starting point rather than a final episode."[80] There still remained the problem of finding the necessary capital for the expansion of productive capacity. Also, the compromise aid agreement could be abrogated with two years' notice, and the Société Générale des Minerais could escape many of its provisions should the Congolese government grow less determined in its policy of economic nationalism and independence. Finally, members of the GECOMIN board of directors found themselves highly vulnerable to outside pressure and influence.

Thus in contrast to such other developing Caesarist bureaucracies as Egypt, the Congolese state has not gained complete control over her means of production. The threat of nationalization has never been effective, for it has been obvious from the very start that the Congo lacks the kind of administrative apparatus that would allow her to institute a planned economy. GECOMIN operates just like any other capitalist enterprise, and the only visible result of the regime's policy of economic nationalism has been the partial, or sometimes total, Africanization of the boards of foreign corporations. In most cases, the government representatives on these boards are unemployed politicians, high civil servants, or trade unionists. Some of them have been designated directly by the central government, while others have been chosen by the companies themselves. Among the new presidents of the Africanized boards of directors are Joseph

Ngalula, a former governor of South Kasai; Joseph Ileo, a former prime minister; Marcel Bisukiro, a former congressman from Kivu; Jean Baptiste Kibwe, a former minister in Tshombe's Katangese government; Michel Colin, a former minister of education in the Adoula government; and Gaston Diomi, a former minister in the Lumumba government.[81] Given their previous occupations, none of these men have any special interest in business. In fact, they represent a small category of prospective middlemen rather than a class of future capitalist entrepreneurs.

 CHAPTER 8

Alternatives to Patrimonialism

In his critique of the concept of development as it is currently used by social scientists, Herbert Spiro argues that it is above all else politics that is developing in Africa:

> Through politics, as the uniquely and supremely human activity, Africans are developing and expanding their awareness of the desirable and realizable. What has been going on in Africa is therefore not as much repetition or innovation, as it is the revival of the pure classic tradition of Western philosophy, according to which politics is the master science.[1]

There is much truth in Spiro's argument that development includes more than economic growth or, for that matter, political engineering and manipulation.[2] Yet one cannot automatically assume that Africa will renew Western traditions of political discourse. The civil wars, coups d'etat, and military take-overs that have marked African politics in recent years are indicative of endemic violence and repression, not of a genuine search for political solutions. Spiro's critique is also disappointing in its failure to ask exactly what kind of politics has evolved in independent Africa.

The present study was undertaken in an effort to answer that question. The explanatory model of patrimonial politics has been used in an attempt to distinguish the basic structures and attitudes underlying the disordered events of Congolese politics between 1960 and 1965. Specifically, appropriation of public offices as the prime motivation of the elite, centrifugal relationships based on a mixture of personal and primordial ties, and the widespread use of private armies are all distinctive features of patrimonialism that have proved very costly in both economic and political terms. The Congo's bankruptcy in 1965 was clearly an immediate consequence of patrimonial politics, for, as we have seen, unrestrained government spending under patrimonialism produced a sharp inflationary spiral. Furthermore, Congolese political leaders had no direct access to national economic resources; no entrepreneurial class ever emerged to spur economic growth; and there was no integration of the public and private sectors. These circumstances accelerated a process of economic and social disintegration that reached crisis proportions during the Tshombe regime.

In the political sphere, patrimonial politics exacerbated personal antagonisms and centrifugal tendencies that neither governmental institutions nor the existing social structure could contain. The key event in this respect was the fragmentation of the six colonial provinces into 21 new ones in late 1962. The central government's inability to control territorial fragmentation had two major causes. First, there really was no "central government" as such in the Congo. The Adoula ministerial team was the end result of a delicate compromise among various moderate regional leaders, most of whom drew no distinction between their duties as public servants and their roles as patrimonial suzerains. Second, even though some measure of political continuity was provided by the so-called Binza group that acted as an invisible government between 1962 and 1964, this secret cabinet gave no attention at all to broad policy issues.

At the same time, the question of tribal cohesion seems to have had little bearing on territorial fragmentation, either before or after the creation of the 21 new provinces. Very few provinces were ethnically homogeneous, and even where some degree of ethnic cohesion existed at the outset, it bore no visible relation to the personal antagonisms that arose within the elite group.

The political system's inability to master environmental constraints and external forces was another fundamental reason for the collapse of patrimonial politics in the Congo. The independent Congo's political institutions and ideology, as well as the belief system of its elite, were copied outright from colonial structures or the Western liberal democracies. The Congolese economic and political infrastructures were totally isolated from one another, and irrational Cold War rivalries colored many events in the political sphere. No political system as inherently fragile as patrimonialism could long resist such disruptive forces; its collapse was plainly inevitable.

The twofold failure of patrimonial politics provides the conceptual framework needed to understand the Congolese uprisings of 1964–65. The causes of any revolutionary movement are ambiguous and complex. In the Congolese case, one may argue that the rebellions were the logical outcome of an institutional breakdown that began in the early days of independence. Alternatively, one may view the rebellions as an attempt on the part of the masses to experience a "second independence" after the failure of the first.[3] However, I have chosen to explain the rebellions in terms of political variables. In such terms, they resulted from popular discontent among key constituencies and social groups (independent peasants, the young, ostracized ethnic groups), as well as from the exclusion of a heterogeneous counterelite from positions of power and influence. I have treated the two main groups involved in the rebellions separately because their motivations and interests were by no means congruent. The discontented social groups openly rejected the kind of politics practiced by the ruling elite. In contrast, the counterelite actively sought a place in the existing political system. Such a fundamental contradiction, together with the other structural and behavioral differences discussed in Chapter 6, explains in part the failure of revolutionary politics in the Congo. In addition, the wholesale violence that marked the rebel campaigns could have only one result: by carrying the rebellions too far to the left, it prompted a strong rightist reaction from the counterelite.

The rightist alternative to patrimonial politics was ushered in by the coup of November 1965. It would be tempting to consider bureaucratic politics as a natural development of patrimonialism, and there are indeed many historical examples that tend to substantiate such a view. As Weber says:

More and more the specialized knowledge of the expert became the foundation for the power position of the officeholder. Hence an early concern of the ruler was how to exploit the special knowledge of experts without having to abdicate in their favor but preserve his dominant position. With the qualitative extension of administrative tasks and therefore with the indispensability of expert knowledge, it typically happens that the lord no longer is satisfied by occasional consultation with individuals and proved confidants or even with an assembly of such men called together intermittently and in difficult situations.[4]

Weber adds that such assemblies of experts as the Conseil d'Etat or the Privy Council were eventually transformed into unified bodies of bureaucratic leaders. At this stage, absolute monarchs were rendered powerless by the expertise of the bureaucrats.[5]

The Congo differs sharply from many other African countries in that bureaucratic politics there did not emerge from advisory bodies attached to patrimonial leaders, but rather from opposition groups that were excluded from positions of leadership. Thus the coup of November 1965 was not simply a military take-over, but more fundamentally a take-over of the state apparatus by such social groups as technocrats, university students, the military, and high civil servants. These were all groups that had developed under patrimonialism but had no future whatsoever under it.

As emphasized above, the concept of bureaucracy does not entirely fit the kind of politics currently practiced in the Congo. The presence of a personalized form of dictatorship calls for a composite concept, that of bureaucratic Caesarism;[6] indeed, there are numerous parallels between the present Congolese regime and Napoleonic France, Nasser's Egypt, or the dictatorship of the Caesars in ancient Rome. Will bureaucratic Caesarism prove to be a mere epiphenomenon, like parliamentary government and provincial reorganization, or a lasting feature of Congolese politics? Is it a viable political form as it stands, or does it mark the transition to yet another one? It is difficult to answer such questions because we are dealing here with "ultracontemporaneous" phenomena. The social scientist can already begin to evaluate the Congo's colonial era (or even its years of patrimonial rule), but he cannot yet do the same with the Mobutu regime. It is therefore tempting to offer the standard conclusion that events now taking place must be evaluated by posterity. Such a conclusion would be too easy, though, since it is possible to draw some logical, if still theoretical, conclusions about the future from what is now occurring in the Congo.

A first possibility is, of course, the reinforcement of the present authoritarian and bureaucratic regime. There are two interdependent conditions that could serve to promote this possibility. First, such key groups as graduate students, civil servants, and army officers might consolidate themselves in such a way as to afford the Mobutu regime greater institutional coherence. Such a condition is most likely to be realized under an authoritarian (Caesarist) regime, since none of these groups has a strong constituency in Congolese society as a whole.

A second condition is that the same key groups maintain or strengthen their existing links with the Congo's external environment. As we have seen, dependence on outside influences is a fundamental characteristic of Congolese politics, since the political elite has had only limited access to economic resources that are still exploited by politically unaccountable foreign trusts. Since bureaucracy derives much of its legitimacy from its efficiency in managing resources, the interdependence between the ruling elite and the foreigners must deepen. Also, the Congo's present rulers find the foreign trusts useful, for they can provide the country with the means to increase its managerial capacity. Thus it is understandable that the Mobutu regime has been more eager than any other to maintain friendly relations both with Belgium in particular and with the West in general, though it has also been the most vocal in its attacks against those "last bastions of colonialism" that still refuse to share their dividends with the ruling elite.

In considering the future of Congolese politics, there is another alternative that cannot be ignored. It is possible that authoritarian and personalistic tendencies will grow stronger, producing a purely dictatorial Caesarist regime. The central government's overreaction to a mild student protest is a case in point. On June 4, 1969, several hundred students from Lovanium University and various technical schools marched through downtown Kinshasa to express their dissatisfaction with the limited financial support they were receiving from the government. The army fired on the marchers and caused about 100 casualties, mostly among innocent bystanders. This event illustrates the strong authoritarian aspect of the Mobutu regime and reveals its inherent vulnerability to nearly any form of opposition.

The central government's extreme care to prevent the emergence of any autonomous center of power or political constituency is quite likely to reinforce Mobutu's present isolation. Such a trend would probably bring regular use of coercion in the public sphere, hinder the process of class formation, and increase the likelihood of the

kinds of coups and political assassinations that are typical of Caesarist regimes. One of the chief unknown factors in Congolese politics is the role of the military. The orientation of the ANC will probably influence future political events, and repeated army intervention and involvement in politics could bring substantial changes in
the ruling elite or the political system as a whole.

Indeed, ANC interventions to date cannot be viewed as isolated
events. Possibly they indicate a trend toward what Huntington calls
praetorianism, a social model that applies to most Middle Eastern
states today.[7] Specifically, praetorianism offers a model of the developing nation as a kind of garrison state. It usually refers to the
establishment of military colleges, an emphasis on specialized training, and the formation of a unified, professional military class. In
praetorian politics, military interventionists are most commonly graduates of military academies. As Perlmutter states in regard to the
Arab nations, significant historical connections exist between patrimonialism and praetorianism:

> In the patrimonial state, the chief obligation of the citizen was the main-
> tenance of the ruler, and the military became a permanent establishment
> as the process of financial rationalization developed. Relations between
> patrimony and conscripts were based on two models: clienteleship and
> slavery. The combinations varied with patrimonial rulers and states. Janis-
> saries were recruited among aliens and pariah castes; at other times, a citizen
> army of peasants was recruited for the same purpose. . . . Military training
> became crucial, the relationship between patrimonial authority and the
> military was altered. . . . The military [became] a formidable bureaucracy,
> proliferating and growing more complex when firearms and cavalry were
> introduced. As a bureaucracy . . . , the military was an active participant in
> politics and, in several of the historical empires, was engaged in an inde-
> pendent political struggle.[8]

Similar trends occurred in many Latin American countries. There,
the national armies first began as private militias hired by powerful
landholders who often acted in cooperation with local political leaders or state governors.[9] Later, the militias became the major means
of protecting the middle class from urban mass movements and political parties based on popular support.[10]

In the Congo, the emergence of praetorianism is still a very distant possibility. Though the ANC is one of the largest armed forces
in Africa, it has neither the attributes of a modern military estab-

lishment (managerial capabilities, a professional and political ideology, the ability to deal with the public or classes outside the military)
nor the tradition of political intervention that characterizes Middle
Eastern or South American armies. Accordingly, military coups are
not likely to occur by way of defending the interests of the middle
class, or in reaction to "the corruption and decadence of democratic
institutions." Coups may take place, though, should the ANC feel
that its veto power or its class interests are threatened by internal or
external factors.

Appendix: Social Profiles and Career Patterns of the Political Class

Pʀᴇᴄᴇᴅɪɴɢ chapters of this study have documented the great importance accorded careers in politics or public service in the Congo. This appendix presents more detailed information on the social origins, educational background, and occupational characteristics of the Congolese political class.

The information presented below* is subject to an important qualification: it does not result from any exhaustive study of the postindependence elite in the Congo, but merely provides raw material from which limited conclusions may be drawn. The survey was aimed at obtaining a minimal amount of biographical information from each of a large number of respondents. An extensive, rather than intensive, approach seemed preferable since this investigation was not conceived as an analysis in depth of the Congolese political class, but merely as a study of processes and structures. At any rate the survey, undertaken a few months before Mobutu's coup, was overwhelmingly successful. The suspiciousness of politicians and the disorganization of the Congolese post office presaged a very low return on the four-page questionnaires used in the survey. Yet of the 1,093 people holding key political posts in 1965 (members of the central government excepted), 584 filled out and returned the questionnaires. Of those who responded, 364 were members of provincial assemblies, 71 were congressmen, 71 were senators, and 78 were provincial ministers. Most of the people in the sample were part of the "second generation" of

* The statistical material related to this appendix is located on pp. 173–77.

politicians who came into office during the national and provincial elections of 1965.

The survey yielded two conclusions. First, it confirmed most prior observations that politics and charismatic standards of honor have a direct bearing on the social status accorded holders of public office in the Congo. Second, it showed that there are no significant variations between the first and second generations of Congolese politicians and high civil servants.

The Congolese political class is relatively homogeneous as far as age is concerned, as most of its members were born between 1930 and 1939. There are only slight differences in the average ages of the various categories. Contrary to what one might expect, for instance, Congolese senators are on the average younger than provincial assemblymen, and are little older than congressmen. Thus the Senate does not conform to its commonly held image as an assembly of elders. On the whole, the relatively young Congolese political class did not experience the pioneer stage of colonization, though it probably has a good recollection of the war years 1940–45. On this point, there seems to be some meaningful contrast between the Congo and the West African countries. According to the sparse information that Levine was able to gather for West Africa, the average age of the founding fathers, incumbents, and successors there was about 48.5 at the time of his study; in other words, most of those men were born around 1920.[1]

More than 80 percent of respondents were born in rural or semirural areas, while 10 to 15 percent of them had parents living in or around large or medium-sized cities. This fact may account for the rapidity and ease with which the countryside was politicized at the time of independence, leading to a greater than 90 percent voting turnout in 1960. Still, most members of the political and administrative class have moved from rural to urban residences since 1960. More than 75 percent of the congressmen, senators, and provincial ministers in the sample have made their homes in Kinshasa or in provincial capitals. It is worth noting, though, that although 57 percent of the assemblymen now live in urban or semiurban areas, notably provincial capitals or other industrial or commercial centers, more than 40 percent of them still maintain larger homes in the country or in predominantly rural areas.

It is difficult to tell exactly when the overall shift from rural to urban residence occurred. The two major periods in which such a shift could most likely have taken place were the period immediately following independence and the one immediately following the creation of the 21 new provinces. Concerning the latter period, the author personally noted during his travels in mid-1963 that the populations of the new provincial capitals had doubled, or sometimes tripled, in a period of four to six months.[2] Presumably, such migrations were spurred by the hope that local patrons (assemblymen, ministers, and civil servants) would be able to furnish their families, relatives, and clients with jobs.

Another salient characteristic of the Congolese political class is its generally limited education. Seventy percent of the people in the sample did not progress beyond the middle level (one to six years of secondary instruction), and the majority in this group actually completed only four years of secondary school.[3] Most frequently, the respondents attended vocational schools geared to train grade school teachers, typists, and agricultural agents. There are significant differences between the educational achievement of provincial assemblymen and senators on the one hand and that of congressmen and provincial ministers on the other. The latter group is generally better educated, with more than 30 percent having attended or completed secondary school. Yet 75 percent of those who received secondary instruction attended religious schools (*séminaires*) rather than high schools as such. Seventy-four percent of the politicians elected in June 1960 had not progressed beyond vocational school, and only 22 percent had attended or completed secondary school. Once again, this educational pattern contrasts strongly with the one prevailing in West Africa. According to Levine, 46 to 48 percent of the founding fathers, successors, and incumbents there had attended some institution of higher learning, either in Europe or in Africa.[4]

This appendix is concerned primarily with determining the exact origins of the Congolese political class. In his study on leadership succession in postwar West Africa, Levine points out that the pioneer generation in African politics was less a generation of revolutionaries than one of "establishmentarians" using revolutionary rhetoric:

The 47 African founding fathers . . . [were] men better suited to operate within the colonial system that produced them than to overthrow it. . . . In the [postindependence] cabinets, 30.5% of the ministers had been civil servants, [as had] 33.3% of the legislators; moreover, 21.7% of the cabinet officers had been educators. . . . The cabinet officers share still another characteristic with their legislative contemporaries: some 70% of the legislators had occupational backgrounds that put them partially or wholly under the rubric of government employee. . . . The point need not be elaborated: the establishmentarians predominated in the cabinets as they had in legislatures and among the founding fathers throughout the continent.[5]

The statistics available for the Congo parallel this general career pattern. Of those who entered politics in 1960, 59.2 percent were previously employed in the colonial administration, 35.9 percent in a teaching capacity; and 33.9 percent in the private sector. Only 4.8 percent were engaged in independent liberal professions, such as journalism, or in running small businesses; only 1.4 percent had no professional background whatsoever. Since those working in the private sector were employed largely as clerks or typists, it is clear that most members of the Congolese political class were previously bureaucrats. A similar pattern appears in the background of incumbents and successors before independence, for those incumbents were of course most likely to have held posts in the colonial civil service.

The trend toward a bureaucratic political class has grown overwhelmingly stronger since independence. The civil service is clearly the most likely starting place for a political career, for it is there that political patronage originates, alliances develop, and political struggles take place. The survey shows that significantly fewer officeholders worked as teachers or clerks in the private sector after independence than before. True, somewhat under 20 percent of the new provincial assemblymen and national deputies worked in industrial firms or grade schools at some time after independence, but most of them also held interim jobs in the civil service before entering politics.

One may ask if employment in the civil service provides sufficient impetus to a political career in the Congo, or whether the aspiring politician also needs support from specific organizations and associations. Table A9 provides some information on this subject. On the whole, associational life has little relevance for the person who wishes to enter politics today. Membership in associations must have been helpful to those who sought public office before independence, however: of those who held office in 1960, only 23.7 percent had not joined any association whatsoever before that year, a percentage that holds true for the sample as a whole. Associational life before independence was not restricted to tribal or ethnic associations, but included a variety of urban groups with varying orientations, such as alumni associations and évolué clubs. The future politicians usually belonged to several associations at a time and often exercised leading functions in them. Such was especially the case with congressmen (71.5 percent), senators (71.7 percent), and provincial assemblymen (65.7 percent), but less so with provincial ministers (54.6 percent). The importance of associational life for the Congolese politician decreased sharply after independence. From 42 to 56 percent of those elected in 1965 no longer participated in any kind of association after 1960. Those who did join associations after that year seldom took leading positions in them.

More interesting and relevant are the data on the relationship between the quest for public office and membership in political parties in the Congo. One might suppose that a politician would need some kind of platform and a measure of backing in order to win the approval of his constituency. Indeed, 94.6 percent of those polled said they were members of some political party. Still, this figure alone does not tell how the Congolese politician uses his party affiliation to achieve his ends.

According to the data in Table A11 the candidate to public office need not climb the party hierarchy in order to gain public office. Between 48 and 58 percent of the respondents who held office at the time of independence exercised some major or minor function in political groups formed at that time. This percentage is much lower for those who were members of the political coalitions and parties that took part in the 1965 national elections (26 percent for assemblymen and 43 percent for senators). Thus the candidate to public office is not usually elected on the strength of his party affiliation. In fact, the term "political party" as it is currently understood makes little sense in the context of Congolese politics; one might better speak of parliamentary caucuses or factions. A chief difference between a party and a caucus (or faction) is that allegiance to a caucus is more fluid and ephemeral than to a party. Also, a party elsewhere has some measure of discipline and a semipermanent organizational structure, characteristics that with few exceptions Congolese political parties have never exhibited.[6] In the survey, 50 to 60 percent of national and local politicians have maintained only nominal affiliations with the parties that helped them enter the political arena. There is no significant difference on this point between the two political generations, as Table A13 shows.

Table A8 gives some significant information about the intraprofessional mobility of the political class. There seems to be little trading of public offices among Congolese politicians. A provincial assemblyman, for instance, is unlikely to obtain a seat in Parliament; among senators and congressmen elected in 1965, only 10.5 percent were previously provincial assemblymen. A provincial assemblyman has a slightly better chance of becoming a provincial minister, though such a position requires higher qualifications than are usually held by ordinary assemblymen. Accordingly, provincial ministers seem to have some success in entering Parliament, especially the House of Representatives. There, 26.7 percent of the members were once ministers in their home provinces.

Finally, there are a few cases of national politicians, notably cabinet ministers and members of Parliament, who were forced to withdraw to local or provincial politics. It is hard to determine exactly what has become of the unsuccessful politicians from the first legislature. It seems likely, though, that most of them withdrew from politics entirely and returned either to employment in private firms or to small businesses of their own.

A familiar stereotype presents the new African political leaders as a group of profiteers. Yet the politicians' actual behavior clearly belies the stereotype. In the Congolese case, the strength of the new political elite is not based on the ownership of property. Very few Congolese politicians have outside occupations that allow them to reinvest the profits accumulated during their political careers. Since they come into contact with foreign business enterprises, members of Parliament probably find more opportunity to enrich themselves than do local politicians. For instance, 21 members of Parliament in the survey also have seats on the boards of foreign companies. Since they live in the capital, these men also have the opportunity to involve themselves in commercial enterprises of all sorts. Yet those who do so never develop their enterprises to a very large or profitable degree, and usually limit themselves to opening bars, restaurants, dance halls, or small construction firms in the city.

Most Congolese politicians have small plantations or other parcels of land in the country and generally leave the management of such holdings to their relatives. A politician's rural holding is never organized as a profit-making venture in the capitalist manner. Rather, it supplements the income of the politician's family or, at most, provides some marketable produce without using outside labor. Thus the survey, though not comprehensive, does seem to support Fanon's observations on the national bourgeoisie in Africa:

The national bourgeoisie of underdeveloped countries is not engaged in production nor in invention nor building nor labour; it is completely channeled into activities of the intermediary level (of which politics is of course a part). . . . It will be quite content with the role of the Western bourgeoisie's business agent. . . . This lucrative role, this cheap-jack's function, this meanness of outlook and this absence of ambition symbolize the incapacity of the national middle-class to fulfill its historic role of bourgeoisie. Here the dynamic, pioneer aspect of the inventor and of the discoverer of new worlds which are found in all national bourgeoisies are lamentably absent.[7]

TABLE A1

Age Distribution Among Congolese Politicians

Year of birth	Assemblymen		Congressmen		Senators		Provincial ministers	
	Number	Per-centage	Number	Per-centage	Number	Per-centage	Number	Per-centage
1940–36	77	20.8%	9	12.6%	—	—	15	19.2%
1931–35	117	30.4	21	29.5	20	29.1%	28	35.8
1926–30	84	22.8	24	33.8	25	35.2	25	32.0
1921–25	41	11.2	14	19.7	15	21.1	7	8.9
1916–20	20	5.4	2	2.8	8	11.2	2	2.5
Before 1915	22	6.0	1	1.4	3	4.2	1	1.2
Unknown	3	0.8	—	—	—	—	—	—

TABLE A2

Birthplaces of Congolese Politicians

Birthplace	Assemblymen		Congressmen		Senators		Provincial ministers	
	Number	Per-centage	Number	Per-centage	Number	Per-centage	Number	Per-centage
Provincial capital	13	3.5%	4	5.6%	5	7.0%	3	3.8%
Territorial chef-lieu	27	7.4	5	7.0	6	8.4	6	7.6
Other urban center	5	1.3	3	4.2	1	1.3	2	2.5
Village	319	88.5	59	83.0	59	84.4	67	85.7

TABLE A3

Residential Preferences of Congolese Politicians

Residence	Assemblymen Number	Per-centage	Congressmen Number	Per-centage	Senators Number	Per-centage	Provincial Ministers Number	Per-centage
Provincial capital	201	55.2%	58	81.6%	56	78.8%	67	85.8%
Territorial chef-lieu	73	20.0	5	7.0	4	5.6	9	11.5
Other urban center	8	2.1	—	—	1	1.4	—	—
Village	38	10.4	2	2.8	2	2.8	—	—
Unknown	44	12.0	6	8.4	6	8.4	2	2.5

TABLE A4

Educational Backgrounds of Congolese Politicians

Level of education	Assemblymen Number	Per-centage	Congressmen Number	Per-centage	Senators Number	Per-centage	Provincial Ministers Number	Per-centage
Completed secondary	66	18.1%	26	36.6%	13	18.3%	25	32.0%
1–6 years of secondary	279	76.6	45	63.3	55	77.4	52	66.6
None	13	3.5	—	—	1	1.3	1	1.2
Unknown	6	1.6	—	—	2	2.6	—	—

TABLE A5

Educational Backgrounds of Congolese Incumbents

Level of education	Number	Percentage
Completed secondary	23	22.3%
1–6 years of secondary	77	74.7
None	3	2.9

TABLE A6

Occupational Backgrounds of Incumbents Before Independence

Occupation	Number	Percentage
Teaching	37	35.9%
Private sector	35	33.9
Administration	61	59.2
Own business	5	4.8
None	2	1.9

TABLE A7

Occupational Backgrounds of Politicians Before Independence

Occupation	Assemblymen		Congressmen		Senators		Provincial ministers	
	Number	Per-centage	Number	Per-centage	Number	Per-centage	Number	Per-centage
Teaching	121	33.2%	19	26.7%	21	29.5%	22	28.2%
Private sector	113	31.0	20	28.1	26	36.6	26	33.3
Administration	192	50.2	28	39.4	49	69.0	49	62.8
Own business	10	2.7	4	5.6	3	4.2	4	5.1
None	30	8.2	5	7.0	1	1.4	6	7.6

TABLE A8

Occupational Backgrounds of Politicians After Independence

Occupation	Assemblymen		Congressmen		Senators		Provincial ministers	
	Number	Per-centage	Number	Per-centage	Number	Per-centage	Number	Per-centage
Teaching	67	18.3%	9	12.6%	4	5.6%	6	7.6%
Private sector	34	9.3	13	18.3	8	11.2	9	11.5
Administration	233	64.0	33	46.4	51	71.8	57	73.0
Own business	16	4.3	7	9.8	8	11.2	3	3.8
Assemblyman	—	—	4	5.6	11	15.4	15	19.2
Congressman or senator	3	0.8	—	—	—	—	5	6.4
Provincial minister	34	9.3	23	32.3	14	19.7	—	—
Cabinet minister	3	0.8	5	7.0	5	7.0	—	—

TABLE A9

Associational Life of Politicians Before Independence

Type of associattion	Number of Assemblymen	Number of Congressmen	Number of Senators	Number of Provincial ministers
Ethnic	101	28	28	28
Alumni	72	15	16	28
Labor	80	22	17	15
Evolué club	32	11	8	8
Other	97	26	19	29
None	113	16	21	19
Percentage not belonging	31.0%	22.5%	29.5%	24.3%
Pct. belonging	65.7	71.5	71.7	54.6

TABLE A10

Associational Life of Politicians in 1965

Type of association	Number of Assemblymen	Number of Congressmen	Number of Senators	Number of Provincial ministers
Ethnic	74	15	13	17
Alumni	17	8	4	4
Labor	17	4	1	3
Other	76	18	12	27
None	206	30	37	39
Percentage not belonging	56.5%	42.2%	52.1%	50.0%
Pct. belonging	51.0	55.5	70.0	39.2

TABLE A11

Party Membership Among Politicians

Party and degree of involvement	Number of Assemblymen	Number of Congressmen	Number of Senators	Number of Provincial ministers
Parties created around 1960				
MNC-Lumumba	50	12	11	14
Other national party	65	11	16	7
Regional party	195	32	37	48
Tribal party	78	18	12	12
Percentage holding responsible positions	48.4%	58.8%	55.2%	51.8%
Parties created around 1965				
Conaco	57	16	7	9
Allied with Conaco	66	10	9	11
Percentage holding responsible positions	26.0%	23.0%	43.7%	40.0%
No membership	17	—	6	8

TABLE A12

Shifts in Party Membership Among Politicians

Have been member of	Number of Assemblymen		Number of Congressmen		Number of Senators		Number of Provincial ministers	
	Number	Per-centage	Number	Per-centage	Number	Per-centage	Number	Per-centage
1 party	200	54.9%	45	63.3%	41	57.7%	42	53.8%
2 parties	130	35.7	21	29.5	24	33.8	26	33.3
3 or more parties	16	4.3	4	5.6	—	—	2	2.5

TABLE A13

Participation in Party Life Among Incumbents

Degree of participation	Number of Assemblymen	Number of Congressmen	Number of Senators	Number of Provincial ministers
Party membership	61	25	10	13
Responsible position	25	18	9	8

TABLE A14

Shifts in Party Membership Among Incumbents

Have been member of	Percentage of incumbents
One party	60.3%
Two parties	34.6
Three or more parties	1.9

TABLE A15

Other Activities Among Incumbents

Type of activity	Number of Assemblymen	Number of Congressmen	Number of Senators	Number of Provincial ministers
Trading	74	17	18	8
Farming	64	16	17	13
Trading and farming	18	12	5	1
Stockholding	6	11	10	1
Other	21	3	2	9
Total involved in commercial activities	134	34	34	26
Percentage involved in commercial activities	36.8%	47.8%	47.8%	33.3%

NOTE: The totals given here are low because categories are overlapping.

Chronology of Events

1960

June 30
: Proclamation of Congolese independence. Some fighting among tribes in Léopoldville and Luluabourg during independence celebrations.

July 5
: Mutiny breaks out in Force Publique.

July 9
: Prime Minister Patrice Lumumba imposes martial law, alluding to assassination attempt by Belgian officers. Northern Rhodesian troops mass along Congolese borders, ready to protect Europeans in Congo from army mutineers.

July 12
: Moise Tshombe declares Katangese independence. Belgian troops arrive in Elisabethville.

July 17
: Belgium rejects Congolese and UN requests to withdraw troops. However, Soviet intervention threats prompt Belgian troop withdrawals in late July, early August. UN troops enter Congo.

August 8
: "Mulopwe" Albert Kalonji announces the creation of the Independent State of South Kasai. In Léopoldville, President Kasavubu arrests Lumumba, replacing him with Joseph Ileo. Lumumba in turn ousts Kasavubu from presidency.

September 14
: Colonel Joseph Mobutu seizes power in Léopoldville, institutes College of Commissioners staffed by university students.

December 3
: Patrice Lumumba arrested, held for trial.

1961

January– February	Central government forces under Mobutu clash with Lumumbist troops from Stanleyville in many parts of Congo.
February 13	Lumumba assassinated in Katanga after escaping from confinement.
February– April	Sporadic talks aimed at reuniting Léopoldville, Elisabethville, Stanleyville regimes.
August 7	Parliament reconvenes at Lovanium University. Government of national reconciliation formed under Cyrille Adoula.
September– October	Violent clashes in Elisabethville between UN and Katangese troops.

1962

January 14	Stanleyville nationalist regime collapses, Antoine Gizenga arrested in Léopoldville. Tshombe's Katangese regime maintains independence.
March 27	Parliament amends Fundamental Law to allow for creation of new provinces.
October	Twenty-one new provinces formed.

1963

January 14	Katangese secession ends as UN troops occupy urban centers in Katanga.
May– August	Mounting parliamentary opposition to Adoula government. Rising tension, political feuding in provinces of Haut Congo, Sankuru, Lac Léopold II, Moyen Congo, Kwango.
July	Pierre Mulele arrives in Kwilu, organizes guerrilla camps in bush.
September 29	Parliamentary stalemate on new draft constitution. President Kasavubu prorogues Parliament indefinitely.
October 3	State of emergency proclaimed in Léopoldville. Committee of National Liberation (CNL) formed in Brazzaville.

1964

February	Growing rebellion in Kwilu. CNL opens new revolutionary front in eastern Congo. Widespread defeat of ANC troops.

June	Constitutional referendum gets under way.
June 30	Last UN troops leave Congo.
July 5	Kasavubu invites Tshombe to join him in forming provisional government of national unity. Tshombe announces Gizenga's release from prison.
August 5	Rebel advances continue, culminating in capture of Stanleyville. First counterattacks by ANC.
November 24	U.S. planes land 1,000 Belgian paratroops in Stanleyville to rescue Europeans there.

1965

March 18	First national elections since independence.
June 24	Kasavubu postpones parliamentary session pending new elections in Kwilu, Kivu, and Cuvette Centrale.
September	First session of Parliament in two years.
October 13	Kasavubu dismisses Tshombe, asks Evariste Kimba to form new government.
November 14	Parliament rejects Kimba government.
November 25	Joseph Mobutu seizes power, displacing both Kasavubu and Tshombe. Colonel Leonard Mulamba named prime minister in government of national reunification.

1966

March	Mobutu assumes all legislative powers without dissolving Parliament.
April 26	Presidential decree reduces number of new provinces from 21 to twelve. Further reduction to eight after some months.
May 5	"Decolonization" decree renames several Congolese cities effective June 30. Léopoldville becomes Kinshasa; Elisabethville becomes Lubumbashi; Stanleyville becomes Kisangani; Coquilhatville becomes Mbandaka; Paulis becomes Isiro; Banningville becomes Bandundu.
June 3	Kimba and three associates executed for alleged plot to kill Mobutu.
September	Army mutiny among Katangese troops stationed in Kisangani.
October 26	Mobutu dismisses Mulamba, establishes one-man rule. Mulamba accused of complicity in Kisangani mutiny.

December   Congolese government cancels UMHK concessions, seizes
                its assets. New Congolese company, GECOMIN, estab-
                lished in its place.

                1967

March 13   Tshombe tried in absentia, sentenced to death for treason.

May   Program of Mobutu's Popular Revolutionary Movement
                (MPR) set forth. MPR manifesto states that "national
                authenticity" is main goal of new regime.

July   Mobutu reports landings by foreign paratroops in Kisan-
                gani, attacks by foreign settlers on the ANC in Bukavu.
                Witnesses state that attackers are dissident elements of
                ANC led by white mercenaries.

October 5   Major cabinet reshuffle. Nine ministers dismissed, eight
                retained with new portfolios.

November   Rebel elements of ANC withdraw from Kisangani to
                Rwanda.

                1968

January   Mobutu accuses Lovanium University students of distrib-
                uting subversive tracts, organizing demonstrations against
                U.S. Vice-President Humphrey. Mobutu threatens per-
                sonal intervention against students.

February 23   Executive committee of General Union of Congolese Stu-
                dents (UGEC) dissolved for allegedly plotting Mobutu's
                assassination.

April   Mobutu announces plot to kill him uncovered by police
                in Luluabourg. Three former deputies from Kasai impli-
                cated.

July 5   Mobutu announces reshuffle of MPR political bureau.
                Fifteen new members added, including several veteran
                politicians.

August   New ministerial reshuffle.

August 29   General amnesty decree affecting all persons convicted of
                political offenses.

September 29   Pierre Mulele returns from Brazzaville to Kinshasa with
                Congolese Foreign Minister Justin Bomboko.

October 2   Mobutu announces Mulele not covered by August am-
                nesty decree.

October 9   Mulele executed following trial by military tribunal.

1969

January	Pro-Chinese exiles meet in Dar es Salaam, Tanzania. Announce formation of Communist party within Congo.
April 24	Colonel Monga, seven other Kisangani mutiny leaders executed. Remaining 250 Katangese soldiers reintegrated into ANC.
June 4	Lovanium University students march through Kinshasa to demand higher government subsidies. Six to twelve students killed, six to eighteen wounded by fire from government troops.
June	Mobutu closes Lovanium University.
June 30	Moise Tshombe dies in Algiers.
August 1	Sweeping governmental reshuffle. Nine ministers ousted, among them Victor Nendaka, Justin Bomboko, Etienne Tshisekedi.
August 8	Mobutu announces projected reopening of Lovanium University in October.
November 3	Mobutu sets off on first Congolese state visit to Belgium since independence.
November	President Ngouabi of Congo-Brazzaville accuses Mobutu of supporting coup against him. Borders between two Congos closed.

1970

March	Increased tension between Congo, Congo-Brazzaville. Minor border incidents.
April 27	Foreign Minister Cyrille Adoula announces deployment of troops on river border with Congo-Brazzaville.
May	With closing of MPR's first congress, Congo becomes one-party state. Mobutu sole party candidate for November presidential election.
June 17–July 1	King Baudouin of Belgium makes first state visit to Congo since independence.
August 5–9	Mobutu visits U.S. Announces from Washington that UMHK allowed to return to Congo. International consortium of mining companies established for Congo.
September 15	Cabinet reshuffle involving interior, finance, justice ministries.
November 1	Mobutu gains popular mandate in presidential election.

November 14–15   Legislative elections.

November 15   Radio Kinshasa announces bank fraud amounting to sev-
                 eral million Zaires. Congolese National Bank, several
                 Belgian banks implicated. Mobutu discharges his minister
                 of finances, Albert Ndele.

December 5   Mobutu sworn in as president by Congolese Supreme
                 Court. Announces general amnesty for all persons in-
                 volved in illegal political activities between 1960 and
                 1970.

Notes

See the Bibliography for complete authors' names, titles, and publication data on items cited in short form in the Notes. The following abbreviations are used in the Notes:

AFP	Agence France-Presse	CRISP	Centre de Recherche et d'Information Socio-Politique
AR	*Africa Report*		
BIT	Bureau International du Travail	*EC*	*Etudes Congolaises*
BM	*Bulletin Militaire*	EDC	Etoile du Congo
CA	*Courrier Africain*	EMFP	Etat-Major de la Force Publique
Cd'A	*Le Courrier d'Afrique*		
CEE	Centre d'Etudes Economiques	IRES	Institut de Recherches Economiques et Sociales
CEP	Centre d'Etudes Politiques	*JMAS*	*Journal of Modern African Studies*
CES	*Cahiers Economiques et Sociaux*	*LB*	*La Libre Belgique*
CIS	*Cahiers Internationaux de Sociologie*	*MC*	*Moniteurs Congolais*
CR	Chambre des Représentants de la République du Congo	*RA*	*Remarques Africaines*
		UN	United Nations
		WP	*World Politics*

Chapter 1

1. Young, p. 607.
2. Zolberg, p. 6.
3. Alexis de Tocqueville, *Democracy in America* (New York: Vintage Books, 1960), p. 447.
4. Zolberg, p. 141.

5. Guenther Roth, "Personal Rulership, Patrimonialism and Empire Building in the New States," *WP*, 20, no. 2 (Jan. 1968): 199.

6. Zolberg, p. 159.

7. This point is particularly well developed by Alex Weingrod in "Patron, Patronage and Political Parties," *Comparative Studies in Society and History*, 10, no. 6 (July 1968): 377–85.

8. Weber, "World Religions," p. 296.

9. Zolberg, p. 144.

10. Weber, "World Religions," p. 296.

11. Weber, *Methodology*, pp. 90–93.

12. Spiro, pp. 4–5.

13. See the bitter racial and political confrontation at the 1969 meeting of the African Studies Association in Montreal. *AR*, 14, no. 8 (Dec. 1969): 16–27.

14. Lucien Goldmann, "Introduction générale," in Maurice de Gandillac, Lucien Goldmann, Jean Piaget, and others, *Entretiens sur les notions de genèse et structure* (Paris: Mouton, 1965), p. 10.

15. See for instance David Apter, *The Politics of Modernization* (Chicago: University of Chicago Press, 1965), pp. 50ff.

16. Human rationality is understood here in the practical sense as opposed to abstract thought or mere empirical observation. See Karl Marx, "Theses on Feuerbach," in Feuer, pp. 243–45.

17. On the significance of this type of explanation, see the perceptive critique by Paul Baran, *Economie politique de la croissance* (Paris: Maspero, 1967), pp. 186–99; and Bettelheim, pp. 27–29.

Chapter 2

1. Weber, *Theory*, pp. 369–70. (Emphasis added.)

2. Georges Balandier, *Sociologie actuelle de l'Afrique noire* (Paris: Presses Universitaires de France, 1963), p. 33.

3. Georges Balandier, "Dynamique des relations extérieures des sociétés archaiques," in Georges Gurvitch, ed., *Traité de sociologie* (Paris: Presses Universitaires de France, 1963), p. 449.

4. In this study, politics in the strict sense will be held distinct from the political realm as a whole. The political realm embraces all the institutions, activities, and interests shared by the members of a national entity. The term "politics" is defined here as any activity associated with individual or group competition for power or advantage. See Sheldon S. Wolin, *Politics and Vision: Continuity and Change in Western Political Thought* (Boston: Little, Brown, 1960), pp. 8–11.

5. Roland Oliver and J. D. Fage, *A Short History of Africa* (London: Penguin Books, 1962), p. 182.

6. Maurice, pp. 25–26.

7. Joye and Lewin, p. 30.

8. R. J. Lemoine, "Finances et colonisation," *Annales d'Histoire Economique et Sociale* (Sept. 1934): 437.

9. André Stenmans, *La Reprise du Congo par la Belgique* (Brussels: R. Louis, 1949), pp. 417–19.

10. Fernand Baudhuin, *Le Capital de la Belgique et le rendement de son industrie* (Louvain, Belgium, 1924), pp. 137–380.

11. Poulantzas, p. 10.

12. Maurice, p. 22.

13. Thomas Hodgkin, *Nationalism in Colonial Africa* (London: Muller, 1956), p. 52.

14. Louis Franck, *Le Congo belge* (Brussels: La Renaissance du Livre, 1930), I, p. 311; II, pp. 208–9.

15. *Plan décennal pour le développement économique et social du Congo* (Brussels, 1949), p. 62.

16. On this point, see Monsignor de Hemptine, *La Politique des missions protestantes au Congo* (Elisabethville: L'Essor du Congo, 1929); Father A. Vermeersh, *Les Missions catholiques au Congo belge: Etude critique de leur action* (Brussels, 1909).

17. *Projet d'organisation de l'enseignement libre au Congo belge avec le concours des missions nationales* (Brussels, 1924).

18. See *Recueil à l'usage des fonctionnaires et des agents du service territorial au Congo belge* (Brussels: Ministère des Colonies, 1930).

19. Interview with P. Bourgeois, former district commissioner for Kivu. Kinshasa, 1964.

20. "L'Administration des indigènes," *L'Essor*, Feb. 17, 1945.

21. Joye and Lewin, pp. 282–83.

22. *Ibid.*, pp. 285–86.

23. Though it was approved by the Belgian Parliament, this charter was in fact an ordinary law that Belgian legislators were free to modify.

24. Jean Stengers, *Belgique et Congo: L'Elaboration de la Charte Coloniale* (Brussels: La Renaissance du Livre, 1963), p. 220.

25. From 1948 to 1952, the number of Belgian civil servants rose from 3,900 to 7,200, an increase of almost 50 percent.

26. Albert Sohier, "La Politique d'intégration," *Zaire*, 5 (Nov. 1952): 902. Quoted from Young, p. 31.

27. John Strachey, *The End of Empire* (New York: Praeger, 1964), p. 218.

28. Young, p. 21.

29. See *Congo: Positions socialistes, 1885–1960* (Brussels: Institut Emile Vandervelde, 1960).

30. Guy Malengreau, "Le Congo à la croisée des chemins," *Revue Noutique sociale au Congo belge* (Brussels: Librairie Encyclopédique, 1952).

31. See Arthur Doucy and Pierre Feldheim, *Problèmes du travail et politique sociale au Congo belge* (Brussels: Librairie Encyclopédique, 1952).

32. Emile Bolaert, "Les Trois Fictions du droit foncier congolais," *Zaire*, 11 (1957): 399–427.

33. Edouard Mendiaux, "Le Comité National du Kivu," *Zaire*, 10 (Oct. 1956): 803–13; (Nov. 1956): 927–64.

34. Théodore Heise, *Congo belge et Ruanda-Urundi: Notes de droit public et commentaires de la Charte Coloniale* (Brussels: Van Campenhout, 1952), p. 53.

35. Young, pp. 26ff.

36. L. Guebels, *Relation complète des travaux de la Commission Permanente pour la Protection des Indigènes au Congo Belge* (Elisabethville: Centre d'Etudes des Problèmes Sociaux Indigènes, 1952).

37. See for instance the pioneering work by James S. Coleman, *Nigeria: Background to Nationalism* (Berkeley: University of California Press, 1963).

38. "Les Cahiers de la politique indigène," in *Dettes de Guerre* (Elisabethville: L'Essor du Congo, 1945), p. 203.

39. UCOL, *Status* (Elisabethville, 1947), in Lemarchand, p. 83. The settlers were always a minority in the Belgian Congo (5,202 Belgians and 4,284 others in 1958). Except in Katanga and Kivu, where they were concentrated, they had a relatively low status in the European community. For more on the settlers, see Emile Dehoux, *Sur le Chemin de la colonisation* (Brussels: Stoops, 1947).

40. Commission du Colonat, *Procès verbaux des séances* (Brussels, 1946), p. 30.

41. Concerning the shift in the Church position, see the Belgian bishops' declaration of June 1956 in Ruth Slade, *The Belgian Congo: Some Recent Changes* (London: Oxford University Press, 1960).

42. Pierre Rijkmans, *Dominer pour servir* (Brussels: Edition Universelle, 1948), p. 12.

43. *Discours du Vice-Gouverneur Général* (Léopoldville: Conseil du Gouvernements, 1952), p. 31.

44. "Intervention de M. Auguste Buisseret," in *L'Avenir politique du Congo belge: Colloque du 22 novembre, 1958* (Brussels: L'Institut Belge de Science Politique, 1959), p. 73.

45. This term is borrowed from Michael G. Smith, *Government in Zazzau: 1800–1950* (London: Oxford University Press, 1960), p. 317. The substantively irrational change is opposed by Smith to the formally irrational change that "repeats or multiplies an established form without promoting further structural change" (p. 316).

46. On the notion of "political tempo" see Georges Gurvitch, *La Vocation actuelle de la sociologie: Antécédents et perspectives* (Paris: Presses Universitaires de France, 1963), pp. 325–430.

47. "African Manifesto Stirs Congo," *Africa Special Reports*, 1 (Oct. 26, 1956): 2.

48. Debacker, pp. 16–19.

49. Lemarchand, p. 187. See also *ibid.*, p. 21.

50. For a very good treatment of this point, see Benoit Verhaegen and Laurent Monnier, "Problèmes concrets et concepts de science politique en Afrique: Application au Bas-Congo," *CES*, 4 (June 1963): 79–91; Monnier, pp. 51–61.

51. CRISP, *ABAKO: 1950–1960*, p. 125.

52. CRISP, *Congo 1959*, pp. 128–35.

53. Monnier, p. 61.

54. CRISP, *Parti Solidaire*, p. 54.

55. Herbert Weiss, p. 191. See also Donatien Mokolo, *Le Parti Solidaire Africain: Introduction à l'étude des problèmes sociaux et politiques du Kwilu* (Kinshasa: Université Lovanium, 1966), pp. 187–90.

56. Weiss, p. 191.

57. *Ibid.*, p. 191.

58. Alan P. Merriam, *Congo: Background of Conflict* (Evanston, Ill.: Northwestern University Press, 1961), pp. 194–203.

59. Ganshof, pp. 524ff.

60. *Les Cahiers Socialistes*, 16–17 (July 1947): 105–7.

61. Patrice Lumumba, *Congo, My Country* (New York: Praeger, 1962), pp. 9 and 60.

62. Michel Crozier, *Le Phénomène bureaucratique* (Paris: Le Seuil, 1963), p. 254.

63. Lemarchand, p. 175.

64. Paul Caprasse, *Leaders africains en milieu urbain.* Unpublished doctoral dissertation (Elisabethville, 1957).

65. Jean de Hasse, *Le Rôle politique des associations de resortissants à Léopoldville* (Université de Louvain, 1965).

66. J. Van Wing, "Quelques Aspects de l'état social des populations indigènes du Congo belge," *Bulletin des Séances*, Institut Royal Colonial Belge, 18 (1947): 189.

67. *La Voix du Congolais*, 128 (Nov. 1956): 825.

68. The tentative reforms were primarily associated with the immatriculation decree, which is analyzed in depth in Young, pp. 75–87.

69. Young, pp. 83–87.

70. Before the expansion and bureaucratization of the colonial government opened new opportunities to the Congolese évolué, the sole access to the modern sector was through the Catholic Church. Thus most Congolese young people began their schooling as candidates to the priesthood.

71. *Enquête par sondage de la main d'oeuvre à Léopoldville, 1958* (Léopoldville: Ministère du Plan et de la Coordination Economique, 1961).

72. This point is particularly well developed in Julius Rohm, *Les Entrepreneurs congolais.* Unpublished study (Kinshasa: Université Lovanium, 1966).

73. For a more precise definition of those terms, see Pascal Mazamba,

Etude comparative sur l'ensemble du statut des agents de l'état congolais.
Unpublished study (Kinshasa: Université Lovanium, 1964).

74. *Loi contenant le budget ordinaire du Congo belge pour l'exercice 1960* (Brussels: Chambre des Représentants, 1960).

75. Dupriez, p. 21.

76. BIT, p. 27.

77. *Ibid.*, p. 26.

78. Young, p. 203.

79. CEP-IRES, *Archives*, doc. MF 160/21: 1–2.

80. *Ibid.*

81. Gérard-Libois, "L'Aide extérieure," pp. 3–5.

82. Verhaegen, "Traitements," p. 10.

83. These facts were gathered during my three trips through the new Congolese provinces between January 1963 and April 1964.

84. Dupriez, p. 21.

85. Fernand Herman, "La Situation économique et financière du Congo en 1962," *EC*, 4, no. 3 (Mar. 1963): 11.

86. The high salaries paid to the military were a direct consequence of the army mutinies of 1960–61.

87. "Congo 1960–1964: Quatre années d'indépendance," *EC*, 7, 8 (Oct. 1964): 5.

88. CRISP, *Congo 1965*, p. 238.

89. Hughes Leclercq, "Analyse générale de l'inflation congolaise," CES, 1 (Oct. 1962): 38–40.

Chapter 3

1. Weber, *Theory*, p. 341.

2. This point is more closely examined in Bendix, *Weber*, pp. 347–48.

3. Gérard-Libois, *Congo 1960*, vol. II; Ganshof, pp. 505–8.

4. *Cd'A*, Apr. 11, 1961, pp. 4–5.

5. *Ibid.*, Jan. 5, 1961.

6. *Ibid.*, Mar. 23, 1961.

7. Verhaegen, *Congo 1961*, p. 14.

8. *Ibid.*, pp. 27–28.

9. The demands of the Katangese delegation forced the expulsion of the chief of state's legal advisor two hours after his arrival in Tananarive.

10. *Cd'A*, Mar. 14 to Mar. 20, 1961.

11. Verhaegen, *Congo 1961*, pp. 64–65.

12. *Ibid.*, p. 75.

13. Of the 27 ministers and 15 state secretaries in the Adoula government, 12 had taken part in the Coquilhatville Round Table.

14. CR, *Compte-Rendu*, Aug. 2, 1961, p. 35.

15. *Ibid.*, doc. 14/1 S.O., 1961–62.

16. *Ibid.*, doc. 20/1.

17. *Ibid.*, Aug. 25, 1961.

18. Sénat de la République du Congo, *Annales Parlementaires*, doc. 15/AP/JPNKLL, Nov. 22, 1961.

19. CR, *Compte-Rendu*, Jan. 29, 1962, p. 20.

20. *Ibid.*, Mar. 27, 1962.

21. CR, *Rapport et projet de loi préparé par le Comité des Affaires Intérieures*, Mar. 23, 1962.

22. CR, *Annales Parlementaires*, Mar. 23, 1962, p. 34.

23. CR, *Rapport*, doc. 21/117/3.

24. *Ibid.*, doc. 21/112/3.

25. Interview with L. Mamboleo, former justice minister in the Tshombe government, 1964.

26. CR, *Rapport*, doc. 21/105/3.

27. Interview with L. Dubois, former district commissioner in Kivu, 1964.

28. Benoit Verhaegen, "Présentation morphologique des nouvelles provinces," *EC*, 4, no. 4 (Apr. 1963): 18.

29. *Rapport de la Mission IRES dans les Provinces du Congo* (Kinshasa: IRES, 1963). Mimeographed.

30. Monnier and Willame, p. 262.

31. Concerning local politics in North Katanga, see Willame, *Provinces*, pp. 120–32.

32. Both were responsible for implementing austerity measures, such as suppression of some parliamentary indemnities, which were applied only to Mwamba Ilunga's followers. See Verhaegen, *Rébellions*, pp. 416–17.

33. In North Katanga, Kabulo and Masengo left their patron around May 1964 and joined the CNL. Verhaegen, *Rébellions*, p. 422.

34. Machiavelli, pp. 16–17.

35. CEP-IRES, *Archives*, docs. MF 1643/50/1; MF 1643/50/40.

36. Interview with Alois Kabangi, personnel minister. Kinshasa, 1964.

37. For additional biographical information about President Manono, see Pierre Artigue, *Qui sont les leaders congolais?* (Brussels: Europe Afrique, 1961), p. 200.

38. Interview with S. Ngoie, provincial secretary of Lomami. Kabinda, May 1964.

39. CEP-IRES, *Archives*, doc. MF 160/21/5.

40. Interview with S. Ngoie. Kabinda, May 1964.

41. When the author was at Lisala, the provincial capital of Moyen Congo, he noted that Laurent Eketebi's name was scarcely known there. By contrast, Jean Bolikango's name exercised a tremendous appeal among the populations of the province, even though he was rarely seen at Lisala.

42. Willame, *Provinces*, pp. 48–58.

43. Maurice Lovens, "Les Elections législatives nationales de 1965 en République Démocratique du Congo: Situation au 15 juillet 1965," *CES*, 3, no. 3 (Oct. 1965).

44. Interview with F. Kahegeshe, former student at Lovanium University. Bukavu, Aug. 1965.

45. Clifford Geertz, "The Integrative Revolution: Primordial Sentiments and Civil Politics," in Clifford Geertz, ed., *Old Societies and New States* (Glencoe, Ill.: The Free Press, 1963), p. 154.

46. For more details on the myth of a unified Bangala, see Young, pp. 242–46.

47. Most Bapende intellectuals were followers of Antoine Gizenga and were Kamitatu's chief opponents after 1964.

48. Interview with Donatien Mokolo, former student at Lovanium University, Kinshasa, Jan. 1968.

Chapter 4

1. Bendix, *Weber*, p. 341.

2. *Manifeste des universitaires congolais* (Léopoldville, 1961), p. 2.

3. See EMFP, vol. 27; and Ermans.

4. Camille Liebrecht, *Léopold II: Fondateur d'empire* (Brussels, 1932), pp. 223ff.

5. CR, *Rapport sur l'administration de la colonie* (Brussels, 1954), p. 49.

6. EMFP, p. 27.

7. Camille Coquilhat, *Sur le haut Congo* (Paris: J. Lebègue, 1888), p. 352.

8. On the mutiny at Luluabourg, see Auguste Verbeken, *La Révolte des Batetela: Textes inédits* (Tervueren, Belgium: Académie Royale des Sciences Coloniales Belges, 1958); Albert François, *Trois Chapitres de l'épopée congolaise* (Brussels: Office de la Publicité, 1949); A. Z. Zousmanovitch, "L'Insurrection des Batetela au Congo belge au XIXème siècle," *Présence Africaine*, 51 (1964).

9. "Mutineries au Congo belge," *BM*, 21 (Mar. 1947).

10. *BM*, no. 4 (1964).

11. Ermans, p. 823.

12. Dupriez, pp. 31–33.

13. Lucian Pye, "Armies in the Process of Political Modernization," in Jason L. Finkle and Richard Gable, eds., *Political Development and Social Change* (New York: John Wiley, 1966), pp. 379–85. "The very fact that the recruit must break his ties and associations with civilian life and adjust to the more impersonal world of the army tends to emphasize the fundamental nature of this process [of modernization] which involves the movement out of the particularistic relationships of traditional life and into the more impersonal and universalistic relationships of an industrialized society" (p. 383).

14. EMFP, p. 27.

15. On May 1, 1960, the Force Publique consisted of 23,900 Congolese soldiers and some 1,100 Belgian officers and noncoms. *CA*, no. 14.

16. *Ibid.*

17. James S. Coleman and Belmont Price, "The Role of the Military in Sub-Saharan Africa," in Johnson.

18. EMFP, p. 27.

19. Gérard-Libois, *Congo 1960*, pp. 334ff. In June 1960, there were some 1,400 Belgian troops stationed in the Congo. They could act only at the request of the governor-general.

20. *Emancipation*, Mar. 19, 1960. Quoted from Gérard-Libois, *Congo 1960*, p. 350.

21. *Le Soir*, July 28, 1960.

22. Ganshof, p. 405.

23. *Emancipation*, Apr. 9, 1960. Quoted from Gérard-Libois, *Congo 1960*, pp. 353–54.

24. Gérard-Libois, *Congo 1960*, p. 1081.

25. *Ibid.*, p. 1076.

26. For the events surrounding the South Kasai secession, see Willame, *Provinces*, pp. 27–74.

27. Roberts, pp. 91–92.

28. *Ibid.*, pp. 102ff.

29. *Cd'A*, Mar. 22, 1961.

30. Interview with a former civil servant of the state of South Kasai. December 1965.

31. UN, doc. S/4557 (Nov. 2, 1960): 27.

32. This machine gun was still proudly displayed in the courtyard of the provincial secretariat long after the end of the South Kasai secession.

33. It should be borne in mind that as a center of the Congolese diamond industry, the province attracted smugglers, adventurers, and the unemployed from as far away as Senegal.

34. Interview with a student from South Kasai. Mar. 1965.

35. Willame, *Provinces*, p. 40.

36. *Rapport sur l'entretien que les membres des deux bureaux ont eu avec Mr. J. Ngalula, président provincial du Sud Kasai, le 31 janvier 1963*, Sénat de la République du Congo, report no. 7, p. 2; interview with Mr. Kabambi, former superintendent of the Bakwanga High School. December 1965.

37. UN, doc. S/4691 (Feb. 12, 1961).

38. Young, p. 453.

39. Gérard-Libois, *Sécession*, p. 178n.

40. Young, p. 454.

41. *LB*, Dec. 17–18, 1960.

42. UN, doc. S/5428.

43. CRISP, *Congo 1964*, pp. 352ff.

44. CRISP, *Congo 1966*, pp. 345ff.

45. Young, p. 451.

46. Gérard-Libois, *Congo 1960*, p. 200.

47. Verhaegen, *Congo 1961*, pp. 197ff.

48. UN, doc. S/4745 (Feb. 2, 1961).

49. Verhaegen, *Congo 1961*, pp. 537ff.

50. Just prior to the formation of the Adoula government in July 1961,

General Lundula stated that he would not object to any government bearing parliamentary approval. His only apparent reason for remaining in Stanleyville was his somewhat obscure relationship with Joseph Mobutu. See Verhaegen, *Congo 1961*, p. 577.

51. Machiavelli, p. 45.

52. *CA*, Feb. 26, 1968, p. 26.

53. Verhaegen, *Congo 1961*, pp. 231–35.

54. Colonel Trinquier never actually assumed his post. This was probably due to pressure from the French government, which was embarrassed by his extreme political views. For more on this affair see Gérard-Libois, *Sécession,* p. 188.

55. *CA*, Feb. 26, 1968, p. 11. According to UN estimates, there were still 300 to 500 mercenaries in South Katanga at that time. See UN, doc. S/5053/ Add. 12.

56. *LB*, Dec. 17–18, 1960.

57. *CA*, Feb. 26, 1968, pp. 16–17.

58. CRISP, *Congo 1965*, pp. 267–68.

59. *Le Monde*, Aug. 4, 1966.

60. For more details concerning the mutiny of the foreign mercenaries see *CA*, Feb. 26, 1968.

Chapter 5

1. For more on Weber's ideal-typical method, see Weber, *Methodology*, pp. 49–112; Weber, *Theory*, pp. 13–17; Talcott Parsons, *The Structures of Social Action* (New York: McGraw-Hill, 1937), pp. 604–5; Gerth and Mills, pp. 55–61.

2. Eisenstadt, *Political Systems*, p. 301.

3. Talcott Parsons, *Structure and Process in Modern Societies* (Glencoe, Ill.: The Free Press, 1960), p. 180.

4. Gabriel Almond, "A Developmental Approach to Political Systems," *WP*, 17, no. 2 (Jan. 1965): 183–214. In this case, the notion of resources covers human behavior, goods, services, honors of all kinds, opportunities, and political support.

5. On this point, see Bendix, *Weber*, p. 350.

6. *Ibid.*, p. 336.

7. In today's emerging nations, democratic political beliefs almost invariably embrace the myth of the welfare state. The term "myth" is used advisedly here, for these nations' political elites do not usually fulfill the expectations that they have aroused in their constituencies.

8. Bendix, *Weber*, p. 336.

9. For a good class analysis of preindustrial England, see Peter Laslett, *The World We Have Lost: England Before the Industrial Age* (New York: Scribner's, 1965), pp. 22–52. The classical work on France remains Tocqueville's *The Old Regime and the French Revolution* (New York: Doubleday, 1965).

10. The most important steps in that direction were taken by the Tshombe government, which organized a national conference of all Congolese paramount chiefs in 1965.

11. Weber, *Theory*, p. 347.

12. Eisenstadt, *Political Systems*, p. 23.

13. See Lucian Pye, *Politics, Personality and Nation Building* (New Haven, Conn.: Yale University Press, 1962), pp. 150ff.

14. Jean Poirier, "Dépendance et aliénation: De la situation coloniale à la situation condominiale," *CIS*, 50 (Jan.–June 1966): 81.

15. Hobsbawm, p. 150.

16. For an analysis of the parliamentary activities in the provinces, see Monnier and Willame.

17. *Ibid.*

18. Laurent Monnier, "Le Kongo-Central: Histoire, institutions, et vie politique." Unpublished doctoral dissertation (Kinshasa: Université Lovanium, 1969), Chapter II, p. 2.

19. Henry Bienen, *Tanzania: Party Transformation and Economic Development* (Princeton, N.J.: Princeton University Press, 1967), p. 5.

20. Gérard-Libois, *Sécession*, pp. 107ff.

21. For details on UMHK subsidiaries, see Joye and Lewin, pp. 220–22.

22. King Léopold offered this company full property rights over one-third of the Katanga district.

23. "Convention du 19 juin 1900 entre l'Etat Indépendant du Congo et la Compagnie du Katanga," *Bulletin de l'Etat Indépendant du Congo* (1900), p. 168.

24. Gérard-Libois, *Sécession*, p. 47.

25. Verwilgen, p. 9.

26. CEP-IRES, *Archives*, doc. 11 (May 11, 1960): Table Ronde Economique Belgo-Congolaise, transcript of the proceedings of May 9 and 10, 1960.

27. Gérard-Libois, *Congo 1960*, p. 92.

28. Gérard-Libois, *Sécession*, p. 47.

29. "Convention du 24 juin 1960 entre le Congo belge et la Compagnie du Katanga," *MC*, 38 (Sept. 1960): 2503.

30. "If the present convention is not approved by the Congolese government, the existing conventions will remain in effect." "Decret du 27 juin 1960 approuvant la convention conclue le 24 juin 1960 entre le Congo belge et la Compagnie du Katanga," *MC*, 38 (Sept. 1960).

31. Thus according to Agence France-Presse, some financial pressure groups may have persuaded Katangese leaders to "come into contact with representatives of the Rhodesian government." AFP dispatch of Mar. 10–11, 1960. This would explain a "sensational" statement made by Sir Roy Welensky in March 1960, according to which some unidentified Katangese encouraged him "to hold out a friendly hand to Katanga in the perspective of a closer association." *Daily Express*, Mar. 2, 1960.

32. CEP-IRES, *Morphologie des groupes financiers* (Brussels: CRISP, 1962), p. 157.

33. Gérard-Libois, *Sécession*, p. 151.

34. *Ibid.*, p. 322.

35. CEE-IRES, *Lettre*, 1 (Feb. 1967): 9.

36. *Ibid.*, pp. 8–9.

37. "Decret-Loi du 29 novembre 1964: Exposé des motifs," *EC*, 8, no. 1 (Jan.–Feb. 1965): 36–43.

38. Verwilgen, pp. 24–25.

39. *Spécial*, Brussels, Sept. 15, 1966.

40. "La République du Congo, la Compagnie du Katanga, et l'Union Minière," *L'Echo de la Bourse*, Brussels, Feb. 12–13, 1965.

41. Wolfram F. Hanrieder, "International and Comparative Politics: Toward a Synthesis," *WP*, 20, no. 3 (Apr. 1968): 480.

42. T. B. Bottomore, "Marxisme et Sociologie," *L'Homme et la Société*, 10 (Oct.–Nov.–Dec. 1968): 7.

43. This term is borrowed from Hoskyns.

44. In a very perceptive article, Ken Post has shown the deep malaise that the Congo crisis, and more particularly Lumumba's assassination, produced among "politically aware citizens" in Nigeria. Ken W. Post, "Nigerian Pamphleteers and the Congo," *JMAS*, 2, no. 3 (Nov. 1964): 405–13. A similar argument has been developed by Jitendia Mohan in "Ghana, the Congo, and the United Nations," *JMAS*, 8, no. 3 (Oct. 1969): 369–406.

45. On Dag Hammarskjold's views regarding the role of the UN in developing countries, see Stanley Hoffman, "In Search of a Thread: The UN in the Congo Labyrinth," *International Organization*, 16, no. 2 (Spring 1962): 331–61; Michel Virally, "Le Testament politique de Dag Hammarskjold," *Annuaire Français de Droit International*, 6 (1960); J. Lash, *Monsieur H.: Huit années de crise à l'ONU* (Paris: Edition du Seuil, 1962).

46. UN, doc. A/4390/Add. 1.

47. *Ibid.*, doc. 5/4405.

48. It should be mentioned that during the civil war in Nigeria, the evident Soviet presence there caused no agonized protests from Washington, no demands for UN intervention, and no threats of a Soviet-American confrontation.

49. Hoskyns, pp. 472–73.

50. Gendebien, p. 47.

51. Hoskyns, p. 472. See also Arnold Rivkin, "The Congo Crisis in World Affairs," *Civilisations*, 10, no. 4 (1960): 473–79.

52. Mahmoud Khiari, personal adviser to Cyrille Adoula, was highly instrumental in helping the prime minister choose the members of his governmental staff and achieve a balanced representation of all major ethnic groups in the central government.

53. Gendebien, pp. 169–91.

54. *Ibid.*, pp. 174–75.

55. *Ibid.*, p. 137.

56. Gérard-Libois, *Sécession*, p. 273.

57. Letter from Paul-Henri Spaak to Cyrille Adoula. June 12, 1964. Quoted in CRISP, *Congo 1964*, p. 158.

58. *Ibid.*, p. 359.

59. Williams, p. 148.

60. Paul-Henri Gendebien, "L'Interférence des politiques nationales dans l'action des Nations Unies," *CES*, 4, no. 4 (Dec. 1966): 439.

61. Williams, pp. 154–59.

62. Ernest Lefever, *Crisis in the Congo: A UN Force in Action* (Washington, 1965), p. 15.

63. Williams, p. 143: "The United States in the interests of African and world peace and harmony is concerned that the Congolese and not the Communists control the Congo."

64. Gérard-Libois, "L'Aide extérieure," p. 3.

65. Ernest Lefever, "The UN as a Foreign Policy Instrument: The Congo Crisis," in R. Hilsman and R. C. Good, eds., *Foreign Policies in the Sixties: The Issues and the Instruments* (Baltimore: Johns Hopkins Press, 1965).

66. Gérard-Libois, "L'Aide extérieure," pp. 1–4.

67. *Ibid.*, p. 19.

68. *Ibid.*, pp. 26–36.

69. See Romain Yakemtchouk, *Assistance économique et pénétration industrielle des pays de l'Est en Afrique* (Kinshasa: IRES, 1966).

70. David A. Baldwin, "Foreign Aid, Intervention, and Influence," *WP*, 21, no. 3 (Apr. 1969): 439.

71. Hoskyns, p. 477.

72. Eisenstadt, *Political Systems*, p. 311.

73. Edward Feit, "Military Coups and Political Development: Some Lessons from Ghana and Nigeria," *WP*, 20, no. 2 (Jan. 1968): 179–93.

74. Verhaegen, *Rébellions*, p. 32.

Chapter 6

1. Hobsbawm, p. 1.

2. *Ibid.*, p. 2.

3. Giovanni Arrighi and John S. Saul, "Socialism and Economic Development," *JMAS*, 6, no. 2 (Aug. 1968): 149.

4. Lacroix, p. 211.

5. See Etienne N'Dongala, "Mutations structurelles de l'économie traditionelle dans le Bas-Congo sous l'impact de la colonisation et de la décolonisation," *CES*, 4, no. 1 (Mar. 1966).

6. Lacroix, p. 208.

7. See, for instance, H. Myint, *The Economics of Developing Countries* (London, 1964), Chapter 3; D. Walker, "Problems of Economic Development in East Africa," in E. A. G. Robinson, ed., *Economic Development for Africa South of the Sahara* (London, 1964), pp. 111–14. Concerning the

Congo, see V. Drachoussoff, "Agricultural Change in the Belgian Congo: 1945–1960," *Food Research Institute Studies*, 5, no. 2 (1965).

8. Coméliau, pp. 43–44.

9. CEP-IRES, *Archives*, doc. MF 1650/23/2.

10. *Ibid.*, "Troisième Conférence des assemblées provinciales" (Boma, Sept. 1963).

11. H. D. Takizala, "Situation de l'enseignement au Congo durant la première législature," *EC*, 7, no. 8 (Oct. 1964): 68.

12. Coméliau, pp. 97–98.

13. Lacroix, pp. 106–7.

14. *Cd'A*, Aug. 7, 1964.

15. *Ibid.*

16. Concerning the Bapende revolt, see Henri Nicolai, *Le Kwilu: Etude géographique d'une région congolaise* (Brussels: Editions Cemubac, 1963), pp. 324–25.

17. Willame, *Provinces*, p. 22.

18. Luc de Heusch, "Autorité et prestige dans la société tetela," *Zaire*, Dec. 1964, p. 109.

19. See Thomas Turner, "Ethnicity and Social Change." Unpublished paper (University of Wisconsin, May 1969).

20. Regarding the feeling of hostility toward the Batetela and Bakusu, see Willame, *Provinces*, vol. 4, pp. 132–33; vol. 5, pp. 94–98.

21. *Ibid.*, vol. 1, pp. 115–16.

22. Verhaegen, *Rébellions*, pp. 483–84.

23. Immanuel Wallerstein, "The Decline of the Party in Single Party African States," in Joseph La Palombara and Myron Weiner, eds., *Political Parties and Political Development* (Princeton, N.J.: Princeton University Press, 1965), p. 207.

24. This caucus was a loose coalition of the PSA, MNC-Lumumba, CEREA (Kivu), and Balubakat. It numbered about 71 members by July 1961. See Verhaegen, *Congo 1961*, pp. 407ff.

25. These were C. Gbenye, R. Mwanbe, A. Eleo, E. Rudahindwa, M. Bisukiro, J. Lutula, E. Kikuyu, and D. Uketwengu.

26. This accusation was substantiated by the fact that the PSA-Gizenga and the MNC-Lumumba were the two best-organized political parties in Léopoldville.

27. Simon Losala (MNC-Lumumba) and Andre Lubaya (UNC-Kasai), presidents of Orientale and Kasai provinces respectively.

28. See CRISP, *Congo 1962*, pp. 71ff.

29. Allegedly, this measure was taken to protect the capital from increasing banditry.

30. CRISP, *Congo 1963*, p. 126.

31. On the CNL, see "Les Regroupements politiques au Congo au 30 juin 1964," *EC*, 7, no. 7 (Aug.–Sept. 1964): 55ff.

32. CRISP, *Congo 1963*, pp. 180–287.

33. Moise Tshombe and two members of the CNL, Sylvain Kama and Assumani Senghie, even signed secret agreements in Madrid. See CRISP, *Congo 1964*, pp. 136–37.

34. Such was the case with the members of Balubakat, CEREA, and CONAKAT.

35. "Les Partis politiques congolais." Unpublished dossier (Brussels: CRISP, 1964).

36. Concerning the conflict between the two tendencies, see CRISP, *Congo 1964*, pp. 31ff.

37. On the concept of the "counterelite," see Raymond Aron, "La Classe dirigeante: Mythe ou réalité, *Association Française de Science Politique: Table Ronde* (Paris, 1963), p. 7; Jean Ziegler, *Sociologie de la nouvelle Afrique* (Paris, Edition Gallimard, 1964), pp. 218–20.

38. Crawford Young, "Significance of the 1964 Rebellion" in Kitchen, p. 119.

39. Marx and Engels, p. 7.

40. Verhaegen, *Rébellions*, p. 107.

41. Both tribes had backed the PSA-Gizenga during and after the 1960 election.

42. Concerning this incident, see Verhaegen, *Rébellions*, pp. 172–73.

43. Thus the Bambunda rebels' offensive into the Bayanzi territory failed primarily because of the Catholic missionaries, who succeeded in coordinating the Bayanzi warriors' defense against the rebels. Interview with Z., a missionary from Kwilu. August 1968.

44. Verhaegen, *Rébellions*, p. 335.

45. CRISP, *Congo 1964*, p. 301.

46. *Ibid.*, pp. 312–13.

47. *Cd'A*, Sept. 21, 1964.

48. Verhaegen, *Rébellions*, p. 134.

49. Hobsbawm, p. 6.

50. Verhaegen, *Rébellions*, pp. 166ff; Fox and De Craemer, pp. 16ff.

51. Fox and De Craemer, p. 19.

52. *L'Essor du Katanga*, Elisabethville, May 22, 1964.

53. Willame, *Provinces*, p. 119.

54. Fox and De Craemer, p. 27.

55. *Ibid.*, p. 30.

56. Verhaegen, *Rébellions*, p. 114.

57. Fox and De Craemer, p. 21.

58. On this point, see Fabian, p. 57n.

59. Max Weber, *Staatssoziologie* (Berlin, 1956), quoted from Fabian, p. 59. The words "can" and "may" are very important here. Their use suggests that Weber did not view the dynamic element in history as consisting of charismatic "breakthroughs" by great men.

60. *RA*, no. 249 (Sept. 22, 1965): 21.

61. *Ibid.*, pp. 21–22.

62. CRISP, *Congo 1964*, p. 316.

63. *Ibid.*, p. 313.

64. At Kabalo, the simba ascribed their defeat to the fact that the witch doctor of the city had sexual intercourse several times just before battle. He was killed on the spot. See *Le Soir Illustré*, Aug. 27, 1964.

65. The first public executions always involved three categories of convict: politicians, civil servants, and thieves. Benoit Verhaegen points out that "political crimes were equated with simple criminal offenses; politicians and civil servants who had enriched themselves were presented as a special kind of delinquent. By killing those guilty of minor offenses, the simba acquired the right to eliminate the 'big crooks,' whom the people identified as the politicians in power." Verhaegen, *Rébellions*, p. 356.

66. *Ibid.*, p. 488.

67. CRISP, *Congo 1964*, p. 288.

68. Those archives were discovered untouched at Gbenye's residence a month after the capture of Stanleyville by the mercenaries and the ANC.

69. CRISP, *Congo 1964*, p. 299.

70. *Ibid.*, pp. 314–30.

71. *Ibid.*, p. 284.

Chapter 7

1. On this distinction, see Poulantzas, pp. 371–82; Edgar Morin, "La bureaucratie," in Edgar Morin, *Introduction à une politique de l'homme* (Paris: Edition du Seuil, 1965), pp. 115–18.

2. Robert Michels, *Political Parties* (New York: The Free Press, 1962); Karl Marx, *Kritik des Hegelschen Staatsrechts*; Max Weber, *Wirtschaft und Gesellschaft*, Part 3, Chapter 6.

3. CRISP, *Congo 1965*, pp. 439–41.

4. *Ibid.*, p. 443.

5. In the provinces, the press used this term to characterize the ideology of the new regime.

6. CEP-IRES, *Archives*, ordonnance no. 67-459 (Oct. 26, 1967).

7. CEP-IRES, *Archives*, "Arrêté du Ministre de la Santé."

8. On the puritanical self-image of the ANC, see *Cd'A*, June 11–12, 1966.

9. Proclamation from the ANC High Command, Nov. 24, 1965.

10. President Mobutu's message to the ANC, Nov. 24, 1965.

11. President Mobutu's speech of Dec. 12, 1965.

12. Assemblée provinciale du Kivu, *Compte-Rendu Analytique*, Oct. 7, 1966, pp. 6ff.

13. On the Popular Revolutionary Movement (MPR), see CRISP, *Congo 1967*, pp. 96ff.

14. *Constitution de la République Démocratique du Congo*, June 24, 1967. Articles 21, 29, 31, and 32.

15. Maurice Lovens, "Le Parlement en 1966," in CRISP, *Congo 1966*, pp. 169ff.

16. Maurice Lovens, "Le Parlement en 1967," in CRISP, *Congo 1967,* p. 132.

17. Banque Nationale du Congo, *Rapport Annuel 1968–1969,* p. 12.

18. *Actualités Africaines,* Kinshasa, Feb. 5, 1966. Before the coup of November 1965, several regional leaders attempted to reunify the provinces, but their efforts were all unsuccessful. See Willame, "Réunification," pp. 74–80.

19. *EDC,* Mar. 25, 1966.

20. Ordonnance-loi no. 205, *MC,* 23 (Dec. 1966).

21. Arrêté ministérial no. 288 (Apr. 11, 1966), *MC,* 15 (Aug. 1966).

22. Ordonnance no. 66-614 (Oct. 31, 1966), *MC,* 22 (Dec. 1966).

23. CEP-IRES, *Archives,* "Conférence des gouverneurs de province" (Kinshasa, Jan. 6, 1966).

24. These were Dominique Diur (Lualaba), Godefroid Munongo (Katanga). Ignace Alamazani (Haut Congo), and Henri Ndala-Kambola (North Katanga).

25. The former vice-governors became provincial commissioners and general secretaries.

26. Ordonnance-loi no. 67-177 (Apr. 10, 1967), "Rapport au Président de la République," *MC,* 23 (Apr. 1967): 27.

27. Interview with Mr. Nakasila, ministry of the interior. July 1968.

28. See CRISP, *Congo 1967,* pp. 175–79.

29. CEP-IRES, *Archives,* "Discours du Président de la République aux étudiants de l'Université Lovanium" (Nov. 1965).

30. CEP-IRES, *Archives,* ordonnance no. 67-462/463 (Oct. 7, 1967).

31. Between July 1966 and October 1967, much harsh criticism of Mobutu's entourage, and most particularly the former university students in the presidential cabinet, appeared in the Belgian press. This unfavorable publicity is understandable in view of the hostility between President Mobutu and UMHK.

32. *Le Monde,* Oct. 7, 1967.

33. Interview with Gérard Nakasila, Ministry of the Interior. July 1968.

34. Interview with Theodore Tshiswaka, former finance minister of South Kasai. Aug. 1968.

35. The writer learned of this phenomenon through various interviews in Kinshasa and the countryside during his visit to the Congo in the summer of 1968.

36. Captain S. Mika, provincial chief of security, followed a hard-line policy against Moise Tshombe's allies in Lubumbashi.

37. Victor Nendaka's influence in Mobutu's entourage exceeded his importance as minister in the central government.

38. See CRISP, *Congo 1966,* p. 25.

39. This essay was the end result of several articles published in *Cd'A,* June 11–14, 1966, under the title "Constitutional Background of Military Regimes."

40. S. E. Finer, *The Man on Horseback: The Role of the Military in Politics* (New York: Praeger, 1962).

41. Young, p. 448.

42. CRISP, *Congo 1966*, pp. 25ff.

43. Such was apparently the case in August 1968 when Cleophas Kamitatu declined the post of education minister that Bernardin Mungul-Diaka had left vacant.

44. Crispin Mulumba and Pierre F. Kasongo, "La Politique africaine du Congo," in CRISP, *Congo 1967*, p. 418.

45. *Le Progrès*, Nov. 26–27, 1966.

46. This was particularly true in the Bakongo area, where 81 percent of the votes were negative, and in the cities of Njili and Dendale (Kinshasa). See Pierre F. Kasongo, "Le Système présidentiel et la politique intérieure," CRISP, *Congo 1967*, p. 30.

47. *EC*, 10, no. 3 (May–June 1967): 66–79.

48. See CRISP, *Congo 1967*, p. 116.

49. "Message présidentiel," *Cd'A*, May 31, 1966.

50. CRISP, *Congo 1966*, p. 437.

51. President Mobutu's press conference of Aug. 14, 1966.

52. AFP dispatch of Oct. 23, 1966.

53. *Ibid.*, Oct. 24, 1966.

54. *Ibid.*, Oct. 26, 1966.

55. Laurent Monnier, "La Province de Bandundu," in CRISP, *Congo 1966*, pp. 329–30.

56. *AR*, Nov. 1968, p. 25.

57. *Le Monde*, Oct. 1, 1968.

58. CRISP, *Congo 1965*, pp. 244–45.

59. Benoit Verhaegen, "Armée et régime militaire au Congo." Unpublished study, p. 32.

60. "L'Armée Nationale Congolaise," *EC*, 10, no. 4 (July–Aug. 1967).

61. Young. In 1964, 276 officers and noncoms were undergoing training in Belgian military academies, against 183 in 1963. By September 1964, a total of 664 ANC personnel had been trained in Belgium. It should be recalled that there were only 900 officers and noncoms in the ANC in 1960. See Willame, "The Military Intervenes," in Kitchen, p. 168.

62. CRISP, *Congo 1966*, p. 39.

63. "Programme d'action du CVR," *EC*, 9, no. 4 (July–Aug. 1966).

64. In Kinshasa, the CVR was the first organization to warn the central authorities about the conspiracy against Colonel Tshatshi, the extraordinary commissioner in Orientale province.

65. In North Katanga and Kasai Oriental, some activists were even arrested and jailed by the military authorities or the local police.

66. See the discussion of urban youth in Chapter 6.

67. Weber, "Bureaucracy," in Gerth and Mills, pp. 230–31.

68. The involvement of women in small retail business in the urban

centers of the Congo might appear surprising. As a matter of fact, in addition to bearing and educating children, African women have always performed a central role as producers in the tribal community. While men spent most of their time in extraeconomic or leisure activities (hunting, house construction), women were responsible for all agricultural work. With the introduction of a money economy, African women became involved in selling and producing goods for local markets, urban as well as rural. On the economic role of African women, see Denis Paulme, *Femmes d'Afrique noire* (Paris: Mouton, 1962), pp. 254–57.

69. *Cd'A*, Apr. 11, 1967.

70. *EDC*, Oct. 20, 1967.

71. Interviews with several civil servants and social workers in Kwilu. Aug. 1968.

72. *Présence Congolaise*, Nov. 18, 1967.

73. *Le Progrès*, Dec. 2–3, 1967.

74. *Ibid.*

75. CRISP, *Congo 1966*, p. 159.

76. *Ibid.*, pp. 163–64.

77. The Institute of Economic and Social Research points out that "if the ownership of mineral stocks were attributed to UMHK, one could only conclude that there had been an export of Congolese goods and merchandise. In this case, UMHK . . . was compelled to pay the value of these stocks in hard currency to the Congolese National Bank." See CEE-IRES, *Lettre*, 1 (Feb. 1967): 12–13.

78. CEP-IRES, *Archives*, ordonnance-loi no. 67-01 (Jan. 1, 1967).

79. Jules Gérard-Libois, "L'Affaire de l'Union Minière du Haut-Katanga," *EC*, 10, no. 2 (Mar.–Apr. 1967): 24.

80. CEE-IRES, *Lettre*, 1 (Feb. 1967): 20.

81. CRISP, *Archives*, "Dossier sur les entreprises du Congo."

Chapter 8

1. Spiro, pp. 143–44.

2. By "political engineering" I refer to a concept that is increasingly fashionable of late, and that views politics as a series of technical or managerial problems to be solved. On the use of such a concept in African politics, see William G. Fleming, "Political Science and African Politics," *JMAS*, 7, no. 3 (1969): 495–511.

3. See, for instance, Fox and de Craemer, pp. 16ff.

4. Gerth and Mills, pp. 235–36.

5. *Ibid.*

6. Reinhard Bendix, "Concepts and Generalizations in Comparative Sociology," *American Sociological Review*, 28, no. 4 (Aug. 1963): 532–43.

7. For an elaborate analysis of praetorianism, see Huntington, *Political Order in Changing Societies* (New Haven, Conn.: Yale University Press, 1968), pp. 193–263.

8. Perlmutter, p. 281.

9. John J. Johnson, "The Latin American Military as a Politically Competing Group in Transitional Society," in Johnson.

10. José Nun, "A Latin American Phenomenon: The Middle Class Military Coup," in *Trends in Social Science Research in Latin American Countries* (Berkeley: Institute of International Studies, 1965), pp. 55–91.

Appendix

1. Levine, p. 9. The founding fathers are the first national leaders of the new African states. The successors are those leaders who, after independence, succeed the founding fathers in national leadership positions. The incumbents are simply founding fathers and successors still in office.

2. CEP-IRES, *Archives*, doc. MF 160/21: 1–2.

3. The percentage may in fact have been higher, since one of the requirements for candidacy in the 1965 elections was the completion of at least four years of secondary instruction. This requirement is known to have been widely violated.

4. Levine, p. 7.

5. *Ibid.*, p. 17.

6. On the principal characteristics of Congolese political parties, see Lemarchand.

7. Frantz Fanon, *The Wretched of the Earth* (New York, Grove Press, 1963), pp. 122–24.

Bibliography

THE LITERATURE on Congolese politics is quite extensive, and only the more important works will be mentioned here. The best source is the documentary series of the Centre de Recherche et d'Information Socio-Politique (CRISP). Between 1959 and 1967, CRISP published all significant documents concerning political events in the Congo. However, much of the material in this book comes from the collection of the Centre d'Etudes Socio-Politiques at Lovanium University in Kinshasa. These materials are now available on microfilm at the Center for African Documentation and Studies (CEDAF), located in Brussels. They include official documents, reports, edicts from provincial assemblies, laws, decrees, official bulletins, information bulletins, and clippings from local newspapers. The majority of these documents are either stenciled or typewritten, making the collection a unique and valuable source.

For many purposes, students interested in the Congo should consult E. Bustin, *Congo Kinshasa: Guide Bibliographique* (Brussels: CEDAF, 1971). This work includes an annotated bibliography on the economic, political, and social history of the Congo, and represents the most serious attempt to date to put together a complete catalog of the many publications about the Congo before and after independence. However, many will find that the bibliography in Crawford Young's *Politics in the Congo* (Princeton, N.J.: Princeton University Press, 1965) is adequate.

Among secondary works, scholars will find Young's book the best aid to understanding the troublesome years of the postindependence period. René Lemarchand's *Political Awakening in the Congo* (Berkeley: University of California Press, 1964) is most valuable for its analysis of the colonial situation and the development of early political groups.

By far the best analytical attempts to explain Congolese politics are found in Herbert Weiss, *Political Protest in the Congo* (Princeton, N.J.: Princeton University Press, 1967); Benoit Verhaegen, *Rébellions au Congo* (Brussels:

CRISP, vols. 1 and 2, 1966); and Laurent Monnier, "Le Kongo Central: Histoire, institutions et vie politique" (unpublished doctoral dissertation; Lovanium University, 1970). Verhaegen's book deals with rural protest in the Kwilu area in the postindependence era. This masterful work represents a unique attempt at an in-depth explanation of the 1964–65 rebellions, and it offers a bright and provocative methodological essay on analyzing contemporary political phenomena in Africa. Monnier's dissertation is an excellent contribution to the understanding of local politics in the Congo.

The following list includes only those sources mentioned twice or more in the Notes. For a source mentioned only once, full publishing information is given in the note in which it appears.

Africa Report. Washington: African American Institute, 1956–   .

Bendix, Reinhard. *Max Weber: An Intellectual Portrait.* New York: Doubleday, 1962.

Bettelheim, Charles. *Planification et croissance accélérée.* Paris: Maspero, 1967.

Bulletin Militaire. Léopoldville: Armée Nationale Congolaise, 1964–65.

Bureau International du Travail (International Labor Organization). *Rapport sur les salaires dans la République du Congo.* Geneva, 1960.

Cahiers Economiques et Sociaux. Kinshasa: IRES, Université Lovanium, 1962–67.

Cahiers Internationaux de Sociologie. Paris, 1946–   .

Centre d'Etudes Economiques de l'IRES. *Lettre Mensuelle.* Kinshasa: Université Lovanium.

Centre d'Etudes Politiques de l'IRES. *Archives.* Kinshasa: Université Lovanium.

Chambre des Représentants de la République du Congo. *Compte-Rendu analytique.* 1961–65.

Chambre des Représentants de la République du Congo. *Rapport fait au nom de la Commission Spéciale des Affaires Intérieures.*

Coméliau, Christian. *Fonction économique et pouvoir politique: La Province de l'Uélé en 1963–1964.* Kinshasa: IRES, Université Lovanium, 1965.

Courrier Africain. Brussels: CRISP, 1960–67.

Le Courrier d'Afrique. Kinshasa, 1960–67.

Centre de Recherche et d'Information Socio-Politique. *Congo 1964.* Brussels, 1965.

———. *Congo 1965.* Brussels, 1966.

———. *Congo 1966.* Brussels, 1967.

———. *Congo 1967.* Brussels, 1968.

———. *Parti Solidaire Africain: 1959–1960.* Brussels, 1963.

Debacker, M. C. C. *Notes pour servir à l'étude des groupes politiques a Léopoldville.* Léopoldville: Infor-Congo, 1959.

Dupriez, Gérard. "Les Rémunérations dans l'ancienne province de Léopoldville," *Cahiers Economiques et Sociaux,* 2 (Dec. 1962).

Eisenstadt, S. N. *The Political Systems of Empires*. Glencoe, Ill.: Free Press, 1963.

Emancipation. Léopoldville.

Ermans, F. "Organization militaire de la colonie," in *Encyclopédie du Congo belge*. Brussels: Bieleveld, 1953.

Etat Major de la Force Publique. *La Force Publique de sa naissance à 1914*. Brussels: Académie Royale des Sciences d'Outre-Mer, 1952.

Etoile du Congo. Kinshasa, 1964–67.

Etudes Congolaises. Kinshasa: CRISP, 1961–67.

Fabian, Johannes. "Charisma and Cultural Change: The Case of the Jamaa Movement in Katanga," *Comparative Studies in Society and History*, 11, no. 2 (Apr. 1969).

Feuer, Lewis S., ed. *Marx and Engels: Basic Writings on Politics and Philosophy*. New York: Anchor Books, 1959.

Fox, Renée, Willy de Craemer, and J. M. de Ribeaucourt. "La Deuxième Indépendance: Etude d'un cas." *Etudes Congolaises*, 7, no. 1 (Jan.–Feb. 1965).

Ganshof Van Der Meersch, Willy. *Fin de la souveraineté belge au Congo*. Brussels: Institut Royal des Relations Internationales, 1963.

Gendebien, Paul-Henri. *L'Intervention des Nations Unies au Congo: 1960–64*. Paris: Mouton, 1967.

Gérard-Libois, Jules. "L'Aide extérieure à la République du Congo," *Etudes Congolaises*, 9, no. 3 (May–June 1966).

———. *Sécession au Katanga*. Brussels: CRISP, 1963. Published in the U.S. as *Katanga Secession*. Madison: University of Wisconsin Press, 1966.

Gérard-Libois, Jules, and Benoit Verhaegen. *Congo 1960*. Brussels: CRISP, 1961.

Gerth, H. H., and C. Wright Mills. *From Max Weber: Essays in Sociology*. London: Routledge and Kegan Paul, 1964.

Hobsbawm, E. J. *Primitive Rebels: Studies in Archaic Forms of Social Movements in the 19th and 20th Centuries*. New York: Norton, 1959.

Hoskyns, Catherine. *The Congo Since Independence: January 1960 to December 1961*. London: Oxford University Press, 1965.

Johnson, John H., ed. *The Role of the Military in the Underdeveloped Countries*. Princeton, N.J.: Princeton University Press, 1962.

Journal of Modern African Studies. London: Cambridge University, 1963– .

Joye, Pierre, and Rosine Lewin. *Les Trusts au Congo*. Brussels: Société Populaire d'Edition, 1961.

Kitchen, Helen, ed. *Footnotes to the Congo Story*. New York: Walker, 1967.

Lacroix, Jean-Louis. *Industrialisation au Congo: La Transformation des structures économiques*. Paris: Mouton, 1967.

Lemarchand, René. *Political Awakening in the Congo*. Berkeley: University of California Press, 1964.

Levine, Victor T. "Leadership Succession in Post-war Africa." Unpublished study. Los Angeles: African Studies Center, 1968.

La Libre Belgique. Brussels, 1960–67.

Machiavelli, Niccolo. *The Prince* and *The Discourses.* New York: Modern Library, 1950.

Marx, Karl, and Friedrich Engels. "Manifesto of the Communist Party," in Lewis S. Feuer, ed., *Marx and Engels: Basic Writings in Politics and Philosophy.* New York: Doubleday, 1959.

Maurice, Albert. *Belgique, gouvernante du Congo: A propos d'un entretien inédit du Baron Lambremont avec S.A.R. le Prince Albert.* Brussels, 1962.

Moniteurs Congolais. Kinshasa, 1960–67.

Monnier, Laurent. "Notes sur l'ABAKO et le nationalisme kongo," *Genèse-Afrique,* 5, no. 1 (1966).

Monnier, Laurent, and Jean-Claude Willame. *Les Provinces du Congo: Structure et fonctionnement.* Kinshasa: IRES, Université Lovanium, 1964.

Perlmutter, Amos. "The Arab Military Elite," *World Politics,* 22, no. 2 (Jan. 1970): 269–30.

Poulantzas, Nicos. *Pouvoir politique et classes sociales.* Paris: Maspero, 1968.

Le Progrès. Kinshasa, 1960–67.

Remarques Africaines. Brussels, 1959– .

Roberts, John. *My Congo Adventure.* London: Jarrold, 1963.

Le Soir. Brussels, 1960–67.

Spiro, Herbert, ed. *Patterns of African Development: Five Comparisons.* Englewood Cliffs, N.J.: Prentice-Hall, 1967.

United Nations. *Documents,* Conseil de Sécurité et Assemblée Générale, 1960–63.

Verhaegen, Benoit. *Congo 1961.* Brussels: CRISP, 1962.

———. *Rébellions au Congo.* Brussels: CRISP, 1966.

———. "Traitements, grèves, et politique d'austérité," *Etudes Congolaises,* 2, no. 5 (1962).

Verwilgen, Michel P. "Les Dissolutions successives du Comité Spécial du Katanga," *Etudes Congolaises,* 7, no. 1 (Jan.–Feb. 1965).

Weber, Max. *The Methodology of Social Science.* Glencoe, Ill.: Free Press, 1949.

———. "The Social Psychology of the World Religions," in H. H. Gerth and C. Wright Mills, *From Max Weber: Essays in Sociology.* London: Routledge and Kegan Paul, 1964.

———. *The Theory of Social and Economic Organizations.* New York: Free Press, 1957.

Weiss, Herbert. *Political Protest in the Congo: The Parti Solidaire Africain During the Independence Struggle.* Princeton, N.J.: Princeton University Press, 1967.

Willame, Jean-Claude. *Les Provinces du Congo: Structure et fonctionnement.* Kinshasa: IRES, Université Lovanium, 1966. Vols. I-V in the Collection d'Etudes Politiques.

———. "La Réunification des provinces du Congo," *Etudes Congolaises,* 9, no. 4 (July–Aug. 1966).

Williams, G. Mennen. "U.S. Objectives in the Congo: 1960–1965," in Helen
  Kitchen, ed., *Footnotes to the Congo Story*. New York: Walker, 1967.
World Politics. Princeton: Center of International Studies, Princeton Uni-
  versity, 1948–   .
Young, Crawford. *Politics in the Congo: Decolonization and Independence*.
  Princeton, N.J.: Princeton University Press, 1965.
Zaire. Brussels-Louvain, 1952–58.
Zolberg, Aristide. *Creating Political Order: The Party States in West Africa*.
  Chicago: Rand McNally, 1966.

Index

Index

ABAKO (Bakongo Alliance), 21ff, 35
ABAZI (Bayanzi Alliance), 35
Actualités Africaines, 135
Adoula, Cyril: formation of his govern-
  ment, 40–41, 48, 196; U.N. and, 95;
  attitude of U.S. toward, 97; and
  nationalist opposition, 112–15, 122,
  152; mentioned, 50, 72, 142, 146, 190
Africa, 1, 3, 62; and Western traditions,
  5, 7, 18, 83–84, 159–60; colonization
  of, 9; westernization of, 18; East, 61;
  decolonization in, 82; one-party
  system of politics, 111; West, 168f.
  See also by country
Africa Special Reports, 21
African Mutual Party, *see* PSA
African Studies Association, 186
Afro-Arab conquest, 110
Afro-Arab traders, 61
AGEL, 138
Agence France-Presse, 148, 195
Agoyo, Minister, 142
Agricultural production, 103–6, 130, 134
Aid, foreign, 75, 96, 98–99
Alamazani, Ignace, 201
Albertville, 72, 119, 126
Almond, Gabriel, 78
Alves, Minister, 142
Anany, Jerome, 49, 53, 146
ANC, 36, 60, 81, 164f; and emergence
  of private armies, 64–72 *passim*; and
  mercenaries, 75f; U.S. and, 98; and
  rebellions, 115, 119–28 *passim*; high
  command, 129, 132, 141, 147–49; and
  Mobutu, 129, 132, 135, 141–49 *passim*;
  reforms of 1965–67, 149; Belgian
  training of, 202

Anekonzapa, Andre, 45
Antislavery campaigns of 1892–94, 59
Apindia, Minister, 142
APL, 115, 119–27 *passim*, 150
Arab nations, 164
Armée Nationale Congolaise, *see* ANC
Army, *see* Military, the
Army of Popular Liberation (APL), 115,
  119–27 *passim*, 150
Assemblies, provincial, 83, 135f
Assemblymen, provincial, 32, 168–77
  passim
Associations: tribal, 26–27, 170; and
  political class, 170–71, 174
Auxiliary agents, 28–32
Azande tribe, 59

Babembe tribe, 119
Bafulero tribe, 119
Bahizi, Minister, 142
Bakongo region, 21–23, 104, 202;
  railways, 11
Bakongo tribe, 21, 48, 67n, 110; Alliance,
  21ff, 35
Bakusu tribe, 119, 125
Bakwa Disho clan, 67
Bakwa Mputu region, 66
Bakwanga, 66ff
Balandier, Georges, 8–9, 29
Baldwin, David A., 99
Baluba tribe: of South Kasai, 35, 65–68;
  of North Katanga, 50, 56, 69, 109–11
Baluba-Kasai tribal group, 110
Baluba-Katanga tribal group, 48, 50, 69
Balubakat, 50, 119, 125, 198f
Balunda tribe, 68
Bamba, Emmanuel, 146

Bambala tribe, 109, 118
Bambala-Kamitatu tribal group, 109
Bambunda tribe, 117f, 199
Bananas, 105
Bandundu, 136f
Bangala, Colonel, 135
Bangala tribe: and private armies, 53, 56, 59, 65, 67n; and the Bakongo, 21
Bangongo tribe, 109
Bank of Brussels, 14
Banyarwanda tribe, 45, 54
Banzyville, 116
Bapende tribe, 18, 56, 192
Bapende-Bambunda tribal group, 109f
Basalampasu tribe, 66
Bashi tribe, 54, 119
Basonge tribe, 51f, 67
Basongomeno tribe, 120
Basuku tribe, 118
Batetela tribe, 50, 59f, 65, 119f, 125
Batetela-Bakusu tribal group, 62–63, 109f
Bayanzi tribe, 118, 199; Alliance, 35
Bayeke tribe, 68
Belgian Congo, 10, 61, 188; colonization of, 1, 8–18; and independence, 18–33
Belgian Socialist Party (PSB), 17
Belgium: colonization of Congo, 1, 8–18; annexation of Congo Free State, 10, 61; Parliament, 15ff, 88, 151; and Congo independence, 18–33; trusts, 18, 86f, 151; army, 62, 64, 193; and Katangese secession, 73, 96; and rebellions, 97; aid to Congo, 99; Economic Round Table, 150–51; civil servants, 187; military training in, 202
Bemba tribe, 65
Bena Tshibanda tribe, 67
Bienen, Henry, 85
Binza group, 113, 143, 160
Bisengimana, Barthelemy, 138
Bisukiro, Marcel, 156, 198
Board of Extraordinary Commissioners, 80
Board of Special Commissioners, 80
Bobozo, Louis, 70, 143, 147f
Boende, 115
Boji, Dieudonne, 54, 137
Bolikango, Jean, 38f, 53, 55–56, 65, 142, 191
Bolya, Paul, 49, 53
Boma, 106
Bombo, R., 137

Bomboko, Justin, 39, 49, 53, 139–44 passim, 148
Bonaparte, Napoleon, 141, 145, 162
Bondekwe, Sylvestre, 37f
Bongoma, Jacques, 138
Bourgeois, P., 187
Brazzaville, 62, 114f, 118, 148
Bréviaire du patriote, Le, 146
British Africa, 62
Brussels, 15–20 passim, 90, 155f
Budget, Congolese, 16–17
Budja tribe, 56
Buisseret, Auguste, 20
Bukavu, 31f, 54, 76, 104; and rebellions, 70f, 116, 119, 147
Bula-Bema island, 113
Bulletin Militaire, 60
Bumba territory, 56
Bunia, 119
Bureaucratism, 129–58, 161–63
Business enterprises, 27–28; small, 154–55, 158; women in, 202–3

Caesarist bureaucracy, 129–58; black, 141–46
Capitalism, 9–15
Caprasse, Paul, 27
Cardoso, Mario, Minister, 142
Catholic Church: and education, 12–13, 169, 189; missions of, 18f, 118, 123–24, 199
CEREA, 198f
Ceulemans, Jacques, 27
Charismatic leadership, 3, 8, 124
Charms, 66, 123–26
Chile, copper in, 155
China, 117, 120ff
Civil service, 28–32, 132, 162, 168, 170, 187; provincial, 137–38
Classes, polarization of, 117–20
Clubs, 26–27, 171
CNL, 114–27 passim, 191, 199
Cobalt, 86
Cold War, 92–100, 160
Coleman, James, 62
Colin, Michel, 142, 158
College of Commissioners, 138, 143, 151–52
Colonial administration, 1, 6–18, 45–46, 84
Colonial Charter, 15, 187
Colonial Council, 15ff
Colonization Union (UCOL), 19
Coméliau, Christian, 106f

Cominière, 14
Commission for Administrative Reform, 139
Commissioners: extraordinary, 54, 80, 127f; special, 80; provincial, 137–40
Committee of National Liberation, see CNL
Committee for the Protection of Natives, 17
Communism, 93, 99f, 117
Compagnie pour le Congo du Commerce et de l'Industrie (CCCI), 10
Conaco, 176
CONAKAT (Katangese tribal confederation), 89, 199
Congo, the: patrimonialism in, 1–7, 34, 48–58, 77–81, 102–28, 159–65; private armies of, 5, 57–76, 159, 164; appropriation of offices in, 8–33, 159; territorial reorganization of, 34–56, 112, 114, 134–37, 160, 169; and environmental constraints, 81–101; bureaucracy in, 129–58, 161–63. See also Belgian Congo; Congo Free State
Congo, My Country, 25
Congo, People's Republic of the, 125f
Congo Free State, 14f, 17, 20; annexation by Belgium, 10, 61; and private armies, 58f, 61; and Katanga Co., 87, 91
Congo-Lux store, 154f
Congo Monetary Council, 90
Congo Oriental, 37f, 40
Congo Radio, 155
Congo-Ubangi, 38f
Congolese Bank for Equipment and Industrial Development (BCDI), 131
Congolese Democratic Party (PDC), 53
Congolese National Army, see ANC
Congolese National Bank, 133–34, 203
Congressmen, 32, 168–77 passim
Conscience Africaine Manifesto, 20–21
Conscription, 59, 164; of medical doctors, 131
Conseil d'Etat, 162
Constitution, provisional, 35, 40
Constitution of 1967, 132, 145
Copper, 86, 90, 134, 155–57
Coquilhat, Camille, 59
Coquilhatville, 31, 116
Coquilhatville Round Table, 38ff, 48, 50, 190
Corn, 130
Cornelis, Gaston, 14

Cotonco, 14
Cotton, 105
Council of Elders, 127
Council of Government, 16
Counterelite, 111–15, 117, 161
Courrier d'Afrique, 37
Crozier, Michel, 25
Cuvette Centrale, 31, 38, 45f, 49, 53
CVR, 150, 202

Dakar, 62
Davidson, Egide Bocheley, 115, 152
De Baker, M. C. C., 21
De Heusch, Luc, 110
Decision-making process, 15f, 140
Decolonization, 1–7, 20, 82
Delvaux, Albert, 49, 53
Democratic forms of government, 7, 83–84
Denard, Robert, 74f
Dendale, 202
Denge, Michel, 38f, 137
Dericoard, M., 38
Dettes de Guerre, 19
Development, concept of, 159
Diamasumbu, Andre, 45, 49–50
Diamond industry, 193
"Dieudonné" sect, 109
Dinanga, Floribert, 67
Diomi, Gaston, 158
District Commissioners, 14, 137–40
Diur, Dominique, 137, 201
Douglas-Home, Sir Alexander, 96
Draft, see Conscription
Dubois, L., 191
Durkheim, Emil, 9

East Africa, 61
Economic Round Table of 1960, 18, 89, 150–52
Education: Catholic, 12–13, 169, 189; under Belgian colonization, 13, 17; compulsory, 107; military, 164; of political class, 169, 174, 204
Egypt, 61, 145, 157, 162
Eisenstadt, S. N., 77f, 81
Eketebi, L., 38, 49, 53, 56, 191
Ekonda faction, 50
Elections: in 1957, 21; in 1960, 63, 65, 168; in 1966, 135
Eleo, A., 198
Elisabethville, 26, 31, 37, 50; and private armies, 61, 66, 68; economic activities in, 89f, 94, 104, 108

Elite, 29–30, 117, 159, 161; and secrecy, 139–41
Empain, 11
Emungania, Minister, 139, 142
Enclosure Movement, 7
Engels, Friedrich, 117
Engulu, L., 49, 137
Environmental constraints, 81–101, 160, 163
Equateur, 45, 55f, 61, 137; ABAKO in, 21; and territorial division, 35, 38f, 42; effects of inflation in, 105
Eswe faction, 50. *See also* Batetela tribe
Ethnicity, concept of, 5, 55–56
Europe, 12, 17f, 90; settlers in Congo, 24–26, 31, 64, 126. *See also by country*
Evolué class, 24–27, 63, 189; clubs, 26, 171
Executions, 112, 126, 200
Executive College, 151
Expenditure, public, 16–17, 33, 134, 160
Experts, reliance on, 138–39, 161
Export duties, 156
Extraordinary commissioners, 54, 80, 127f

Fage, J. D., 9
Falu, Major, 135
Fanon, Frantz, 3, 173
Fariala, Tshombe, 55
Fataki, Gilbert, execution of, 112
Feudalism, 4, 36f
Feuds, political, 48, 51
Finance, public, 16–17, 33, 134, 160
Finant, Jean-Pierre, 38, 112
Food taboos, 123
Force Publique, 58–62, 81, 109, 141, 149; mutinies in, 1–2, 62–65, 68, 93
Foreign aid, military, 75, 96, 98–99. *See also* Mercenaries
Foreign capitalism: corporations and trusts, 11, 139, 146, 154, 156f, 163, 172; Belgian trusts, 18, 86f, 151; economic dependence on, 85–92; UMHK, 86–92, 96, 155–57, 201, 203
Forminière, 11, 14
Fragmentation, *see* Provinces
France, 9, 16, 78, 162
Franck, Louis, 11
Francqui, Emile, 14
French West Africa, 62
From Legality to Legitimacy, 140
Fromm, Erich, 93
Fundamental Law, the, 40–42, 48

Gandajika territory, 67
Gbenye, Christophe, 41, 126–27; and rebellions, 112, 115, 118f; mentioned, 152, 198, 200
Geertz, Clifford, 55f
Gendelbien, Paul-Henri, 95f
General Executive College, 151
General Mining, 90
General Secretariat to the Presidency, 138
General Society of Belgium, 87, 91
General Union of Congolese Students, 152
Gérard-Libois, Jules, 64f, 90
German army, 61
German Federal Republic, 99
Ghana, 62
Gillet, Colonel, 66
Gizenga, Antoine, 37, 40, 71f, 112–15, 192
Goldmann, Lucien, 6
Governing Council, 15ff
Governors, provincial, 135ff, 140
Great Britain, 9, 16, 87, 96, 99; Enclosure Movement, 7
Greek traders, 28
Grenfell, Georges, 113
Gross national product, Congolese, 29, 133–34
Guerrilla warfare, 117–18, 123
Guggenheim, 11
Gullion, Edmund, 96
Gungu region, 56

Hammarskjold, Dag, 48, 94f
Hanrieder, Wolfram, 92–93
Harriman, Averell, 98
Hausa, 59
Haut Congo, 49, 135; creation of, 38, 45f; and private armies, 54–55; nationalist opposition in, 113, 119, 127f
Heenen, Gaston, 14
High Planning Commission for National Reconstruction, 131
Hobsbawm, E. J., 83, 120–21
Hodgkin, Thomas, 12
Holland, 10
Hoskyns, Catherine, 94f, 99–100
House of Representatives, 41–44, 112, 133, 172
Huntington, Samuel P., 164

Idiofa territory, 117f
Ileo, Joseph, 36, 39, 142, 156

Ilunga, Minister, 142
Imperialism, 7, 16
Income, 32, 130, 134; of industrial enterprises, 11
Independence of Congo, 8, 18–33, 35, 63–64
Industrial revolution, 85–86
Industries: income of, 11; UMHK, 86–92, 96, 155–57, 201, 203; production of, 133–34
Inflation, 33, 103–5, 160
Inga, 131
Ingende, 116
Institute of Economic and Social Research (IRES), 90–91, 157, 203
Interior, Ministry of the, 43, 138, 140
Internal Affairs, Committee on, 42ff
International Company, 73f
International Labor Office, 29
Iron curtain, 7
Isia-Amundala, Minister, 142
Isombuma, Paul, 55
Italy, 99
Ituri, 127f, 135; creation of, 38, 45ff, 49, 53f
Ivory, 11
Ivory Coast, 59

Janssen, General, 62
Japan, 7

Kabalo, 200
Kabange Numbi, F., 51
Kabangi, Alois, 31, 37ff, 45, 49, 51–52, 191
Kabinda district, 67
Kabulo, Roger, 51, 191
Kahamba, Minister, 142
Kahegeshe, F., 192
Kalonda, Minister, 142
Kalonji, Albert, 38, 58, 65–68
Kalumba, Joseph, 37
Kama, Sylvain, 199
Kamanda, Gerard, 138
Kamanga, Gregoire, 38, 45, 49–51
Kamina, 75
Kamitatu, Cleophas, 109, 192, 202; and territorial reorganization, 38, 40, 49, 53, 56
Kande, Jean-Jacques, 139f, 142, 144f
Kande, V., 142
Kankolongo, M., 67
Kanyoka troops, 67
Kasai, 21, 105, 110; and évolué class, 24;

and territorial reorganization, 38f, 42, 44, 51, 136; and rebellions, 61, 71, 81
Kasai Occidental, 136f
Kasai Oriental, 136f, 202
Kasavubu, Joseph: and territorial reorganization, 36, 40; and rebellions, 63, 65; and Katanga Co., 91; support by Western powers, 95, 97; mentioned, 122, 129, 149, 151
Kashale, Minister, 142
Kashamura, Anicet, 112
Kasongo, Joseph, 41
Kasongo, Pierre, 135, 144
Katanga, 17, 137, 195; and territorial reorganization, 36–39, 42, 48, 55; and secession, 36, 40, 58, 65–73 passim, 95, 114; and private armies, 68–74 passim; and UMHK, 86–87, 89–90, 96; national opposition in, 109, 111ff, 116; mentioned, 80f, 188
Katanga Company, 87ff, 91, 195
Katanga Oriental, 38, 46
Katanga Special Committee (CSK), 14, 86–91
Katshi, Mutombo, 66
Kavunzu, P., 49
Kazadi, Minister, 142
Khiari, Mahmoud, 196
Kibassa-Maliba, Minister, 142
Kibwe, Jean Baptiste, 158
Kidisho, Minister, 142
Kikangala, Minister, 142
Kikuyu, E., 198
Kilo-Moto, 14
Kimba, Evariste, 146, 149
Kimbanguism, 109, 146
Kimpiobi, Vyon, 53
Kimvay, Felicien, 40, 143, 154
Kindu, 72, 119, 125ff
Kinshasa: and Mobutu, 135, 140, 143f; youth in, 149–50, 163; business in, 154–56; mentioned, 148, 168, 202
Kisangani, mutiny in, 70, 76, 136f, 147f
Kishiba, Minister, 142
Kitanta, L., 137
Kitawala movement, 110
Kithima, Minister, 142
Kititwa, Minister, 142
Kivu, 71f, 80f, 98, 137; and territorial reorganization, 38, 42, 44f, 53f; national opposition in, 110, 112f, 118f; settlers in, 188
Kivu Central, 38, 46, 49, 53–55, 135
Kivu-Maniéma, 40

Kivu Volunteer Corps (CODOKI), 75
Kole, 120
Kongo Central, 85, 106, 137; creation of, 35, 37f, 44–49 *passim*
Koumoriko, V., 38, 49
Kulumba, Joseph, 49, 53, 142
Kupa, F., 49, 137
Kwango, 38–40, 45f, 49, 53, 80
Kwango-Kwilu, 21–24, 37
Kwilu, 135, 137, 148; creation of, 38, 40, 45f, 49, 56; national opposition in, 109, 115, 117–18, 121–25

Lac-Kwango-Kwilu, Democratic Assembly of, 35
Lac Léopold II, 37, 45f, 49
Lacroix, Jean Louis, 104, 108
Land, right of ownership, 28
Latin America, 164f
Le Monde, 148
League of Young Vigilantes, 149
Leclerq, Hughes, 33
Lejeune, E., 124
Lemarchand, René, 26
Lemoine, R. J., 10
Lengema, Marcel, 140
Leninism, 93
Lenze tribe, 55, 65
Léopold II, 9–15 *passim*, 60, 195
Léopoldville (city): education in, 13; and colonial administration, 15f, 20f, 26f, 31; economic development of, 47, 48, 104, 108; and uprisings, 63f, 112f, 116; mentioned, 72, 94, 141
Léopoldville (province): and colonial administration, 23; and territorial reorganization, 35, 38, 40, 42
Léopoldville government, 151f; and national reconciliation, 36–37, 40; and Stanleyville secession, 70–71; and uprisings, 74–75, 96f, 113–14; mentioned, 51, 54, 80
Leta, Norbert, 49, 53, 56
Lever, 11
Levine, Victor T., 169–70
Lihau-Kanza, Sophie, 142, 144
Lingala, the, 60
Lisala, 116, 191
Litho, Jean-Joseph, 142, 144
Loango, Minister, 142
Lodja, 50, 119, 122
Loliki, Evariste, 138, 142
Lomami, 38f, 46–53 *passim*, 135
Lomami-Maniéma, 44

Losala, Simon, 198
Loso, Major, 71
Lovanium Students, General Association of, 138
Lovanium University, 40, 52, 90, 95, 112; student protest in, 163
Lualaba, 38, 46, 50
Luba tribe, 65ff, 73, 119; and Sendwe, 50, 55
Lubaya, Andre, 49, 198
Lubumbashi, 140
Lulonga-Ikelemba, 37
Luluabourg, 37f, 45f, 49; and évolués, 24; mutiny of 1944, 60, 63f, 66; mentioned, 116, 135
Lumanza, Congressman, 44
Lumumba, Patrice, 23, 126, 151; *Congo, My Country*, 25; and Kasavubu, 36; and military, 63, 66, 70f; U.N. opposition to, 95; death of, 99, 110, 112, 196; mentioned, 58, 93, 146, 148
Lumumba's Congolese National Movement, *see* MNC-Lumumba
Lumumbism, 114, 118, 153
Lundula, Victor, 70–72, 194
Lusambo, 50
Lutete, Gongo, 110
Lutula, Eugene, 38f
Lutula, J., 198
Luxury goods, 155
Lwakabwanga, F., 49, 137
Lwango, Minister, 139

Machiavelli, Niccolò, 51, 72–73, 75
Madudu, Minister, 142
Magic, 66, 123–26
Mahamba, Alexandre, 146
Mahdists, 61
Maindombe, 37
Malago, Simon, 49, 54, 118
Malila, Ferdinand, 148
Mambaya, P., 49
Mamboleo, L., 191
Maniéma, 23; and territorial reorganization, 35, 37f, 40, 44ff, 49, 54–55; and uprisings, 113, 119
Manifesto, *Conscience Africaine*, 20–21
Manioc, 105, 130
Manono, Dominique, 49, 51–52
Manzikala, Jean-Foster, 49, 54, 137
Mao Tse-tung, his Red Guard, 122–23
Marandura, Mussa, 118
Marxism, 93, 117, 120f, 130
Marzorati research team, 17

Masengo, Ildephonse, 51, 191
Masikita, P., 49, 137
Massa, J., 45, 49
Massamba-Deba, President, 150
Matadi, 61
Matobo, Minister, 142
Matriculation decree, 20, 26f, 189
Mauss, Marcel, 9
Mayala, Minister, 142
Mayi-Ndombe, 38
Mbariko, Laurent, 38, 40
Mboyo, Mrs., 154
Mbunda clans, 118
MEBECO, 155
Medical assistants, school for, 13
Medical doctors, draft, 131
Mercenaries, 57f, 72–76, 126, 128;
    mentioned, 66, 116, 194
MIBEKA, 65
Michels, Robert, 130
Middle East, 164f
Midiburo, Senator, 45
Mika, S., 140, 201
Milambo, Jules, 44
Military, the, 190, 192; private armies,
    5, 57–76, 159, 164; mercenaries, 57f, 66,
    72–76, 116, 126, 128, 194; recruitment
    by, 57–60; and patrimonialism, 80–81,
    162, 164; education of, 164. See also
    ANC; Force Publique
Militias, private, 5, 57–76, 164
Millenarian movements, 120–21, 124
Minerals, 11, 156
Mingabengele, Francois, 49ff
Mining firms, 65, 156
Ministers, 32, 132, 169–77 passim;
    1965–70, 142
Miruho, J., 38
Missions: Protestant, 13; Catholic, 18f,
    118, 123–24, 199
MNC-Jeunesse, 66f, 71, 108–9
MNC-Lumumba, 23, 45, 176, 198; and
    the military, 65, 70; and nationalist
    opposition, 110–15 passim, 122, 125,
    127; and Mobutu, 141
Moanda, Vital, 37f, 45, 49, 137
Mobutu, Joseph, 36, 194, 201; and mer-
    cenaries, 75; and U.S., 97; his regime,
    129–58, 162f; and economic rational-
    ity, 130, 133; mentioned, 30, 113, 167
Moeler, Alfred, 14
Moke, General, 69
Mokolo, Donatien, 192
Moley, Benezeth, 49, 54

Monetary stabilization, 1967 plan for,
    133
Mongo, 38
Mongo tribe, 56
Monguya, D., 137
Monnier, Laurent, 85
Moulaert, Georges, 11, 14
Moyen Congo, 38, 44ff, 49, 53, 59
MPR, 132, 155; manifesto, 145f;
    Presidium, 145–46
Muhona, P., 137
Mukamba, J., 137
Mukenge, Barthelemy, 37
Mukongo tribe, 65
Mulamba, Leonard, 70, 132, 142f,
    147–48
Mulele, Pierre, 115, 117–18, 123–24, 148
Mulelenu, Minister, 142
Mulelism, 120, 122ff
Mulumba, Crispin, 144
Mumbunda tribe, 118
Munganga, 125
Mungul-Diaka, Bernardin, 140, 142,
    144, 202
Munongo, Godefroid, 58, 68, 201
Mupende tribe, 71
Mushiete, Minister, 139, 142
Mutinies, 58, 62–65, 70, 72
Mutshungu, Senator, 45
Muyeke tribe, 69
Mwamba, Minister, 142
Mwamba Ilunga, Prosper, 50f, 191
Mwanbe, R., 198
Mwanzambala, General, 68
Mwenda Munongo, Antoine, 69
Mwene-ditu area, 67
Mwenga territory, 119

Nagelmackers, 10f
Nakasila, Gerard, 201
Namwizi, Minister, 142
Nasser, Gamal Abdel, 141, 145, 162
National Association of Tradeswomen
    (ANAFCO), 154
National College of Law and Adminis-
    tration, 139
National Office for Agricultural Cooper-
    atives (ONACA), 131
National Office for the Management
    of Real Estate (ONAGI), 131
National Security Department, see
    Secret police
National Youth Council, 149
Nationalist opposition, 5, 109, 111–15,

122, 162. *See also* Rebellions of 1964–65
Ndala, Minister, 142
Ndala-Kambola, Henri, 201
Ndele, Minister, 142
Ndjoku, E., 38, 137
Ndjoli, Minister, 142
Ndongala, Minister, 142
Ndudry, Senator, 45
Nendaka, Victor, 113, 140, 142, 144, 201
Ngaie, Major, 135
Ngalulu, Joseph, 49, 67f, 157–58
Ngoie, Sebastien, 52, 191
Ngombe tribe, 44
Ngwenza, Minister, 142
Ngweshe region, 54
Nigeria, 61f, 196
Njadi, Minister, 142
Njili, 116, 202
Nkokolo, Adjutant, 65
Nonintervention, principle of, 99–100
North Kasai, 38
North Katanga, 136, 202; and territorial reorganization, 38, 44–51 *passim*, 56; and private armies, 69, 72; and nationalist opposition, 110, 118f
North Kivu, 38, 45ff, 49, 53f, 116
North Sankuru, 38
Notre Kongo, 63
Nsinga, Joseph, 139, 142, 144
Nyembo, Kasongo, 69
"Nzambi-Malembe," 109
Nzeza, Minister, 142
Nzondomyo, 49

Offices: appropriation of, 8–33, 159; competition for, 78
Okuka, Minister, 142
Olenga, Nicolas, 115
Oliver, Roland, 9
Omari, Adrien, 37
Omari, Antoine, 38, 40
Opepe, Major, 71
Operation Roll-Up-Your-Sleeves, 131
Oppenheimer group, 87
Organic law, 42ff
Organization of African Unity, 155
Orientale, 23, 71, 137; and territorial reorganization, 37f, 40, 42; Stanleyville secession, 37, 40, 65, 70–72, 95, 108, 115; and nationalist opposition, 105f, 112f, 115, 119, 126
Orts, Pierre, 14

Paluku, D., 137
Parliament, 32, 112ff, 133, 135; and fragmentation, 40–44; House of Representatives, 41–44, 112, 133, 172; Senate, 41ff, 112, 133, 135; institutions of, 83–84, 132–33; mentioned, 122, 172
Parsons, Talcott, 78
Pashi, A., 49
Patriarchalism, 4
Patrimonialism, 57–58, 129–34; defined, 2; and decolonization, 2–7; and appropriation of offices, 8; and territorial reorganization, 34, 48–56; instability of, 79–81, 100–101; breakdown of, 102–28; alternatives to, 159–65
Paulis, 119, 125
Peasants, 57, 104–7, 121, 124, 161
Pende tribe, 109, 118
Pene-Sengha, Emery, 39
Pentecost Conspiracy, 146–47
People's Cooperative, 131, 154–55
People's Republic of the Congo, 125f
Perlmutter, Amos, 164
Pétillon, Governor, 20
Plebiscite, 145
Poirier, Jean, 82
Political Round Table, 35, 151
Political system, 159–65, 186; and independence, 8, 18–23; power politics in, 23–33; factions of, 51; outside influences on, 81–101, 160, 163; condominial situation of, 82; parties of, 111, 132, 150, 171–72, 176–77; and Mobutu, 131–32, 150; secrecy in, 139–41; class of, 167–77. *See also* Bureacracy; Patrimonialism
Politics in the Congo, 1
Popular Revolutionary Movement (MPR), 132, 145–46, 155
Population growth, 134, 169
Portuguese traders, 28
Post, Ken W., 196
Poulantzas, Nicolas, 12
Praetorianism, 164
President of Congolese Republic, 132, 136
Presidential Advisory Board, 138–39
Private armies, *see under* Military, the
Privy Council, 162
Protestant missions, 13
Provinces: creation of 21 new, 35–47, 112, 114, 169; colonial, 38, 160; as of

1961, 38; and patrimonial relationships, 48–56; Mobutu's reorganization of, 134–37; reduction to 12, 135; reduction to 8, 136; as of 1967, 137. *See also by name*
PSA, 22f, 109, 112, 198; Gizenga wing, 45, 113f, 198f; Kamitatu wing, 114
Pye, Lucian, 61

Quipe, 123

Racism: in colonial situation, 19; in Force Publique, 62, 64
Radium, 86
"Raubwirtschaft," 10
RDLK (Democratic Assembly of Lac-Kwango-Kwilu), 35
Rebel army, *see* APL
Rebellions of 1964–65, 102–11, 161; and mercenaries, 58, 116; and U.S., 97f; reasons for failure of, 115–22; mentioned, 23, 74, 112
Recruitment, army, 57–60
Resources, 77–79, 163, 194
Revolutionary movements, *see* Nationalist opposition; Rebellions of 1964–65
Rhodesia, 69, 73, 195
Rice, 130
Rijkmans, Pierre, 20
Roberts, John, 66
Roelens, Monsignor, 13
Rome, ancient, 145, 162
Roth, Guenther, 3
Round Tables: Economic, 18, 89, 150–52; Political, 35, 151; of national reconciliation, 36–40, 45, 48, 50, 190
Rubbens, Antoine, 19
Rubber, 11
Rudahindwa, M., 198
Rural life, 103, 121–22; and political class, 168–69, 172–74
Rwakabuba, Cyprien, 54
Ryan, 11

Sakombi, D., 137, 142
Salaries, 104; civil service, 28–29; administrative, 134; military, 190
Sankuru, 38, 45–51 *passim*, 135; and rebellions, 109, 116, 119–20
Sankuru-Lomami, 37, 39
Sankuru-Maniéma, 110
Saul, John, 103f

Scheyven, Raymond, 150
Schoeller, acting Governor-General, 21–22
Schram, Jean, 75
Secessions, 113; Katangese, 36, 40, 58, 65–73 *passim*, 89, 95, 114; Stanleyville, 37, 40, 65, 70–72, 95, 108, 115; South Kasai, 65–68
Secret police, 113, 140, 144, 150
Secretaries, provincial, 138
Self-determination, principle of, 17
Self-employment, 27
Senate, 41ff, 112, 133, 135
Senators, 32, 168–77 *passim*
Sendwe, Jason, 45, 48ff, 55
Senghie, Assumani, 199
Sexual intercourse, taboo on, 125, 200
SHCB, 11
Simbas, 115f, 122, 150, 200
Singa, A., 140
Sita, A., 137
Smith, Michael G., 188
Société Générale, 11, 14
Société Générale Congolaise des Minerais (GECOMIN), 157
Société Générale des Minerais, 157
Solidarité Africaine, 63
Songhe regions, 66
Soumialot, Gaston, 118f, 122, 125–28
South Africa, 73, 90
South Kasai: army, 5, 65–68, 71; secession of, 65–68; and territorial reorganization, 35, 37f, 44ff, 49; and mining industry, 35, 65, 193
South Katanga, 35, 38, 136, 194; army, 5, 68–71; secession of, 36, 40, 58, 65–73 *passim*, 89, 95, 114
South Kivu, 132
South Kwilu, 38
Spaak, Paul-Henri, 96f
Spain, 10
"Speaking Snake" sect, 109
Spiro, Herbert, 5, 159
Stalin, Joseph, 7
Stanleyville, 23, 31; Nationalist Army of, 5, 70–72; secession of, 37, 40, 65, 70–72, 95, 108, 115; economic development of, 47, 108; and nationalist opposition, 112f, 115, 119, 125f, 128
States, *see* Provinces
Statutory workers, 28–33
Stengers, Jean, 15
Stevenson, Adlai, 96

Strikes, 61, 138
Students: in government, 139, 150–53, 162; protests, 163
Subsistence farming, 103
Sudan, 47
Sumbu, Paul, 49ff
Suzerainty, 37, 40, 160; direct, 48f, 50f; indirect, 51–53

Taboos, 123, 125, 200
Takizala, H. D., 137
Tananarive Round Table, 37, 39f, 48
Tanganyika Concessions, 87, 157
Taxes, 12, 156
Territorial administrators, 13, 137–39
Territorial reorganization, see Provinces
Tetula-Kusu value system, 110
Thant, U, 69, 96
Third World, 7, 93f
Thys, Albert, 14
Tippu-Tib, 110
Tocqueville, Alexis de, 2
Trade, 10f, 27; illicit, 47; unions, 113, 138
Traditionalism, 4
Transport, 11
Tribalism: and ethnicity, 5, 55; and associations, 26–27, 170; and new provinces, 44f, 160; and politics, 55–56, 132, 152; and military recruitment, 59–60; and nationalist opposition, 109, 117–20
Trinquier, Claude, 74, 194
Trotsky, Leon, 16; his Red Army, 122
Tshamu, Minister, 142
Tshatshi, Colonel, 135, 143, 202
Tshibamba, Louis, 66
Tshibangu, Minister, 142
Tshipola, Colonel, 70
Tshisekedi, Etienne, 136, 139f, 142, 144
Tshishimbi, Minister, 142
Tshiswaka, Theodore, 201
Tshombe, Moise, 89–92, 129; and public finance, 33, 160; and territorial reorganization, 35–39, 53, 55, 96; and private armies, 58, 68–75 passim; and nationalist opposition, 97, 114; return to power, 149, 153, 195; mentioned, 144, 199
Tshuapa, 37
Tumba, Minister, 142

Ubangi, 38f, 44ff, 49, 53

Uélé, 80, 135; and territorial reorganization, 38, 46f, 49; and nationalist opposition, 106f, 119, 127f
Uélé-Ituri, 38
Uganda, 47
Uketwengu, D., 198
Umba-di-Lutete, Jean, 138, 143
UMHK, 86–92, 96, 155–57, 201, 203
Union Minière, 11, 14
Union Minière du Haut Katanga, see UMHK
Union Minière Métallurgique, 156
Union of Soviet Socialist Republics, 93, 99, 121f; in Nigeria, 196
Unions, trade, 113, 138
Unité Kasaienne, 38, 45f, 48–51
United Nations, 98, 101; and Katanga secession, 68, 72, 74, 94–96, 194; and UMHK, 90; Security Council of, 94; mentioned, 40, 48
United States, 87, 93, 96–99, 116; in Nigeria, 196
University students, 139, 150–53, 162f
Uprisings, see Rebellions of 1964–65
Urban life: workers, 103; criminals, 107; youth, 107f, 149–50; and political class, 168–69, 174
Uvira, 122

Van Bilsen, Joseph, 17, 20
Verhaegen, Benoit, 46, 64f, 101, 117–20, 149, 200
Verwilgen, Michel, 88
Vicicongo, 14
Vidibio-Mabiala, Clement, 108
Voix du Congolais, La, 26
Volunteer Corps of the Republic (CVR), 150, 202

Wages, see Salaries
Wallerstein, Immanuel, 111
Warega tribe, 119
Weber, Max: on patrimonialism, 2–5, 34, 77–80; on appropriation of public office, 8; on military forces, 57–58, 72; on charisma, 124, 199; on bureaucratism, 130, 153–54, 161–62
Weiss, Herbert, 23
Welensky, Sir Roy, 195
Welfare state, 194
West Africa, 168f
Western traditions, 5, 7, 18, 83–84, 159–60
Williams, 11

Williams, Mennen, 98
Witch doctors, 123, 125, 200
Women, role of, 202–3
Wrengen, Colonel, 98

Yangara, Camille, 71, 112
Young, Crawford, 1, 68, 161; on Belgian
    colonial policy, 9, 16–17; on elite, 27,
    29–30; on ANC, 71, 149; on rebellions,
    115–16

Youth, 66f, 71, 107ff, 139, 149–53, 162f
Youth of the National Revolutionary
    Movement, 150
Yumba-Lemba, Joseph, 106

Zagambie, P., 49
Zambia, 155
Zamundu, Minister, 142
Zanzibar, 59
Zolberg, Aristide, 1, 3f